Problem Solving in Primary Schools

Edited by
Robert Fisher

16

Basil Blackwell

© Robert Fisher 1987
First published 1987

Published by Basil Blackwell Ltd
108 Cowley Road
Oxford OX4 1JF
England

British Library Cataloguing in Publication Data

Problem solving in primary schools.
  1. Problem solving – Study and teaching
  (Elementary)
  I. Fisher, Robert, *1943–*
  001.4'2   LB1590.5

  ISBN 0-631-15374-8

Typeset in 11pt Plantin
by MULTIPLEX techniques ltd, St Mary Cary, Kent.
Printed in Great Britain

Acknowledgements

Thanks are due to the many contributors who have shared their experiences of problem-solving in this book. I am most grateful to all who have offered ideas, advice and support, and in particular to Professor Keith Jackson, Bob Jeffrey, Heather Govier, Benita Pamplin, Robert Thornbury, Michael Whalley and Professor A.M. Wilkinson. Grateful acknowledgement is also due to the editors and publishers who have given permission to reproduce copyright material in this book.

Special thanks are due to Celia, my wife, for typing the manuscript. Thanks also to the many children and teachers who have created and responded to the problem-solving challenges presented in this book, to Margaret Mears and the staff of St. Luke's C.E. Primary School in Oldham, and to the staff and children of Archdeacon Cambridge's C.E. Primary School in Twickenham.

The publication of this book was also made possible by a grant from the School Curriculum Development Committee. The views expressed are, however, those of the authors, and not necessarily those of the Committee.

Contents

Introduction

'The accuracy of the work in standards 1 and 2 is all that can be desired, and in many cases marvellous; at the same time the oral test shows that the children are working in the dark. In these years, at least, far too much time is given to the mechanical part of the subject. The result of this unintelligent teaching shows itself in the inability of the upper years to solve very simple problems.'

HMI Report 1895

We live in a changing society, a society that is making increasing demands on the problem-solving skills of its citizens. The school curriculum is also changing in response to these new demands. Emphasis is moving away from the transmission of facts, the *products* of knowledge neatly packaged into separate subject areas, towards an approach which focuses on the *processes* of study, investigation and problem-solving. This approach moves from simply teaching children the facts of language, mathematics, history, geography, science and the other 'disciplines', towards encouraging children to be scientists, historians, geographers, linguists and mathematicians, through the use of appropriate problem-solving skills and processes. Such change is slow to take place, and it needs to be planned with care if it is to be effective. However it is a change which many of those involved in maintaining and evaluating the education system see to be one of profound importance.

The system of primary education in this country is widely regarded as being among the best in the world, with its emphasis on curriculum development and a 'child-centred' learning approach. But no system, or school, is perfect; many official reports on primary education produced in the last 50 years have repeated similar criticisms of primary school practice. These include that:

- Children are offered few opportunities to engage in problem-solving activities, and to apply basic skills in new contexts;
- Children are rarely required to use 'higher-order' thinking skills such as inference, deduction, analysis and evaluation;

- Children are given insufficient opportunity to develop the social skills of co-operation and communication through discussion and group work;
- Brighter children are frequently given work which is not sufficiently demanding.

One way teachers may respond to the need to provide stimulus and challenge across the whole ability range is by introducing a problem-solving approach to class activities. The aim of this book is to show how problem solving can be used to enliven and enrich all aspects of the primary curriculum. The book does not present a full analysis of all the cognitive benefits of problem solving. Rather, it is a collection of thoughts and experiences which can provide starting points for investigation and problem-solving work in primary classrooms. The contributors cover many different aspects of the curriculum and show how good ideas can be translated into practical classroom experiences. We hope this will be of interest and practical value to all concerned in primary education.

What does *problem solving* in primary schools mean? Problem solving is an activity that can be defined in a number of ways, for example 'dealing with a difficult situation', 'overcoming an obstacle', 'bringing about a desired effect', 'resolving a puzzling question', or 'getting a required result'. What problem solving involves is *thinking and doing*, or acting for some purpose. It is a way through which we can learn, practise and demonstrate essential skills and knowledge – and it can give purpose to a whole range of curriculum activities.

The book begins by asking the question *Why problem solving?* and offers a rationale for the introduction of problem solving across the primary curriculum. *Skills and strategies* presents an account of the work being done in Oldham schools, based on the Bulmershe-Comino Problem-Solving Project, offering starting points for teachers who may wish to introduce this approach into their own classrooms. Other chapters explore problem-solving through different areas of experience in the curriculum – through discussion, writing, mathematics, the use of computers, science and technology (CDT), environmental studies, aesthetic development, moral education and the use of games. The final chapter explores ways of introducing problem solving into the primary classroom.

Each chapter offers ideas and activities that can be adapted to suit a variety of teaching styles and class situations. An index to major themes can be found at the end of the book.

1 Why problem solving?

'There are no such things as problems, only opportunities'
Motto of modern management

The opening sequence of Stanley Kubrick's film *2001- A Space Odyssey* shows bands of our ape-like ancestors roaming a rocky landscape, squabbling over their scant resources in a primitive struggle for survival. In the midst of a dispute between rival groups, one of these primitive creatures finds a bone. After examining it carefully the creature experiments by throwing it. The streamlined bone flies high in the air. The first missile has been launched, and as it travels it becomes transformed cinematically into a space vehicle – and time moves on to the year 2001.

The human animal is the most adept of living creatures at learning to control its environment. This s/he does by:

- *Coping with changes:* adapting behaviour to changing circumstances, being able to answer the question 'What would you do if. . .?'
- *Communicating:* using symbols to convey meaning to others – language, maths, pictorial signs
- *Predicting:* being able to look ahead, to visualise events and anticipate the future; seeing what may happen next

These capacities enable us to generate options, to work together towards agreed ends; they give us the power to choose the most effective solutions to problems. We do not need the Thames to overflow before we build a barrier.

The human animal has survived because s/he is a problem-solving animal. The whole of human evolution can be seen as the history of problem solving. 'All organisms are constantly day and night engaged in problem solving'.[1] The organisms that fail to survive are those that fail to make the necessary or appropriate changes in the face of a changing environment. If problem solving is, and must be, an essential activity for humankind, then it must have an important part to play in human education.

Education in schools is about teaching and learning. The focus of problem solving is not so much to do with teaching as with the child as learner. In Arabic there are two words for teaching: one, *daras*, means literally 'to teach'; the other, *t'allam*, means 'to make to learn'. The latter describes the phenomenon that takes place in problem solving, that of learning through experience, learning as a part of living.

Learning by doing

All successful human activities, be it cooking a meal or learning to read, can be divided into three elements:

1 *Knowledge* – to understand the context of the activity and the concepts which underlie it;
2 *Skills* – with which to act and to get results;
3 *Attitudes* – which provide the motivation to achieve successful outcomes.

The traditional concern of schools has been to promote knowledge and understanding. But, as a recent HMI report says

> 'There is so much knowledge that is potentially useful or of intrinsic interest that syllabuses are often overladen with factual content. . . and because knowledge itself continues to expand rapidly schools need to be highly selective when deciding what is to be taught'.[2]

Knowledge needs to be relevant to the tasks in hand, it is in using knowledge that we make it our own. As the Chinese proverb says 'I hear and I forget, I see and I remember, I do and I understand'. In itself, knowledge is not enough to overcome the problems that life presents to us. Even the largest computer data base cannot tell us how the knowledge it contains is to be used. Teaching needs to be directed not only at the sources of knowledge but also at the uses of knowledge. Problem solving is a process through which children can learn to use their knowledge, building on skills and concepts, for themselves. As one girl said when she constructed her first bridge, after several unsuccessful tries, 'I dunnit, I dunnit'.

Problem-solving skills are the basic skills, the know-how of everyday

life. They are skills that can enhance general competency regardless
of ability level or potential. Problem-solving skills are complemen-
tary to the traditional curriculum, they are the skills of successful
living. These skills include *general thinking skills*, both creative and
critical, and *specific strategies* such as observing, designing, decision-
making, team-working, 'brainstorming', implementing and evaluating solutions and so on. Problem solving relies on a blend of skills
in a creative approach to the learning process. When the girl made
her first bridge, she remarked afterwards, 'I didn't know I could
do it until I done it'. Her success was a product of some knowledge
and skill, but it was also a question of *attitude*, of wanting to do it.

Children often find a problem-solving approach to learning exciting and stimulating. It aims to give them greater responsibility for
their own educational progress – to make them independent learners.
It emphasises the development of qualities like curiosity, resourcefulness, independence, tenacity and patience, and – when successful
– it promotes a growth in self-confidence and self-esteem. The following are some comments from children on why they like problem-
solving:

> '*It gives you a chance to look and look for answers.*'
> '*I like working with others, you get better ideas.*'
> '*You can try things out and it doesn't matter if it goes all wrong.*'
> '*You don't have to write everything, you can draw and make things.*'
> '*You can decide how to do it yourself.*'
> '*It makes you think.*'
> '*I like it because you work out your own way of doing things.*'

Problems offer opportunities for children of all ages to play with
ideas and materials, and provide purpose and structure to their play.
Problem solving makes use 'of the impulses inherent in childhood
itself, allied with the spontaneous activity that is inseparable from
mental development'.[3]

From their first demanding cries as babies, human beings have
an urge to master the environment and to control their personal
worlds. They are engaged in real problem solving. Both in and out
of school, children can see *the value of tackling real problems*. Meeting
a real human need can stimulate not only intellectual interest but
also emotional involvement. Whether the problem is a personal one
– like trying to find a lost pet; a community one – like trying to

safeguard a local beauty spot; or a school problem – such as how to prevent bullying in the playground, what really matters is that it should be an interesting problem which we are genuinely trying to solve. Problems start from the given materials of life, from where we are, and from what is relevant to us at the time. Real problems can make the school curriculum relevant to our own needs, to the needs of children in the school and to the needs of the wider community.

Focusing interest on problems not only stimulates our own efforts, it can also help us appreciate the efforts of others. Problem solving is often most successful when it is a shared enterprise, demonstrating *the value of working with others* towards a common objective. It can help develop communication and cooperation in a spirit of enquiry. It can be fun too, even when the results are unsuccessful – the boat that sank, the recipe that failed, the building that collapsed. Sometimes we learn more from our failures than from our successes (success only serving to confirm us in our errors!). Problem solving can help children develop the confidence to make mistakes and to try again.

Asking questions

'*Where do the days go when they are over?*' (Three-year-old girl)

Most problems begin as questions, and one of the key notions connected with problem-solving is that of *questioning*. Young children are by nature questioners. They approach the world wondering about it, with theories they are eager to check. Their questions are directed not only at others but also at themselves; they give themselves the job of finding out about the world by direct exploration. They build models of the world in their minds and need to test these models through first-hand experience. Such models become powerful problem-solving tools, enabling children to anticipate events and to be ready to deal with unforeseen circumstances.

We need to nurture children's natural curiosity by developing a spirit of enquiry in the classroom – an atmosphere of questioning in which questions are respected for themselves, whether or not we know or can even find out the answer. Sometimes questions will arise at inconvenient times – so we need to devise a way of storing them for later investigation, such as a question board, box-file or book kept by a teacher or a child. The harvest of questions arising in any classroom can be a rich and fascinating one. . .

> *'If I have two eyes why don't I see two of you?'*
> *'How can we be sure that everything is not a dream?'*
> *'Can flowers be happy or sad?'*

What children often lack is the skill of asking the right question, of identifying and formulating the problem they are trying to solve.

A formal curriculum can rapidly repress children's natural curiosity. Traditional education has tended to present knowledge as a set of answers to other people's questions. With such an approach, getting the right answers is what educational achievement is all about; the *Mastermind* type of brilliance, in which speed of recall of factual information is the criterion, is much admired. Certainly such skills are impressive. But feats of factual memory can be regarded, in the title of the popular game, as *Trivial Pursuits*. Such skills are unlikely to equip the learner with problem-solving ability. When the answer is taught, the question – the reason for finding out – is lost.

Asking questions is an important method of enquiry and one that a problem-solving approach actively encourages. In this the child is at one with the philosopher. Aristotle remarked that the search for wisdom begins in wonder. Bertrand Russell wrote that philosophy,

> 'if it cannot *answer* so many questions as we could wish, has at least the power of *asking* questions which increase the interest of the world, and show the strangeness and wonder lying just below the surface even in the commonest things of daily life'.[4]

Young children's natural curiosity and sense of wonder about the world is often lost as they grow older, but it is something that problem solving can help to keep alive.

There are, of course, different kinds of questions. Conceptual problems like 'What is a number?' and 'Where is tomorrow?' depend on analysing the meaning of a concept, and sorting out what Wittgenstein called 'the bewitchment of our intelligence by means of language'. Children enjoy puzzling over questions such as 'Is that apple on the table alive?' and 'If I were you would I still like bananas?'. Such wordplay has an important role in cognitive development. It encourages exploration of the meaning of words, and of concepts like time, personal identity and what it means to be alive. Children are able to discuss these meanings with a surprising degree of sophistication.[5] Karl Popper, however, argues that the important questions are not conceptual ones like 'What is time?' but practical ones like 'What do we do in these circumstances?'. For Popper, important questions are those which pose a problem and have outcomes that can be put into practice. Interesting as word-meanings and the analysis of concepts are, they cannot be tested by experience. The most fruitful questions invite a problem-solving approach that goes beyond words, and enters the real world of the child's experience.

The following case study by Leone Burton shows how a young child's question was turned to good account:

> Richard, aged four, carries his father's briefcase downstairs each evening in preparation for the next day. One evening, his mother puts a large quantity of coins into the briefcase for his father to bank the following day. Richard is unable to lift the briefcase. This, for Richard, is a problem that provokes investigation. When presented with this scenario, teachers in training respond by saying, 'Explain to Richard that there is something heavy in the briefcase' or 'Show Richard the heavy coins in the briefcase.'

> Here is an alternative approach. First, pose the problem. Well, Richard, *what has changed*? Now, conjecture:

> - Perhaps Richard has changed, that is, he is no longer strong enough to lift the briefcase.
> - Perhaps the conditions surrounding the briefcase have changed, that is, the briefcase has become glued to the floor.
> - Perhaps the briefcase itself has changed, that is, it is no longer the same briefcase, or something about it is no longer the same.

> Next, test each conjecture:

> - Is Richard feeling ill?
> - Is the floor different?
> - Has Richard's father changed his briefcase?

> What remains? Something different about the briefcase. Let us then examine the briefcase and its contents, starting with the briefcase empty, refilling it item by item, and testing each time. What does Richard find out?

1   He can investigate his problem.
2   He can conjecture and test his conjectures.
3   He can construct an argument step by step.
4   His curiosity can be fed in different ways.
5   He can create his own resolution of the problem.
6   Heaviness has meaning because of the process Richard undergoes to establish that meaning.

The most gentle explanation, the most sensitive 'showing', cannot encourage Richard's mathematical thinking, and it kills his problem stone dead![6]

What a child investigates and finds out for himself has a quite different status, in his mind, from what he has been told by an authoritative adult. In solving his own problem the child's learning becomes his own, in being fed knowledge the child is merely the passive receiver of another's teaching. Plato gives a famous example of how a great teacher can help in this process of a pupil's 'coming to know' by the use of subtle questioning. In a dialogue called the *Meno*[7], Plato shows how Socrates gave a slave boy a problem-solving lesson in geometry – not by 'teaching' him but by leading him on through a series of questions. Socrates starts by drawing a square 2 feet by 2 feet, and gets the boy to work out the area, 4 square feet. Socrates then asks the boy if he can draw a figure double this size. The boy says he must double the length of each side, ie draw a square 4 feet by 4 feet. 'You see, Meno' says Socrates, 'I am not teaching him anything, only asking him questions'. Socrates has revealed the slave boy's false belief that doubling the length of its sides will double the area of a square. Socrates continues with a series of questions which lead the boy to contradict himself. The boy admits he is wrong, and that he does not know how to double the area. Socrates observes that the boy is now perplexed, he knows it can be done but does not know how to do it. 'We have helped him to some extent to find the right answer', says Socrates 'for now not only is he ignorant of it, but he will be quite glad to look for it'. Socrates succeeds in showing the slave boy how to double the area simply by questioning him. 'At present these opinions, being newly aroused, have a dream-like quality' says Socrates, 'but if the same questions are put to him on many occasions and in different ways, you can see that in the end he will have a knowledge on the subject as accurate as anybody's'.
Socrates called himself a 'midwife' of ideas, helping people to

pursue the struggle for meaning, awareness and understanding through the medium of questioning. Examples of the kinds of questions that can be used to help children reflect on what they are saying and doing are:

> *'Why do you think that?'*
> *'What do you notice when. .?'*
> *'What do you mean by . .?'*
> *'Is there another way?'*
> *'What would happen if. .?'*
> *'Can you show me how. .?'*
> *'Will it always work?'*
> *'What might explain it?'*
> *'Which explanation is best?'*
> *'How can you test it?'*

In questioning children we are also demonstrating one of life's most important skills – the skill of learning to ask. Our aim as teachers is to get children to tell us when they do not understand and to ask for more information when it is needed. Questioning can help in this process, it will help in the growth of self-awareness, and in our awareness of children's needs. Questions can help us clarify exactly what we are trying to achieve in any activity. They can challenge our underlying assumptions, make us re-examine what we take for granted, and so awaken our sense of wonder in the world.

Meeting a challenge

Recent reports from Her Majesty's Inspectors for Schools have been critical of teaching methods in some schools. They found that children were not being sufficiently challenged and stretched by classroom work. There was little evidence of children being encouraged to exercise initiative or to work towards their own problem-solving solutions.

In secondary schools the reasons for this may lie in the tradition of following a syllabus full of facts and information, much of which has to be reproduced at exam time. In the past this has proved a great deterrent to curriculum change at the secondary stage, and it is not surprising that the most innovatory education has occurred in primary schools. This pattern, however, is changing. With the onset of GCSE, secondary schools are engaged in developing a curriculum which aims at providing students with more challenge and opportunity, placing greater emphasis on continuing assessment of course work.

Primary problem-solving skills can now be seen within the context of a pattern of education continuing through nursery, infant, junior, secondary and tertiary stages, which is aimed at developing mental autonomy, decision making, and problem solving. At each stage education should be concerned not just with competency in lower order 'basic skills' – important as these are – but with providing a series of challenges that will stimulate and motivate children's use of high order problem-solving skills.

How do children react to the challenge of problem-solving? With every problem there are two kinds of response. We may meet it with fear and suspicion, defending ourselves against the challenge and complexity of the task by withdrawal. Or we may meet the problem as a challenge to be overcome, to be resolved to the best of our ability with all the means at our disposal. With such a response, we positively seek a solution to things that challenge our resources and intellect.

The difference between these two responses is of critical importance in education. The aim of teachers should be to encourage a readiness to come to grips with problems, to seek out ways of overcoming obstacles, to foster the enjoyment of challenge. Children need opportunities to exercise their capacities for initiative and decision-making, and for achieving results. Meeting a challenge will enhance a child's self-image and encourage that sense of competence which is so vital for future progress.

Ideally the teacher should seek to maintain a consistent level of *appropriate challenge* for every child in the class – but this is no easy job. To match the challenge to the child takes a high level of professional skill and understanding; there is no general formula that will guarantee success. With older primary children the use of specialist teachers may help in achieving a sustained level of challenge in particular subject areas. Throughout the primary range, teachers need to work as a team, to share their interests and enthusiasms with as many children as possible. Children respond in different ways to different challenges, and there is no one teaching style that will suit all children. An advantage of the problem-solving approach is that it enables teachers to set different levels of challenge to suit children's varying needs and abilities. The teacher also has a vital role in sustaining the child through his or her particular learning process, helping him or her to meet the challenge and to think things through.

Thinking things through

THOUGHT

Thought, I love thought.
But not the jiggling and twisting of already existent ideas
I despise that self-important game.
Thought is the welling up of unknown life into consciousness,
Thought is the testing of statements on the touchstone of the
  conscience
Thought is gazing on to the face of life, and reading what can
  be read,
Thought is pondering over experience, and coming to a conclu-
  sion.
Thought is not a trick, or an excercise, or a set of dodges,
Thought is a man in his wholeness wholly attending.

DH Lawrence

By the time they enter school all normal children are language-users and have some ability to reason for themselves. Many are skilled and practical thinkers. They know that the world is a system that contains options, for example that people can walk, cycle or go by car. They have a sense of situations where more than one possibility is open, ie they realise that successful living requires the making of choices. Young children are also capable of making informed choices themselves. But they are not likely spontaneously to postulate hypotheses or reasons for action, and neither are older children unless they are trained and encouraged to do so. If children are deprived of opportunities to make choices they will not grow up as autonomous thinkers and decision-makers. They need to be trained in critical thinking and in decision-making, since success in life will largely depend on their ability to make the right choices at the right time.

'Teaching children to think for themselves' has often been seen as a prime aim of education. But how is this to be achieved? People often regard thinking as rather like breathing, walking, talking, seeing and hearing – a natural function that hardly needs to be taught. However we *do* teach children to be creative through language, the arts, physical activities . . . The trouble with thinking is that it cannot be done in isolation.

> The centipede was happy quite
> until the toad in fun
> said, 'Pray which leg comes after which?'
> This wrought her mind to such a pitch
> she lay distracted in a ditch
> considering how to run.

Like the centipede's, our thinking must always be about something.[9] There must be an object of thought, a reason for thinking. Thinking is related to doing and essentially to problem solving. It is through problem solving that thinking and doing, theory and practice, are united.

It is said that there are two sorts of people connected with teaching – the teachers and those who talk about how to do it. Thinking can also be divided into two aspects – the *critical* and the *creative*. The critical or analytical approach involves seeing the different parts of a problem and the ways in which they are related (also called *convergent thinking*); the *creative* side of thinking is concerned with how to generate a variety of possible solutions, and the ways in which the problem might be tackled (which may involve *lateral or divergent thinking*) (Figure 1.1).

Critical thinking

The critical aspect involves a readiness to reflect on experience (do we give children time for reflection, to explore the consequences of their preferences, and are children taught to value that time?). It involves suspending judgement; a readiness to consider alternative explanations; refusing to take anything for granted; ensuring that judgements are supported by evidence; and being aware that evidence can support different judgements. Critical thinking

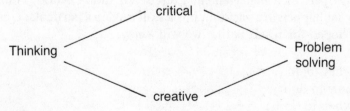

Figure 1.1

emphasises the need to justify what one is saying (a challenge to both teacher and child); it frequently challenges conventional and 'accepted' ways of thought and action. Experience of critical thinking will help children to avoid some of the common errors of thinking:

- errors of perception (it's right because part of it is right)
- egocentric thinking (it's right because I think it is right)
- trusting first judgements (it's right because it looks right)
- trusting others' judgements (it's right because he/she says so)
- distrusting others' judgements (it's right because you're wrong!)
- errors of logic (faulty arguments, moving from the part to the whole, arguing from the irrelevant.)

Creative thinking
Creative thinking aims to help children think more widely, consider other possibilities, look at the same situation in different ways, extend their range of options, and to explore ideas for their own sake – as *possible* courses of action.[8] For example, choose a subject or object and try to look at it from many different angles (as in Wallace Stevens' *Thirteen Ways of Looking at a Blackbird* from his *Collected Poems*, Faber) or think of how many uses it could be put to. How many uses can you think of for a brick, a length of string, or a handkerchief? Children enjoy playing with ideas and possibilities. Their thinking tends to be fresher and more vigorous than our own. What they lack are our years of knowledge and experience. The primary child is at a creative stage in thinking; s/he does not have to be right all the time as we do! If children are encouraged to be critical and creative thinkers it will help them to see more in any situation, including the factors most relevant to their problem solving.

A major company once put the message '*Think!*' on every office wall as part of a management exercise. It didn't work. Thinking does not happen in a vacuum, it is a skill used in a particular context. The hoped-for result is that we will know:

1 what to do;
2 how to do it;
3 when to do it;
4 what the consequences will be.

Like all skills, thinking will improve with practice, what we need to do is to provide the context in which it can be exercised. We also need to demonstrate thinking in action; to show children openly our own ways of approaching problems; to invite children to work alongside us in joint problem-solving exercises; to encourage children to join 'the club' as valued members of a problem-solving community. We need to build up the child's image of him/herself as a thinker and doer, able to think both critically and creatively; and we must emphasise that this enterprise is worthwhile. Problem solving can help in this process by making children's thinking more focused, flexible and effective.

Developing the curriculum

Problem solving can provide an impetus for development across the whole primary curriculum. Many of the primary child's experiences are fragmentary; there is a need to unify these experiences, to establish a *continuity* across the whole curriculum. Problem solving can be implemented as part of:

- *the language programme:* stimulating language skills in the four modes of listening, speaking, writing and reading, providing a link between thought and communication;
- *mathematics:* providing a basis for investigation and the application of maths to real-life situations, with a link to logic and methodology (the step-by-step approach);
- *computer studies:* through the use of problem-solving programs and programs which stimulate children to pose their own problems;
- *science and technology:* through the exploration of craft and design problems, observation and experiment, the formulation and testing of theories;
- *study of the environment:* providing a structure for topic work and integrated studies (including history, geography, social and environmental studies);
- *moral and religious education:* investigating moral questions and social problems, sharing ideas and differing viewpoints, looking at consequences of thoughts and actions;
- *aesthetic experience:* through the use of drawing and modelling to express ideas, the stimulus of problem solving in aesthetic and physical education.

As adults we tend to work within boundaries of subject matter whereas children are largely unaware of these distinctions. They happily work in two or three disciplines at once – creating a map, for example, might involve maths, geography, art and perhaps history. What unites these activities is the task in hand, the problems that need to be solved.

Large and important areas of a child's life may not be touched by the subject matter s/he encounters in school. Problem solving can provide a vehicle through which the private concerns of children can be explored. Older primary children become increasingly conscious of 'adult' and controversial issues such as lifestyles, sex-roles, jobs, racial discrimination, religious beliefs and social morality. Areas of experience which are of increasing importance to children may be left untouched by academic school work. Problem-solving can be a way of introducing topics that are relevant to a child's needs which might otherwise be ignored.

Finally, problem-solving activities may help to break down the rigid distinction that sometimes exists between the 'practical' and the 'academic' or intellectual. When working on practical problems the solution requires reflection and deliberation as well as the use of concrete materials. Problem solving requires the weighing up of alternatives, the making and testing of hypotheses, investigations by trial and error, as well as know-how with tools and materials. Here at last we may break down the age-old barriers between art and science, between thinking and doing, between activities suited to one sex or another – and embark on a joint venture with our children in which we can work alongside each other in tackling the problems of the present and in preparing ourselves for the problems of the future.

Summary

Problem solving is an essential activity for humankind. Human progress has depended on successful adaptation to a changing environment. The human animal has been able to control its environment through the ability to adapt, communicate and predict. Problem solving therefore has an important role in education. It is a process whereby children can use their knowledge, concepts and skills for relevant and practical ends.

Problem solving nurtures a child's natural curiosity, it develops confidence in decision making and the ability to work with others. Problem solving can make learning fun. It develops a questioning attitude and thinking skills that are both critical and creative. Problem-solving activities can unify and enrich every aspect of the primary curriculum.

Notes and references

1   *Objective knowledge* Karl Popper (Oxford University Press, 1972) p 42
2   *The Curriculum 5–16* HMI (HMSO, 1985)
3   Jean Piaget, quoted in *The Enquiring Classroom* by Stephen Rowland (Falmer Press, 1985) p 148
4   *The Problems of Philosophy* Bertrand Russell (Oxford University Press, 1912)
5   *Philosophy and the young child* Gareth B Matthews (Harvard, 1980)
6   'Mathematical thinking: the struggle for meaning' Leone Burton, in *Journal for Research in Mathematics Education* 1982, 15, No 1, p 47
7   *Meno* Plato (various translations exist, eg 'Protagoras and Meno', translated by W K C Guthrie, Penguin Classics 1956, p 130ff)
8   *Teaching thinking* E de Bono (Temple/Penguin, 1976)
9   *Learning to be a critical thinker* Frank Smith (Centre for the Teaching of Reading/Abel Press, Victoria, BC, 1984)

Further reading

Donaldson, M. *Children's Minds* (Fontana/Collins, 1978)
Lipman, M., Sharp, A. M. and Oxanyon, F.S., *Philosophy in the Classroom* (Temple University Press, Philadelphia, 1980)
Tuma, D. T. and Reif, F. *Problem Solving and Education* (Lawrence Erlbaum, 1980)

2 Skills and Strategies

What are the skills and strategies of problem-solving, and how can they be taught? One scheme, devised by teachers in Oldham, is to introduce – to children as young as five – a systematic approach to the solving of everyday problems. This programme has been inspired by the Bulmershe-Comino Problem-Solving Project, as described in Professor Keith Jackson's book, *The Art of Solving Problems* (see page 19).

The strategy teaches children to tackle problems in a logical sequence of steps, which Oldham teachers have translated into five questions:

1 What is my problem?
2 How can I explain it?
3 What can I do about it?
4 Which way is best?
5 Have I finished successfully?

This process can be drawn up as a table by the child or teacher with gaps to fill in for each stage of the problem as it is tackled, including the outcome. To help younger children, one school uses a five-colour rainbow as an aid. Another teacher has written a book about Splodge, a starfish who wanted to look like other starfish. In the story a wizard taught Splodge the five questions he must ask to overcome the problem.

Any problem from a child's home or school situation can be tackled in this way, whether it be having to sit next to an incompatible classmate, planning a nature trail or resolving a family argument. It is important for children to consider a variety of possible courses of action. Indeed, it comes as a surprise to some that there *are* several choices. Children are not restricted to the conventional, expected answers but are free to explore apparently bizarre and impractical solutions. Faced with the problem of how to get water out of a ditch one child suggested 'bringing in an elephant to suck it out'. Instead of thinking only in terms of draining the ditch, children suggested a variety of solutions which led on to the concept of pumping water – an example of the creativity that problem solving can inspire.

The Oldham teachers help children to apply the strategy not only in academic situations, but to other aspects of their everyday lives. Children are encouraged to be open to sharing their real-life problems. One approach is to provide a *Problem box* in the classroom into which they can pop an anonymous description of their personal problems and questions. For example:

- My sister is always fighting me at home
- I can't reach my train set which is kept on top of the wardrobe and my Mum and Dad won't get it for me
- My brother always rips up letters from school before I get home
- I would like a copy of Roald Dahl's *Revolting Rhymes* but I can't afford it

The problems can be tackled cooperatively or individually, and much lively discussion often ensues about possible plans of action. Some children keep a record of the problems they have tackled which can be used to monitor the quality and depth of their insights. In this way children develop resourcefulness and confidence in decision making.

Teachers in Oldham have introduced strategic thinking to children as young as five by using practical illustrations – for example, explaining how a problem has a purpose and an obstacle by 'planting' a sweet on an out-of-reach sill and asking 'How do we reach it?' Classes of seven-year-olds have been introduced to the terms 'strategy', 'strategic thinking', 'obstacle' and 'outcome'. Children are expected to use the problem solving strategy not only in special lessons but whenever the need arises – during class work and in everyday situations. Just as children learn to look for their own ways of tackling a problem so teachers find their own way of teaching problem-solving and incorporate it into their everyday teaching.

As in all aspects of teaching children vary in their response and in their ability to understand a problem-solving strategy. We know from experience that abstract rules are far harder to understand than practical ones. These skills and strategies aim to make the abstract practical. The approach aims to make children partners in the learning process, and to give them more control over what they are doing. Whatever the situation, once a problem arises our control and mastery of the situation will first depend on identifying and defining the problem.

In the following extract from *The Art of Solving Problems* Professor Keith Jackson gives guidance on 'Identifying and defining the problem'. Jean Dowson then offers some practical starting-points for teachers who wish to introduce this approach to problem solving, in 'Getting results and solving problems', based on her Oldham experience. Finally, Betty Pedley concludes with some 'Practical examples of problem-solving work from Oldham schools'.

Identifying and defining the problem

Keith Jackson (*Professor at Bulmershe College of Higher Education*)

Having detected that we have a problem, the next step is to identify it in order to single it out for investigation. If it is a simple problem that is an easy matter, but if it is a complex one its identification may be a task of great difficulty.

However, it is easy enough to make a start in the right direction towards identifying the problem. All we have to do is to ask suitable questions, according to the type of situation in which we have detected the problem.

1   What is it that we dislike? What are we trying to get away from?
2   What is it that we desire? What are we trying to achieve?
3   What is it that we dislike and what do we desire instead? What changes do we wish to make?
4   What is preventing us from getting away from the situation that we dislike?
5   What is preventing us from achieving what we desire?
6   What is preventing us from changing from what we have now to what we want to have?

When we have found the answer to the appropriate one of these questions we shall know in which direction the solution lies.

Defining the problem

But the first stage of problem solving is not finished until we have defined the problem clearly and made quite sure that our definition is both correct and complete.

Here are some of the advantages of having a clear definition of a problem.

1   It enables us to concentrate on what really matters.
2   It helps to avoid wasting time on irrelevances.
3   It gives us a better chance to evaluate the success of our achievements because it helps us to be clear about what we are trying to do.
4   It helps us explain to other people what we are trying to do.
5   It helps us to avoid working at cross-purposes with other people.
6   It gives us confidence.

7　It gives us a clear aim.

8　It gives us a choice of strategies, for example either to avoid the obstacle or remove it.

9　It often gives us a direct clue as to what kind of course of action will be successful in solving the problem. For example, if the objective is to reach a certain standard of performance then we may recognise that this is a problem of control, and there are certain well-established principles for solving problems of that kind.

Objective and obstacle

All problems have the two outstanding features of an objective that someone is trying to reach and an obstacle that is preventing them from reaching it. The key to the solution of any problem can be found in a clear definition of the problem in terms of the objective and the obstacle. In recent years I have been able to observe a considerable number of managers (and teachers and pupils, since the book was originally published) at work on the solution of problems during training courses. It has been obvious that those who really try to define their problems in this manner tend to make good progress towards their solution, whereas those who do not try or who cannot define them in this way tend not to get very far.

From *The Art of Solving Problems* Bulmershe-Comino Problem-Solving Project. Available from: Bulmershe College of Higher Education, Woodlands Avenue, Earley, Reading, Berks RG6 1HY

Getting results and solving problems

Jean Dowson (*Primary Adviser, Oldham LEA*)

In the Oldham Education Authority's project *Getting results and solving problems* the theoretical model of Professor Keith Jackson has been used. The model can be overwhelming when looked at in its entirety and so we have found it advantageous to find an exciting, stimulating starting point and then to develop the rest of the strategy in appropriate ways. This article is addressed to the development of one such possible *starting point* (see Figure 2.1).

Definition

The definition of a problem, as proposed by the Bulmershe-Comino Problem-Solving Project, uses the formula:

Problem = Objective + Obstacle

We consider that:

> The fact that in any problem there is an objective that is sought and an obstacle that prevents someone from reaching the

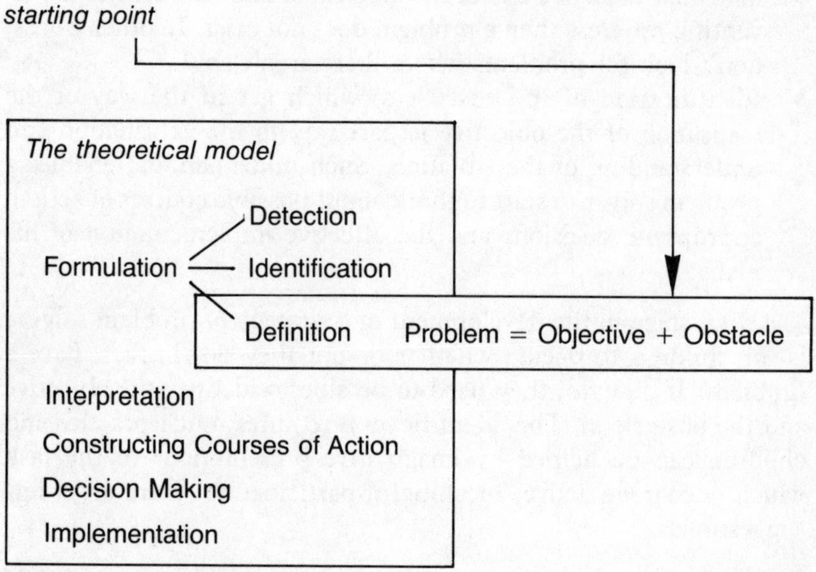

starting point

The theoretical model

Formulation —— Detection

Formulation —— Identification

Definition   Problem = Objective + Obstacle

Interpretation

Constructing Courses of Action

Decision Making

Implementation

Figure 2.1

objective, provides us with an effective formula for stating the definition of all problems . . . *Simply to state what the objective and the obstacle are is sufficient definition for any problem.*

This statement rests on the following definitions:

- *Objective:* the result we intend to get or to avoid in order to meet a need.
- *Obstacle:* that which prevents us from achieving our objective.

In presenting this formula to children, discussion and explanation of the words 'objective' and 'obstacle' steers the children into formulating questions which enable them to identify their objective and any obstacle which may be getting in the way of the realisation of that objective. One group of children, after discussion, decided to use these questions:

1 What do I want to do?
2 What is stopping me from doing it?

If this formula is applied to various situations during the day children realise that:

- It is vital to have established one's purpose for an activity; short-term and long-term objectives enable purposeful activity to be monitored and evaluated.
- When an objective has been established and no obstacle is preventing progress then a problem does not exist. In other words, don't look for problems where there aren't any!
- Identification of the obstacle(s) which get in the way of the realisation of the objective is part way to the explanation and understanding of the situation. Such understanding enables a problem solver to start to think about possible courses of action, appropriate decisions and the effective implementation of his plans.

A vital stage in the development of a strategy of problem solving is for children to decide whether or not they do, in fact, have a problem. If they do, they need to be able to identify the objective and the obstacle(s). This identification requires much practice and children can be helped by imaginative presentations of the task which encourage active, meaningful participation. Here are a few suggestions:

1 When a child identifies a situation he is asked to discuss it or record it in writing. (See Figure 2.2). From a statement of the

situation he is asked to identify the objective and the obstacle
and tick the box on the right hand side when appropriate. This
visually demonstrates that for a problem to exist there has to
be an objective *and* an obstacle. A tick in one of the boxes only
does not show the presence of a problem.

Situation	David is doing his homework. He can only work well when it is fairly quiet. His younger sister is banging on a drum in the same room.

	RING	
Objective	✓	X

Obstacle	✓	X

PROBLEM	YES	NO

Another example for you to try.

Situation	Debbie has 10p to spend. She goes to the sweet shop. She wants a packet of chewing gum. Chewing gum costs 12p.

	RING	
Objective	✓	X

Obstacle	✓	X

PROBLEM	YES	NO

Figure 2.2

2   If children are discussing their situations and do not wish to record them in writing they can use cards to signify the successful identification of the objective and obstacle. (Figure 2.3).

3   An interesting and valuable experience can be for a group of children to discuss the *same* situation – each looking at it totally from his or her own position. The pattern quickly emerges that what is a problem to one person is not necessarily a problem to another (Figure 2.4).

Once children can effectively formulate the problems which arise in their own experience they are well on the way to being able to use a strategy for problem solving, quite independently, and thus to becoming more effective managers of their own school and everyday life situations.

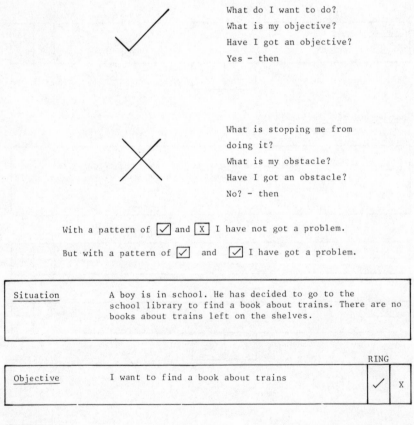

What do I want to do?
What is my objective?
Have I got an objective?
Yes – then

What is stopping me from
doing it?
What is my obstacle?
Have I got an obstacle?
No? – then

With a pattern of ✓ and X I have not got a problem.

But with a pattern of ✓ and ✓ I have got a problem.

Situation	A boy is in school. He has decided to go to the school library to find a book about trains. There are no books about trains left on the shelves.

		RING	
Objective	I want to find a book about trains	✓	X

Figure 2.3

Figure 2.3 (cont)

Obstacle	There are no books about trains left in the library	✓	X

	PROBLEM	YES	NO

Some other examples for you to try

Situation	A girl in school says, 'I want to get on with my work as quickly as I can but Simon, who sits next to me, keeps on copying from me and this puts me off my work.'

RING

Objective		✓	X

Obstacle		✓	X

	PROBLEM	YES	NO

SITUATION	More sewing thread is needed to enable us to finish our work.

Objective   I will obtain more sewing thread.

Obstacle   None

             No Problem   ✓ + X

OR

Objective   I will obtain more sewing thread.

Obstacle   I cannot reach the tin on the shelf where it is kept.

             Yes I have got a problem ✓ + ✓

Figure 2.4

Situation	Carol has hair that always flops forwards and gets in her eyes. She wants to grow her hair longer.

RING

Objective		✓	X

Obstacle		✓	X

PROBLEM | YES | NO

SITUATION	John and Paul are building a model on the floor in Paul's house. Scamp, Paul's dog, keeps on running through and around their half-finished model.

RING

OBJECTIVE		✓	X

OBSTACLE		✓	X

PROBLEM | YES | NO

Figure 2.5

Practical examples of problem-solving work from Oldham schools

Betty Pedley (*Advisory teacher, Oldham LEA*)

The following are just some examples of the kinds of situations in which problem-solving methods can be employed.

1 Tackling organisational and resourcing problems in the classroom or school:
- I want to get on with my work but _____ is distracting me . . .
- We want the school to look good but the playground is full of litter . . .
- We want to play on the school field but people walk their dogs out on the field and it's not fit for us to play on . . .
- I want to find out about _____ but I cannot find any information . . .

2 Planning for a school visit:
- We want to go to London for the day and must find the quickest, cheapest, most interesting way of getting there.

3 Within a curriculum project:
- We are making a nature trail in a nearby 'wild area . . . '

4 In a real crisis situation:
- Our school has been on fire and we are looking for ways of operating as normal a school life as possible in half of the building . . .

5 Within a practical activity:
- We want to spray these balls with gold paint in order to make Christmas decorations but we don't want to hold the balls as we spray them . . .

Children recorded situations in which a problem-solving method was used. These situations were recorded in pictures and words for sharing and discussion with groups. They were then included in a problem-solving diary or 'problem box'. Figures 2.6–2.9 show some of the pupils' records of how they tackled planning a visit to London (see point 2 above).

DECISION MAKING

* qualities
* criteria

I want to go to London by the transport which is <u>CHEAPEST</u>
and will get me into London for <u>9.30 am</u>

Name _____

List of criteria	Car	Bus	Train	Air
Cheap	✓	✓	✗	✗
Fast	✗	✗	✓	✓
Convenient for John Adam St.	✓	✗	✓	✗
I could go direct from Oldham	✓	✓	✓	✗
I could go direct from Manchester	✓	✓	✓	✓
Can arrive for 0930	✓	✗	✓	✓

Figure 2.6

Extract from MY PLANNING AND ACTION Sheet

What is involved in the planning?	Have I got the result I require?	I have identified my problem	I have made my plan	I have used my plan	I have been successful in solving my problem	I have not been successful in solving my problem
			I have got a problem			
1 I (we) must get my parents permission.	✓					
2 I (we) must get my head-teacher's permission.	✓					
3 Has our teacher got permission to go?	✓					
IF WE HAVE ALL GOT PERMISSION TO GO, WHAT ELSE IS INVOLVED?						
1 Where is London?						
2 How far is it?	I used a grid which told me that from London to Manchester is 184 miles.	I want to know the distance to London but I do not know how to find out.	✓	✓		
3 How can we get there?						
4 Which route will we take?		I want to know which route to take but I don't know which is best.	✓	✓	I have chosen to take a route by rail from Manchester	
* by road?						
* by rail?						
* by air?						
5 How much would it cost		I need to know how much it will cost but at the moment I don't know.	✓	✓	Road £48 for 2 cars. Bus £35, Rail £54 Air £400	
* by road a) car? b) bus?						
* by rail?						
* by air?						

Figure 2.7

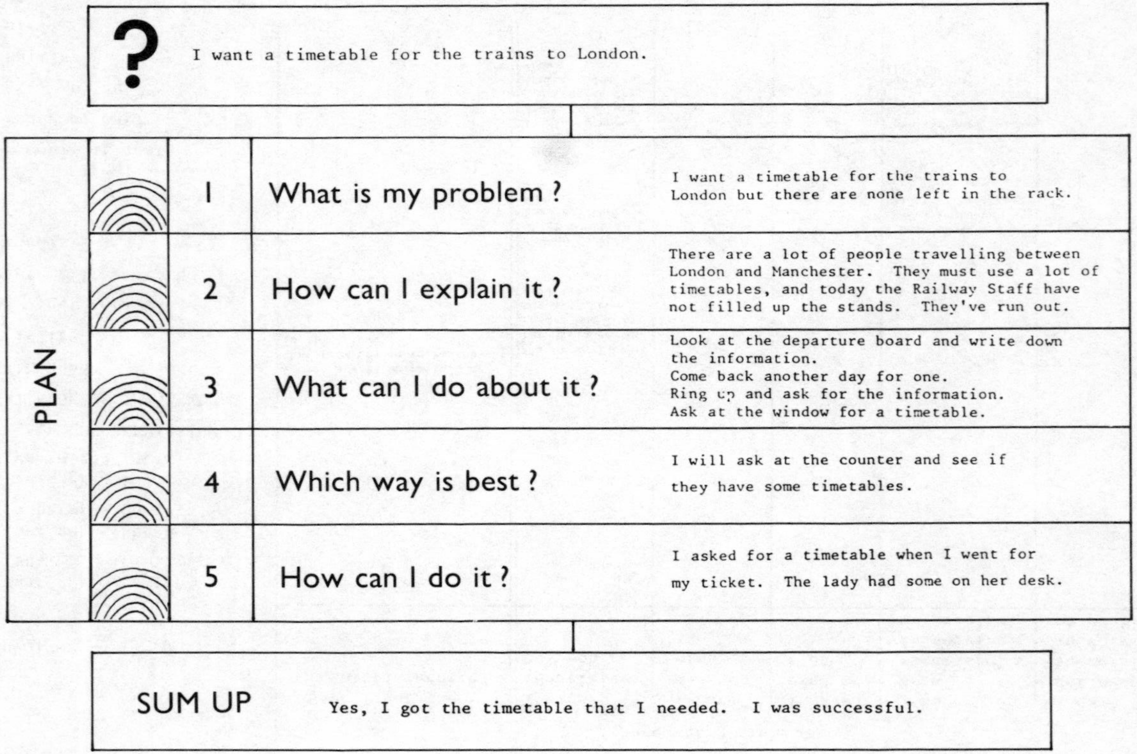

❓ I want a timetable for the trains to London.

PLAN

1	What is my problem ?	I want a timetable for the trains to London but there are none left in the rack.
2	How can I explain it ?	There are a lot of people travelling between London and Manchester. They must use a lot of timetables, and today the Railway Staff have not filled up the stands. They've run out.
3	What can I do about it ?	Look at the departure board and write down the information. Come back another day for one. Ring up and ask for the information. Ask at the window for a timetable.
4	Which way is best ?	I will ask at the counter and see if they have some timetables.
5	How can I do it ?	I asked for a timetable when I went for my ticket. The lady had some on her desk.

SUM UP   Yes, I got the timetable that I needed. I was successful.

Figure 2.8

Figure 2.9

Problem I want to use the box from the top shelf but I cannot reach it.

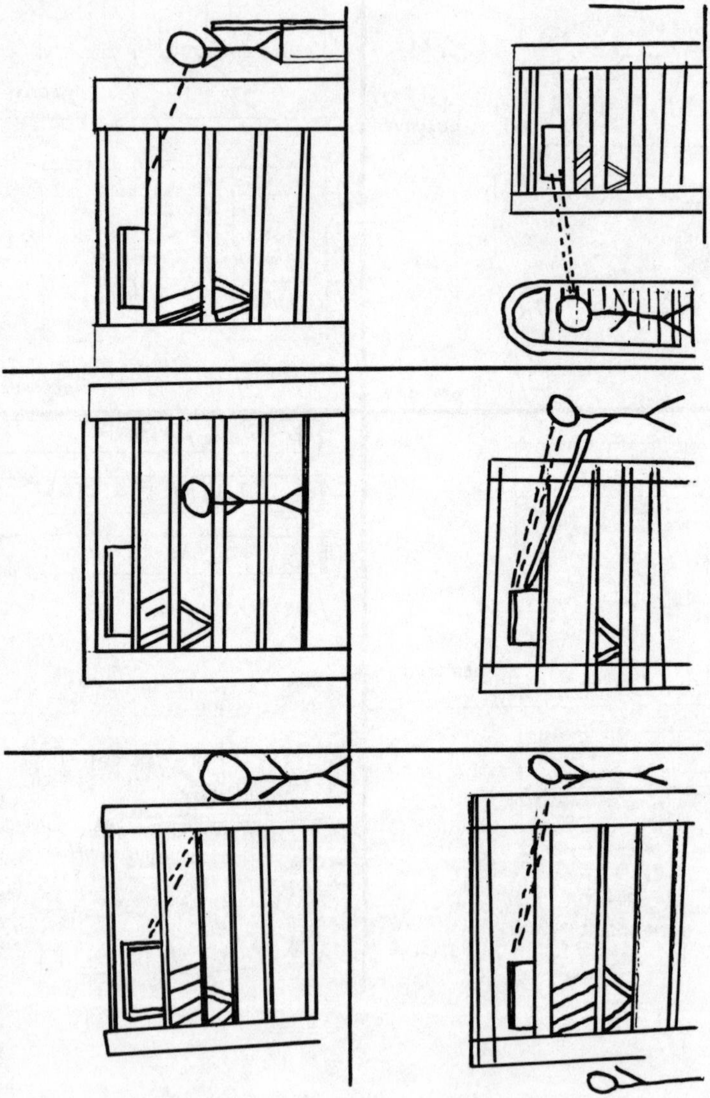

Figure 2.10 A pictorial way of recording alternative courses of action

Further reading

Jackson, K.F. *The Art of Solving Problems* (Bulmershe-Comino Problem-Solving Project, Bulmershe College of Higher Education, Woodlands Avenue, Reading, Berks) (1975, compact edition 1983)

Problem-Solving News (the Newsletter of the Bulmershe-Comino Problem-Solving Project)

3 Discussion and investigation

'Why is a raven like a writing desk?'
'Come we shall have some fun now!' thought Alice, 'I'm glad
they've begun asking riddles. I believe I can guess that!' she
added aloud.
'Do you mean you think you can find out the answer to it? said
the March Hare.
'Exactly so,' said Alice.
'Then you should say what you mean', the March Hare went on.
'I do', Alice hastily replied; 'at least – at least I mean what I
say – that's the same thing you know'.
Lewis Carroll, *Alice in Wonderland*

There are tools of the hand and tools of the mind. Talk is our most
important tool of communication. It serves many purposes, but it
is essentially about the exchange of meanings – our inner meanings
and our thinking. Through discussion children become involved in
different ways of thinking. In her book *Intellectual Growth in Young
Children*[1] Susan Isaacs tells of some children who were discussing
the beginning of the world. Eventually they decided that the earth
was once part of the sun. Then arose the question 'But where does
the sun come from?' Silence. Tommy, aged five, who had said
nothing until then, suddenly spoke: 'I know where the sun comes
from'. The children turned to Tommy, 'Tell us!' they begged. Tommy
smiled – 'Shan't tell you'. Talk serves many purposes, and to get
the best out of it children need help. Interaction through dialogue,
and discussion with adults, will help children to express their meaning more fully, extend their thinking and overcome their 'Can't tell
yous' and 'Shan't tell yous'.

Talking begins with listening. A teacher who wishes to get to
know a child and find out how that child is learning needs to listen

and observe. As Stephen Rowland found, 'a few such insights into their learning were worth more than a battery of objective measures of their performance.'[2]

In listening to children Joan Tough has identified seven characteristics of children's use of language.[3]

1   *Self-maintaining* – referring to the needs and wants of the self or group, the use of language as a competitive and critical instrument
2   *Directing* – to guide and control our own and others' actions, to instruct, demonstrate or demand
3   *Reporting* – commenting on past or present experiences
4   *Reasoning* – explaining events and actions, recognising problems and justifying solutions, not just using words as labels
5   *Predicting* – using past experience to anticipate and predict the future
6   *Projecting* – imagining ourselves in other situations, with other experiences; or empathising with the feelings and reactions of others
7   *Imagining* – inventing stories or imaginary situations.

These uses of language may overlap, and all may be called into play during the problem-solving process. Through listening to the way children use language we can gain an insight into their learning processes, and so be in the best position to help them.

Education depends on children's ability to use language in particular ways – and children without this ability may not succeed in school or life situations. The Bullock Report of 1975[4] recognised the essential role of the teacher in this process when it emphasised that demands should be made on children's language 'by the nature of the problem, and the process of arriving at a solution to it'. Therefore the teacher must 'structure the learning so that the child becomes positively aware of the need for a complicated utterance, and is impelled to make it'. One means of doing this is through dialogue.

Dialogue

Learning to use language effectively and learning how to solve problems successfully depend on interaction (dialogue) with others – and 'learning *by doing*' applies equally to both areas. Children are best helped to learn to think if they are encouraged to talk and express their thinking. Dialogue encourages children to listen closely, to reflect, to consider alternatives, and to engage in other kinds of mental activity. Successful dialogue is that which extends a child's thinking and his/her ability to express ideas through questions and comments.

Achieving the sort of relationship with a child where dialogue will flourish is not always easy. A dialogue is a relationship, and successful dialogue is a two-way process involving respect for what both the teacher and the child are offering. Much depends not only on what is said, but also on the manner of saying it: tone of voice, stress on words, facial expression and gesture. It is important that the child's form of talk is not rejected, what matters is the *meaning*, not the manner of speech. The following strategies have been found helpful in getting children to express and extend their thinking.

1   *Opening strategies* – open initiatives for a child to think in a particular way about a topic, inviting a report, eg 'What is happening here?' 'Tell me about . . . ' 'What is the problem . . . ?' or calling for a reasoned explanation eg 'Why would you need to . . . ?' 'Can you explain . . . ?' 'What are the reasons for . . . ?' These kinds of questions offer a wide choice of possible responses within an intended range, and open the way for a range of strategies which encourage the child to pursue thinking and communication of meanings further.

2   *Sustaining* – asking for a more detailed explanation, justification or reasoned response, by inviting the child to continue talking, to follow up and build on ideas. This can be achieved through the use of both verbal and non-verbal cues (facial expressions, gestures, smiles, grunts of appreciation, looks of surprise) aimed to prevent fade-out.

3   *Focusing* – concentrating on a feature which may be a clue to a more effective and reasoned response. It is important that such questions are open, not closed, (ie requiring a pre-determined response).

4   *Checking* – not correcting, but asking the child to clarify meaning. Try to get the child rather than you to clarify it if possible.

5   *Informing* – making a summary, adding relevant facts and knowledge to the discussion.

6   *Concluding* – drawing the contribution to a close or changing the topic of discussion without indicating that interest in a child's ideas has been withdrawn.

Class discussion

Dialogue will often take the form of class discussion. There are some important constraints on free discussion in the classroom setting. These include gaining and keeping the pupils' attention, controlling the group, sticking to the point, and ensuring balanced participation. Dialogue with classes of children will need direction and control if interaction is to be effective and productive. Not all dialogue encourages thinking; quite the opposite effect may arise from chattering, giggling, talking at once and talking without listening. Certain constraints and clearly agreed guidelines (eg no-one is to put up their hand while someone is speaking) are needed. Good group discussion is not easy to maintain, even among adults. Effective dialogue, however, will develop a child's problem-solving ability, building up attitudes and ways of thinking that will support a child's learning throughout his education and in later life.

Discussion with children should be aimed at:

1 *Finding out what they think,* their expectations and assumptions. Many of the hypotheses used by children are unconscious or inarticulated. The sorts of question they need to be asked are 'What would happen if . . . ?' 'What might explain it . . . ?' 'Which explanation is best?' 'How can I test this?' 'Will this explanation fit all cases?'
2 *Helping them to express their ideas clearly,* by seeking consistency in what they are saying, requesting definitions, revealing assumptions, helping them to develop reasons and examining alternatives.

Children need help if they are to become thinking adults. They need help in asking questions – not merely *what* happened but *why* – and in listening to others. They need to reflect on their own needs – the problems *they* wish to discuss – and the needs of others. They need to learn how to share in decision-making, including decisions about the rules of discussion. They need to learn how to contribute to the well-being of the community – the school community and the wider community – through working towards agreed ends.

In the problem-solving process the whole class may cooperate to define the challenge, develop a coordinated plan of action, review progress and take overall decisions. The class may then divide into small groups to investigate different aspects of the problem, or to achieve their task, then to report back and share their findings with other groups.

Children can get used to planning and making decisions together, and entrusting particular tasks to smaller groups, but it will remain the task of the teacher to provide overall structure and control with teaching strategies that will foster independent reasoning, and to make available the resources necessary (facts, techniques, materials) for successful problem solving.

Group discussion

Whenever learning takes place some form of interaction or communication is needed. Thinking requires some kind of internal speaking (sometimes thinking aloud). The advantage of group discussion is that there is, or should be, more interaction and communication going on than in class discussion. Children will need to talk to each other, explain to each other, to listen and to work with each other. No longer will it be a quiet classroom. If the classroom is quiet during group activity it probably means that not much work is going on!

Group discussion is a rule-governed activity, not a free-for-all. The major rules will need to be discussed, practised and understood.

Points for discussion might include:

1 how the group is to be formed;
2 whether to have a chairperson and/or reporter;
3 how to provide opportunities for all members to contribute;
4 how and when the teacher can be asked for help;
5 how the group is to present its conclusions.

If group discussion is a new departure from the normal routine of the classroom it is likely there will be some restlessness and bustle in the early stages. Teachers concerned about the initial impact of using small group discussion may prefer to ask only one group at a time to work together, while the rest of the class works as usual. A useful rule is that matters under discussion can only be heard by members of that group!

Groups may be of any size from two to eight or more. In practice three is generally not a good number, as someone inevitably gets left out of the interaction. Four is a more successful grouping number. As Figure 3.1 illustrates, the lines of communication between four can provide for optimum interaction.

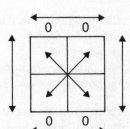

Figure 3.1

The teacher will need to decide whether the groups are to be chosen at random, by childrens' choice or by other factors. Group discussion can be important for social interaction, and children should have experience of working in a variety of groups, not just with their chosen friends. There will usually be some shy, introverted children reluctant to speak in any group situation. One way to overcome this is for them to work with equally shy children. Another way is to rotate the job of chairperson and make it that person's task to ensure that every member of the group has a say. Groups should function as open, supportive units in which each member feels safe to contribute.

Investigation

Children need to be given opportunities to extend their thinking through discussion and investigation. But where does investigation begin? The immediate environment can often provide stimulating starting points. The following is part of a taped discussion between a teacher and a group of five-year-old children who can hear the sound of a machine coming from a nearby street:

Teacher   *What's that noise you can hear?*
James   *A digger in ground.*
Teacher   *A what James?*
James   *A screw going under the ground.*
Teacher   *What do they do that for James?*
James   *Mending the pavements.*
Teacher   *Right. What do you think Rebecca?*
Rebecca   *Um, bulldozer?*
Teacher   *A bulldozer. Listen, makes a lot of noise doesn't it –*
Darren   *I think I know what it is –*

Rebecca   *Something with a yellow pipe and it goes in the ground.*
James   *Goes in the ground and shakes.*
Rebecca   *And it digs up the ground.*
Teacher   *Ah, why do you think they want to dig up the ground?*
Hugh   *'Cos maybe the pavements were smooth . . .*[5]

This sort of discussion, arising from an experience in the real world, will often stimulate a wealth of ideas and speculation. However there is no need to have a special stimulus to start investigation. All situations where children and teachers are together will present opportunities for investigation through dialogue, exploring what children think and why. Even the most ordinary and mundane of objects and activities can hold their own fascination. As Wittgenstein said, the true mystery of the world lies in the visible, not the invisible. If the everyday objects that surround you seem rather uninspiring, bring in *mystery objects*, and encourage the children to bring in some of their own. These might include historical items, objets d'art and objets trouves, parts of machinery, any object 'washed up from the shipwreck of time' which children can discuss and investigate. What is it? How was it made? What could it be used for? All – or almost all – ideas welcome!

People and their opinions are also well worth investigating. One way to introduce this sort of discussion with older children is to hold a 'Speakeasy'. Place a chair at one end of the room. This is the Speakeasy chair. Announce a subject for discussion – for example, 'If I had £100.' Volunteers come in turn to the Speakeasy chair and begin 'If I had £100 I would . . . ' This is an orderly way of giving everyone a chance to have their say, and to practice good listening habits.

Here are some suggested subjects for discussion, drawing on a child's own experience of life. Children may think of many more.

- *Who am I?* Describe a friend/teacher/person you all know/someone famous.
- *My hobbies* Talk about an out-of-school activity, collection, sport or club.
- *My family* Describe the whole family, or one member – good and bad points.
- *If I ruled the world* What laws would you pass? How would you prevent war, hunger etc?
- *If I had one wish/three wishes* What would you ask your fairy godmother for, and why?

- *My gifts* What are the best presents you have given/received? What would you like to give to special people and why?
- *My happiest* /saddest/funniest/most memorable/magic moment.
- *When I grow up* What would you like to do and why?
- *The most beautiful/ugly* things in life.
- *About me* What makes me mad/glad/sad/laugh . . . what I like/ don't like about me.
- *Where I'd like to live* If you could move to another place, where would you like to be?
- *If I wasn't born human* What animal would you like to be and why?
- *If I wasn't born me* Who would you like to be, and why?
- *My dream holiday* Where would you go? What would you do?
- *If my house was on fire* What would you do? What would you try to save?
- *My favourite* book, film, TV programme.
- *If I were marooned on a desert island* What persons/things would you most like to be with and why?
- *Accident!* Describe a real or imaginary accident and its consequences.
- *The school I would like* What would you change in your school and why?
- *A day in my diary* Describe a real or imaginary day – its pleasures and problems.

The Speakeasy is a way of introducing discussion in depth about broader subjects in which children have a natural interest – exploring such concepts as friendship, truth, the environment, war and peace, the good and the bad . . . It can be used to encourage children to reflect on their own life situations and relate them to broader social issues, such as *education* (Why go to school? Who should run schools? Should schools be compulsory? . . .) and *rules* (stealing, lying, crime and punishment – what should be done?) (See also 'Moral problems' on page 186 of this book.)

A variation is to have an *Any Questions* panel (as in the BBC Radio programme) of about four people, to whom the class puts questions of topical interest. Children can extend their range of investigation by using a tape recorder or video camera – recording on-the-spot reports, opinions and impressions from a variety of locations for future reference. Visitors can provide a stimulating focus of inquiry. With preparation, children can also role-play interviews between 'visitors' related to a current topic and members of the class. Canvassing opinion, opinion polls and surveys are other ways of investigating what people think and feel. Finding out about other people, their personalities and problems, can help us to understand ourselves better. It can lead to a growth in empathy, whether the investigation is of real people, or of characters in literature.

Stories for thinking

A teacher was reading *Winnie the Pooh* to a group of children and reached the part where Piglet's grandfather is said to have two names 'in case he lost one'. The teacher paused, and enquired 'Can you lose a name?' There was a pause for thought and the shaking of heads. Suddenly a hand went up, 'You could if you forgot it'.

A good story is a kind of investigation, an adventure in thinking and imagination. Stories invite us to consider situations different from our everyday experience, they are thought experiments about different worlds. We respond to stories, good stories, because of their emotional significance *and* their intellectual adventure. All stories need thinking about, need to be recreated in our own imaginations. The response we have to stories tells us as much about ourselves as it does about the story; it offers us clues about our own lives.

In *The Uses of Enchantment* Bruno Bettelheim[6] argues that the purpose of literature, like the purpose of education, is to provide meaning in our lives. Finding this meaning, he says, is the greatest need for human beings in any age – and the most difficult to realise. We all face the questions 'Who am I?', 'Why am I here?', 'What can I be?' In attempting to answer these questions we most often seek help from parents/teachers and from literature.

The essence of a good story lies in some form of conflict, problem or series of problems. Each story is the start of an unknown journey, and reflects in part the journey of life that we are all on. 'Once upon a time' could be any time and the story could be ours. If it is a good story we had better listen carefully for there will be much to work out on the way, and perhaps we can help in reaching a happy ending.

The teacher is there as a guide to help children stop and reflect and perhaps talk about what the story means to them. A good story contains not only many different objects but also many different relationships between objects, characters and events. Thus it will present a more complex challenge to a child than objects in the immediate environment. For a young child to grasp and digest a story requires a great amount of attention and a major effort of understanding. Not only is the child engaged in assimilating its complex fabric, he or she is also confronted with the equally puzzling problem of separating reality, representations of reality, possibility and fantasy.

A good story or novel is at first a strange country which the child gradually explores and in which new discoveries are always possible. This is why children tend to go back to good books and want the story repeated, and why it is important to allow time to reflect and respond to a story. Every renewed encounter may reveal new aspects and lead to deeper understanding. It is comparable to the relationship between an adult and a work of art, piece of music or poem. The possibility of this kind of meaningful encounter is very different from the story-reading or listening that just has the purpose of killing time or of being passively entertaining. A real encounter with a work of art involves an active response, and possibly several contacts, as does a child's attempt gradually to assimilate a story.

One group of stories that young children in general never tire of hearing are fairy stories.[7] According to Bruno Bettelheim the message of the fairy tale is this: if you have courage and persist you can overcome any obstacle, conquer any foe and achieve your heart's desire. Fairy tales reflect a child's daily fears (the world is an unpredictable and dangerous place). The story addresses itself to the child's sense of courage and adventure and offers the hope that problems can be met and successfully resolved. The true fairy tale has a hero, a problem solver who, in the end, succeeds in getting the desired results – the happy ending.

Fairy tales tend to have turning points when crucial decisions are made, and often what seems to be the wrong decision turns out right in the end. In *The Sleeping Beauty* one of these turning points concerns the decision of the parents – should they tell their daughter about the danger of spinning wheels in the hope that she will avoid them, or should they not tell her and simply destroy every spinning wheel they can find? This is the sort of question that can fruitfully be discussed at all ages, and one that can be applied to many of life's dangers. In *Jack and the Beanstalk* – would you have swapped a cow for a handful of magic beans, or climbed a beanstalk into the sky? In *Hansel and Gretel* – how would you have found your way out of an unknown wood, and would you go into a stranger's house even if it were made of sweets? There is a wealth of material in traditional tales to stimulate discussion and problem solving. Could you, like the *Three Little Pigs*, build houses out of straw, wood and brick and how would they stand up to the wolf's fierce breath? How would you have raised the *Enormous Turnip* from the ground? How would you have rescued *Rapunzel* from the Tower?

Many modern writers and illustrators have extended and developed the challenge and adventure to be found in traditional tales. Good illustrations can be of great value in stimulating the search for meaning and the discussion of possibilities – though they are less easy to use in a group or class setting. Pictures that are well integrated with the text provide opportunities for reflection ('What is happening?') and can encourage prediction ('What will happen next?'). The best books, including picture books, have something to offer all ages. For example Professor Gareth Matthews uses fables written by Arnold Lobel as a basis for discussion with his philosophy students.[8] He regards Lobel's '*Frog and Toad Together*' as a philosophical classic.

Each of the stories presents a problem of philosophy. In the first story 'A List', Toad writes a list of *all* the things he will do that day. The problem arises when the wind blows the list away. He complains that he cannot run after the list since running after the list was not on the list.

In the next story, 'The Garden', Toad plants some seeds, becomes impatient about their growth and shouts at them to grow. Frog warns Toad that he is frightening the seeds. Toad tries other strategies – burning candles, singing songs, reading poetry, playing music. When these produce no visible results Toad laments,'These must be the most frightened seeds in the whole world'. Trying to work out the relationship between cause and effect can be as hard as growing seeds, but as this story shows it can also be fun.

In 'Cookies' Frog and Toad are eating cookies that Toad has baked. Each agrees to eat one last cookie. They do. Then they eat one very last cookie. Frog says what they need is will power. Toad asks 'What is will power?' Frog answers, 'Will power is trying hard not to do something that you really want to do' and sets out to show Toad how it works. But can you really try hard not to do what you really want to do?[9]

The story 'Dragons and Giants' explores the idea of bravery. How can I tell whether I am brave? Must I do something dangerous? But supposing I am scared the whole time, or don't realise how dangerous it really is, or think it is dangerous when it really isn't? The last story, 'The Dream' suggests the familiar problem – How do I know when I am not living in a dream world? Frog asks Toad after a dream, 'is that really you?'

Discussion of stories, especially with young children, will depend largely on the teacher inviting a comment or asking the appropriate question. Older children are able to hold group discussions for themselves. In the extract below a teacher had set up an experiment with a class of seven-year-olds.[10]

They had been reading '*The Shrinking of Treehorn*', a book by Florence Parry Heide, about the problems of a boy called Treehorn who shrinks; eventually he returns to his normal size, but then he starts to turn green while watching TV. The children were split up into groups of four, with a tape-recorder, and given the simple instruction – 'Ask each other questions about the book'. On transcribing the subsequent discussion the teacher, Martin Coles, was startled by the complexity of the interaction revealed.

> Time and again the power of a child's imagination was evident. Often the discussion just became an explosion of ideas, as in this passage where the group is discussing why Treehorn started to go green:
>
> Lyn: *The room was green.*
> Jonathan: *Mirror was green.*
> Sophie: *Something reflecting on him.*
> Jonathan: *What about the elephant on the television.*
> Brett: *The light, the light. The light might be reflecting on the mirror and the mirror on him.*
> Lyn: *He may of ate something that made him turn green.*
> Sophie: *Something poisonous.*
> Johnathan: *He ha ha. He might of drunk some green washing up liquid.*
> Sophie: *He might have had a green counter.*
> Brett: *I've got an idea. Listen Listen. When he was small he wasn't green. Right? But when he played that game he probably stretched and that made him go green.*
> Jonathan: *He isn't Incredible Hulk you know.*
> Sophie: *I think he went green because the counter was green.*
> Lyn: *The lightening made him turn green.*
> Jonathan: *Yeh, the sun probably shining down on that and reflecting up into his face.*

This discussion went on for four minutes and eventually collapsed into giggling when a suggestion about green underpants was made . . .

The Treehorn tapes convinced me that young children are capable of the whole range of human thinking if the context is right. They can produce imaginative ideas, attempt to solve problems, explore implications, explain, predict, interpret, express feelings, reason logically, justify an opinion, and unselfconsciously find it all fun, if only they are given proper opportunities.

At the end of this section (on page 55) is a selection of the vast range of books that can help stimulate thinking and discussion with children, with a general guide as to age level. These books can be read aloud to children for pure enjoyment, whether or not they result in discussion. There will probably be other books you would add to this short list. Whatever the story, class discussion will permit the thoughts, emotions and discoveries aroused by the books to be shared. Some children may prefer to do this through written or artistic expression. Whatever the medium, the aim is to enrich the child's experience both of the book and of life.

Another approach is to create a story yourself as a stimulus for discussion and investigation – or to develop ideas presented by the children. A third-year junior class were studying 'water' as a topic, and had got onto the study of tropical islands.[11] They discussed various Caribbean islands which some of the children had visited. They were told the story of St Brendan's voyage of discovery (one island he landed on turned out to be a whale) and learnt of Thor Heyerdal's expeditions from television programmes. They then created their own story about being on a tropical island on which only bananas grew. The island was slowly sinking, so they would have to escape (with sufficient bananas to sustain life). Modes of leaving were discussed. Helicopter rescue and Giant Albatross lift were ruled out. They eventually agreed to construct something that would enable them to leave by sea. A Fairy Godmother named Flotsam was called in to provide a selection of materials for use in making an escape machine, and so the investigation continued . . .

The following case studies indicate how stories can be used to prompt enquiry-based and problem-solving approaches in the primary school. In *King Kong and the Pirates* the teacher, Hilary Tunbridge, created a story as a stimulus for scientific investigation with her class of top infants. With *How to get Piglet off an island*, Valerie Irving used characters from *Winnie the Pooh* in a problem-solving exercise with her infant class.

King Kong and the pirates

Hilary Tunbridge

King Kong's problem

King Kong was a big man with a long black beard. He wore a velvet cloak with jewels all over it. He lived in a big castle on an island all on his own – except for his prisoners.

He had a secret cave where he kept his ship. There was a secret tunnel from the cave to a trap-door in the floor of his bedroom in the castle, but the walls of the tunnel were covered in slippery wet sea-weed.

King Kong wanted to be able to escape up the tunnel if his enemy, the Pirate King, discovered the cave. How could he get up the slippery slope? Could the children help him?

Testing the ideas

Ian's idea – glue strips of wood to the walls to make a ladder. He wrote 'We wanted to know if glue would stick to a wet surface. We wet one piece of paper and put glue on the paper and put another wet piece of paper on top.' They did the same with dry pieces of paper 'We put the same amount of glue on and spread it out the same'.

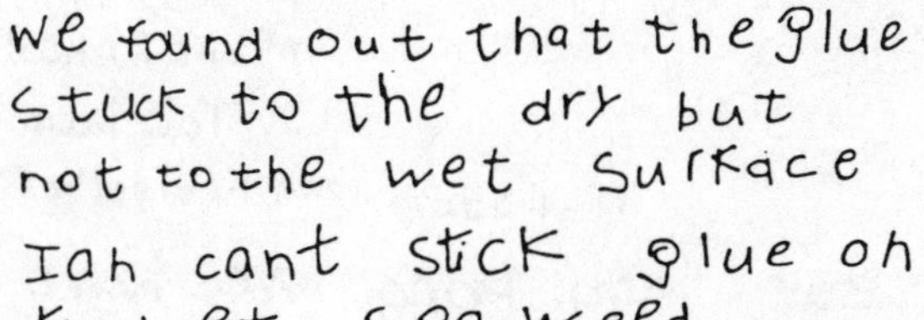

> We found out that the glue
> stuck to the dry but
> not to the wet surface
> Ian cant stick glue on
> to wet sea weed. Liam

Figure 3.2

Kerry's idea – King Kong could climb up a rope ladder and pull it up behind him. We thought this was the best of many ideas for using ropes. *What sort of shoes do you need to climb up a rope ladder?* 'With a strong grip'. We made rubbings of the soles of all our shoes, and put them into sets of those we thought had a good grip, those we thought not so good, and those which were smooth. We tested each shoe four times on a 3m long varnished PE plank. Stuart wrote 'We put the plank by the wall and we put the shoe on the end of the plank and Miss Tunbridge moved the end of the plank up until the shoe slipped. Then we put (a length of) wool up the wall and the wool measured how high the end of the plank was.' We then stuck the lengths of wool on a chart. (Figure 3.3).

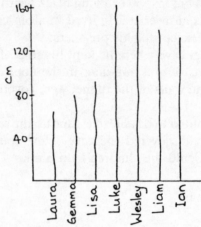

160
120
cm
80
40
Laura
Gemma
Lisa
Luke
Wesley
Liam
Ian
Lukershoe had the strongest grip
Sarah

Figure 3.3

The answer

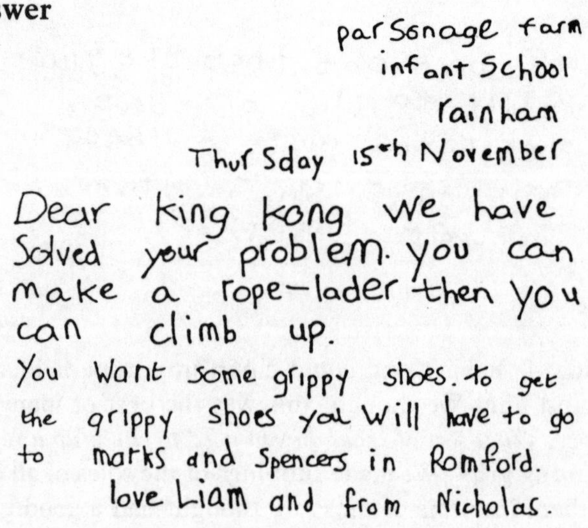

parsonage farm
infant School
rainham
Thursday 15th November

Dear King Kong we have Solved your problem. you can make a rope-lader then you can climb up.
You Want some grippy shoes. to get the grippy shoes you Will have to go to marks and Spencers in Romford.
love Liam and from Nicholas.

Figure 3.4

Also

The children became really involved with the story and made a collage of the characters, performed a play in a toy theatre, sang pirate songs and used co-ordinates on maps of the island and on plans of the castle.

The Pirate King's problem

King Kong loved to collect gold and treasure and jewels. Most of the treasure came from the pirates, and King Kong had a lot of pirate prisoners in his nasty dungeons.

The Pirate King badly wanted to get back his gold, so one day he sailed his ship near to King Kong's island, But he could not think how to get onto the island. There were lots of sharks in the water, so they could not just swim, and they did not want to leave· wet footprints in the castle or King Kong would know they had been there.

The idea

We decided that King Kong would see any ropes or bridges the pirates used, so they would have to go under water. They needed dry suits, and the Pirate King sent us several pieces of material from his treasure chests for us to choose the best.

A strong sharkproof suit

Each child added its picture to the set it thought best (Figure 3.5).

Figure 3.5

How could we find out who was right? We cut pieces of material about 70cm × 100cm. Lisa and Gemma explain what happened next:

we used drawing pins for pining
the Material (between 2 tables) and
we pyled weights on top of the
material. we used weStley's
cardigan so when (the material
tore and...) the weights fell in to
the box they didn't make a bang.

Lisa

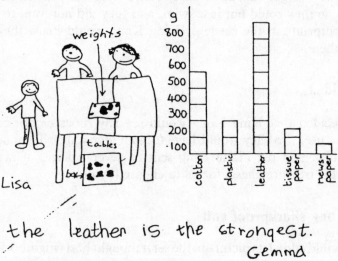

the leather is the stronqest.

Gemma

Figure 3.6

.... and a waterproof one

On a large chart the children wrote their names beneath the material they thought most waterproof and we discussed their reasons. For our test we wanted to fix discs of the materials stretched over plastic pots. After trying various ways of doing this the children decided to use sellotape.

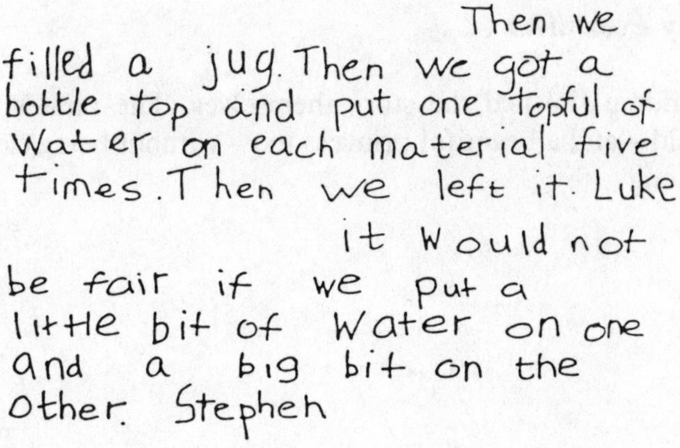

Then we
filled a jug. Then we got a
bottle top and put one topful of
water on each material five
times. Then we left it. Luke

it would not
be fair if we put a
little bit of water on one
and a big bit on the
other. Stephen

Figure 3.7

After about half an hour we looked inside the pots and found that
the plastic was the only material which had not let any water through.
We put the rest in order of waterproofness.

The answer

The strongest material was not the most waterproof and we had to
think carefully about how the pirates should make their suits. We
finally decided that they needed two materials – leather and plastic
– but which should they put inside and which outside?

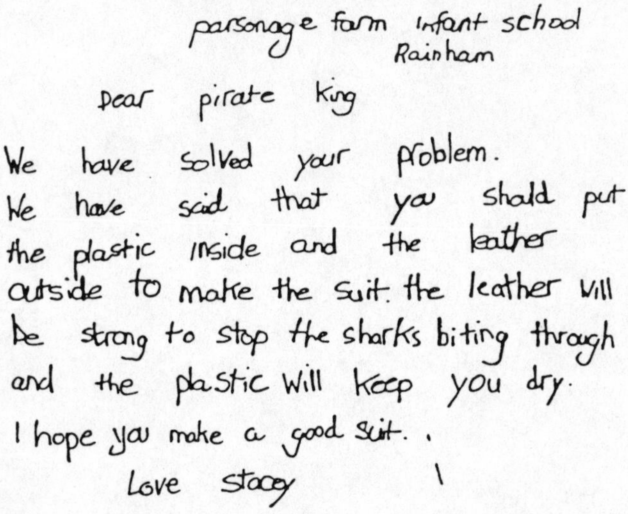

parsonage farm infant school
Rainham

Dear pirate king

We have solved your problem.
We have said that you should put
the plastic inside and the leather
outside to make the suit. the leather will
be strong to stop the sharks biting through
and the plastic will keep you dry.
I hope you make a good suit. .
Love stacey

Figure 3.8

Happily ever after . . .

The children finished the story themselves. The pirates rescued
their gold – and a beautiful princess too – without being caught by
King Kong.

From *Primary Science* Summer 1985 (Association for Science Education)

How to get Piglet off an island

Valerie Irving

Kingsley Infants and St Mary's Infants took part in a problem-solving exercise as part of a curriculum enrichment project.

At Kingsley school the intention was to extend the children's ability to work through a scientific approach relevant to work already in progress in the classroom – in this case a topic on 'Islands'.

It was decided to present children with a problem and to give them investigative work in order to develop skills which they would need to solve that problem. They would need to discover the relationship between land, water and possible means of transport.

Talk centred around the island's vegetation, animal life, climate and the influence of water. Drama, escape stories and messages in bottles, eventually led on to the writing of individual log books. The use of television programmes reinforced the children's interest in and knowledge about water.

After three weeks of working in this way, a group of six of the most able children was withdrawn and invited to investigate buoyancy. This gave further opportunities to hypothesise about the relationship between water and materials put into it.

In response to open-ended questioning from their teachers, the children were led to conduct their own research. In all this activity, the behaviour of water was being observed.

The story of piglet was then told to the whole class. Arising out of their interest in the story, the groups of six children decided to attempt the rescue of piglet from the island. A 'treasure chest' of useful articles provided some of the materials which might help to solve the problem.

Most of the children looked for a means of conveyance by water but one thought of flight. A paddle boat, sailing boat, balloon boats, rafts and propeller-driven boat were made and tried out. It was interesting to note the children's varying responses to failure and success and their ability to tolerate uncertainty.

Translation of ideas from the design to the final working models involved solving many problems and taking lots of decisions. The development of one particular craft will serve as an example; a raft.

The raft was made of straws. The first problem was to fix them together in some way. Glue proved unsuccessful, so tape was tried. The raft was then launched. It floated quite well until Piglet was put on it, whereupon it sank!

Discussion of the cause resulted in the remedy of stopping up the ends of the straws with Blu-tac. The relaunching of the raft with Piglet on it was once again a disaster, with the small furry creature now becoming very sodden!

It was necessary to arrange the straws to make a stronger support for Piglet. The idea of placing some straws crosswise together as a second layer on top of the raft was suggested and carried out. This carried Piglet, but only just.

Looking around for ways to increase the floating capacity of the raft, the children decided to stick corks to its base. One type of glue proved unsuccessful but another did the job. The raft then carried Piglet very well and the problem of propulsion was solved by taking the ideas of another child who had a 'balloon boat'. Balloon propulsion, by means of balloon, cork and straw worked for the raft too and Piglet was transported right across the paddling pool. Piglet was rescued!

From 'Children as decision makers' (London Borough of Croydon, Summer 1985)

Story books for problem solving

The Great Flood by Peter Spier (World's Work) a wordless picture book illustrating some of the problems Noah had to face on the Ark (3–11)

Alfie Gets in First by Shirley Hughes (Bodley Head; Picture Lions) Aflie returns home from shopping first and manages to lock himself inside the house. What would you have done as Alfie, or as Mum left outside? (3–6)

Winnie the Pooh by A A Milne (Methuen) Problems for a bear with very little brain. Can you help Pooh devise a Cunning Trap for a Heffalump? (4–7)

Cloudy with a Chance of Meatballs by Judi Barnett (Gollancz) A fantasy in which the weather changes three times a day, supplying food from the sky. Suddenly the weather takes a turn for the worse, bringing big problems. (5–8)

Don't Forget the Bacon by Pat Hutchins (Bodley Head/Puffin) How do you remember all the things you went to the shop to buy? (4–7) Also *The Surprise Party*, same author, in which an important message becomes confused when whispered from one animal to another – something to try out in class!

Fables by Arnold Lobel (Cape) Comic and thoughtful commentaries on the human condition by the author of the *Frog and Toad* books, *Mouse Tales* and *Owl at Home* (4–7)

Little Tim series by Edward Ardizzone (OUP/Picture Puffin) Rescues by children in a variety of situations against great odds. (5–9)

Clever Gretchen and Other Forgotten Folk Tales by Alison Lurie (Heinemann) Fifteen feminist folk tales with active heroines outwitting, overcoming and rescuing others from all kinds of evil (8–11)

The Tenth Good Thing About Barney by Judith Viorst (Collins) How a child and his parents cope with the death of the child's cat, called Barney (4–7)

The Big Red Barn by Eve Bunting (Harcourt Brace Jovanovich) How a farm boy comes to terms with his mother's death, and how families, like barns, can be rebuilt (6–9)

A Taste of Blackberries by Doris B. Smith (Heinemann) shows how a child comes to terms with the death of his best friend.

Tuck Everlasting by Natalie Babbit (Chatto & Windus/Fontana Lion) What would it be like to live forever? A family has found the fountain of youth but problems follow (9–12)

The Battle of Bubble and Squeak by Phillipa Pearce (Andre Deutsch/Puffin) What do you do when your mother is determined to get rid of the pet gerbils that you love? (7–10)

Flat Stanley by Jeff Brown (Methuen/Magnet) Poor Stanley Lambchop is flattened to a thickness of half an inch – what problems and advantages might this entail? (7–10)

Littlenose by John Grant (BBC/Knight) A small Neanderthal boy accidentally discovers many useful principles (6–9)

The Owl who was Afraid of the Dark by Jill Tomlinson (Methuen/Puffin) How do you overcome your fear of the dark? (5–7)

The Real Thief by William Steig (Hamish Hamilton) An animal story of theft and friendship, and the problem of owning up to your mistakes (8–11)

The Shrinking of Treehorn by Florence Parry Heide (Kestrel/Puffin) A young boy begins to shrink. Ignored by parents and teachers he must solve the problem himself (7–10)

The Children of Green Knowe by Lucy Boston (Faber/Puffin) A meeting in an old house with children who had died in the Plague of 1665. Problems of time and place. First of a series (9–12)

Conrad by Christine Nostlinger (Anderson Press/Beaver) The problems of a factory-made boy who has to be re-programmed (8–11)

The Eighteenth Emergency by Betsy Byars (Bodley Head/Puffin) What do you do when you have angered the school bully? (10–12) Other books by Betsy Byars include *The Midnight Fox* and *The Pinballs*.

The Turbulent Term of Tyke Tiler by Gene Kemp (Faber/Puffin) Schoolmate Danny's problems challenge the resourceful Tyke (10–12)

Tales of a Forth Grade Nothing by Judy Blume (Bodley Head/Piccolo) Family problems with brothers can be fun (9–11)

Notes and references

1   *Intellectual growth in young children* Susan Isaacs (Routledge and Kegan Paul, 1930)
2   *The Enquiring Classroom* Stephen Rowland (Falmer Press, 1985)
3   *Talk for teaching and learning* Joan Tough (Ward Lock, 1976)
4   *A Language for Life* (The Bullock Report) (HMSO, 1975)
5   *Children Talking* Andrew Folker and Martin Coles (Cherwell 'Learning about learning' booklet) Available c/o Pat D'Arcy, County Hall, Trowbridge, Wilts
6   *The Uses of Enchantment: the meaning and importance of fairy tales* Bruno Bettelheim (Thames and Hudson, 1976)
7   For a fresh slant on the traditional fairy tale see *Don't Bet on the Prince*, a collection of contemporary feminist fairy tales, ed. Jack Zipes (Gower, 1986)
8   See 'Thinking in stories' Gareth Matthews, in *Thinking, the Journal of Philosophy for Children* Vol 6, No 2 and Vol 1, No 1
9   St Paul struggles with a similar problem in *Romans* 7:20
10 For a full account see 'Hearing a pin drop' in *Children Talking op cit*
11 See 'Approaching primary science through a problem' by Sue Dale Tunnicliffe in *School Science Review,* June 1985

Further reading

Matthews, G.B. *Dialogues with Children* (Harvard 1984)

4 Problem solving in writing

'Language is the dress of thought'

Dr Johnson

Writing helps children to represent and shape their experiences. It provides an opportunity for them to reflect, recollect, anticipate, investigate, argue, report on thinking, and experiment with ideas. Unlike talking, writing forces a child to stand back from experience and so to shape it into a symbolic form – written words. It is an important tool, but not an easy one to use. In writing the child needs to stop to consider not only what to say but how to say it. Difficulties are created by the great number of things that have to be done at once – handwriting, organisation of ideas, clarity of meaning, spelling, punctuation, considerations of length, reader awareness etc. Writing presents for many children the greatest single set of problems they have to face in school.

Adults use writing to explore the perennial problems of the human condition – problems of freedom, conflict between individuals and between individuals and societies. Children also use writing to express their own view of the world. There are two ways in which we can arrange our experience – chronologically, through narrative and story-telling, or logically, through argument, discussion and explanation.

Narrative, or story-telling, is the primary act of the mind – we dream, gossip and remember in narrative forms. Story-telling is a natural means of communicating and organising one's experience. This is why children find story-telling easy, and often do it well. We live in a world of chronological time, a succession of events with beginnings and ends; this chronological experience is the basis of narrative and becomes the form and function of much creative writing. No wonder then that the creating of stories and poems is often the major source of writing activity for children in school.

The other way of ordering our experience, the logical, is more difficult. Here we need to abstract from experience connections between events, people and things. When the apple fell on Newton's head it provided a story of some interest, but it took Newton to perceive the connection between the fall of the apple and the laws of gravity. This kind of writing can be called *cognitive writing* since it involves such processes as abstracting general principles, making inferences and deductions, speculating on reasons, organising information, critical thinking etc. Through writing ideas become visible. Writing frees us from the here-and-now. It casts thought into permanent form, allowing us to share our thinking over a length of time. Writing can be reproduced and viewed critically by a wide range of audiences. It is an important means of helping us to learn how to think, and how to use our thinking to solve problems.

There has been a great emphasis in primary schools on creative writing, on story telling and narrative. More attention should perhaps be given to the use of writing as a means of developing a child's powers of reasoning, thinking and problem solving. More cognitive writing goes on in secondary than in primary schools, but often this is at a low level of note-taking, copying and the completion of exercises. Given the choice, children usually prefer the easier option of narrative or story writing to the challenge of argument and analysis. Likewise teachers and examiners tend to enjoy and reward 'creative writing' more highly than 'cognitive writing'.

Professor Wilkinson, at the University of East Anglia, suggests that 'part of the problem lies in the range and nature of the written tasks used in schools, which are too narrow to train the minds of the pupils adequately'. We need to stretch the intellectual powers of children through the use of writing, to give them a balanced diet of both creative and cognitive forms. Problem solving can provide a stimulus to both creative (imaginative) and to cognitive (logical) writing. Written language can become the dress of real and extended thinking.

Many teachers are now using writing as a *means* of learning – offering it to their children as a discovery process and helping them, through writing, to reflect on their own thinking and learning. The following articles illustrate some of the ways in which this can be put into practice. In *Writing to recollect, ask questions, reflect* . . . Pat D'Arcy shares some experiences from the Wilts/Somerset 'Write to Learn' Project. Steve Bicknell describes how he used *Think Books* to encourage his children to express their thinking and learning. *What if?* offers some starting points to stimulate thinking and writing.

Writing to recollect, ask questions, reflect. . .

Pat D'Arcy (*English Adviser for Wiltshire*)

Writing isn't just a medium, words penned across the page or typed up on a screen; writing is also an activity generating thoughts, feelings, memories, questions and ideas inside the writer's head as the hand pauses, then scribbles, then pauses again. . .

Just as talking can make thoughts audible, writing can make our thoughts visible so that we can literally 'have a look' at them as they appear in front of us. Even more usefully, writing doesn't disappear into thin air like speech. Consequently we can take a second look – come back to reflect on the meanings which lie behind, or beyond, the words on the page. Because correct handling of the medium receives so much attention in our schools, children who are slow to grasp the code correctly often come to think that they are 'no good at' writing. They stop trying to 'learn to write' and never discover how powerfully they could perhaps 'write to learn'. Writing that enables us first of all to find out what we already know and then to extend and clarify our knowledge must surely be relevant to learning across the curriculum for pupils of all ages, from reception class infants to research students.

Recently, teachers involved in the Wilts/Somerset 'Write to Learn' Project have been exploring how to offer writing inside their own classrooms as an activity which can help learners to learn more. Think-books and learning logs which free pupils from the constraints of product-making and allow them to 'think onto paper' without having to shape their thoughts into a particular *form*, are proving to be highly successful. A boy in a top junior class who had recently been introduced to this notion of writing as a reflective activity wrote: 'The Think Book is a good idea. I think it sort of kickstarts your brain like a motor bike.'

One of my favourite activities which directs the writer's attention to how writing can trawl below the surface of the mind and come up with an interesting catch, is brainstorming (or brainwaving, as one child put it). In essence, this means programming the brain to search its memory for material relevant to the task in hand. You can brainstorm for information or for personal memories (about people, places, events, feelings); you can brainstorm for visual images (mental snapshots, sometimes whole films); you can brainstorm for words and, because you are using writing as your medium, you brainstorm *in* words. These may pop up singly into the conscious mind, in twos and threes, or in whole sentences. Having programmed the topic into the head, all the writer has to do at this stage is to become an attentive listener as her brain searches the memory, jotting down whatever she hears just as she hears it.

The first 'information retrieval' brainstorm that a class of 7-year-olds in one of Wiltshire's smallest primary schools tried out led to the following responses. We first talked together for several minutes about the amazing things that *any* human brain can do. Then, as a way of finding out whether we could actually 'make our brains work' we gave ourselves about five minutes to jot down anything that we already knew about *blood*.

William wrote:
The body yousis it a lot
Keeps you alive
Mum skreems at it!
a red liquid that vampires and Dracular likes

Roy:
Its red runney keep(s) a human body going It run by the heart
Pumping it the human body contains 9 pints of blood If you lose
about 3 pints of it you die.
There are different blood groups
Even babys can have a pace-maker
It needs oxygen

Oliver:
Contains lots of water
Underneath our skin
Liquid
dangerus if lost
cells
clots
warm
circleatage
dead blood turns into a wart

Josephine:
it keeps us kleen
we live on it
everyone have it
it is different shades of red
we serviv on it

Nicholas:
red
there are sells in it
is it warm or cold?
thick
thers lots in our body
can be lost

When I asked the children to brainstorm on paper to find out what they knew about blood I also let them know that for this kind of writing, correct spelling and neat handwriting were not important. What was important was to be able to see, there in front of you, the information your brain had come up with. Think-writing is used to help you to think and to see what you have thought. The time and place for conscious attention to be brought to the mechanics of writing comes at the editing stage of a continuous final draft.

In this initial brainstorm many children were already raising questions, as Nicholas did in the last example. Several of the girls wrote down questions *about* blood as their initial response to 'find out what you know':

Kerry
Why do we have blood
What dus it do
Why is it red
Why dus vampiers like it

Anna:
Why does our blood help us?
Will we survive with no blood?

Becky:
Red
Some people have blue
How does it come?
Why is it red?

We shared some of the fragments of information that had 'come back' to us and listened to some of the initial questions. Then I invited everyone in the class to brainstorm for anything they *didn't* know about blood. Here are some examples of the questions they came up with:

How much blood have we got inside us?
Why dosent blood come when you are burnt? (from a boy with a

bad burn on his arm)
Why does it come out when you fall over?
Why does blood come out of your ear when you have a fractured skull?

Next I asked everyone to choose either one of the questions that by now I had written up on the board, or one of their own, to see whether they could come up with a possible 'answer'. I was interested to find out whether any of them could think speculatively about the topic.

Some couldn't move beyond *Do insects have blood? Yes I think so.*

But several were more specific:

Do insects have blood?
I don't think so because when I step on an ant I don't see any blood.
Do insects have blood?
Yes I think they have blood in them
But is it red like ours
and is it thick?
How does blood clot?
To make our blood clot there is probably a chemical in your blood that thickens. If you don't have a particular blood it could be dangers because not many people have that kind of blood so I think they should try chemicals in the blood to change the rare blood in to blood that most people have so if they lose blood people could put blood from some other person and pump it back in.

I spent about an hour with the class. During this time we moved back and forth continuously between *writing* (to ask questions, to reflect) and *talk* (sharing whatever facts, feelings or thoughts emerged on paper). The class found out that between them they knew many interesting facts about blood and they were certainly able to formulate their own questions about it.

At the start of any new topic, finding out what is already lodged inside all those heads, however fragmentary it may be, is a good way to create an attitude of mind that wants to find out more. The less children know the more likely they are to find the voices inside their heads asking questions – not the teacher's questions but their own. What better way to set in train a whole series of mini-investigations which pupils can research, either individually or in pairs, in order to add to the information that is already 'known' by the class group?

At the end of this session I asked everyone to jot down how they would set about finding out more. They were not short of sensible ideas:

> *I would look in books about blood and encycloprediea*
> *I could go to a hospital*
> *I would go to the natrue history museum*
> *I would go to a spellist*
> *I would look in an animal dicsionary*
> *I would go to a special Doctor to see if he new.*

And Milo wrote:
If you wanted to right about stamps you could do the think writing and when you have done it you could right a topic about what you've found out.

Learning to write or writing to learn? I am convinced that Milo will be far more likely to develop his capacity to handle writing as a means of shaping meaning if he continues to use the strategies that we had been trying out in his class that morning.

(*With thanks to the children, Head and staff of Crockerton Primary School, Warminster, for making this particular mini-investigation possible.*)

Think books

Steve Bicknell

I think Think Books are alright because I can write about what I don't understand, like why does the world go round.

Alan, 10

Children most often produce writing concerned with the things they don't understand or have just discovered – their new ideas. To begin with, the children whose Think Books are almost exclusively concerned with this type of entry produce writing largely to do with asking questions, such as this piece from another ten-year-old, Michelle.

Is the earth really moving round? Why is there so much crime and violence? Why can't we be perfect? How does the sun shine? How does the moon control the sea tides? How come a rainbow is all different colours? What causes diseases? How can fish breathe underwater? Why have camels got a hump? How is sand formed? Why do we have to drink water? How does the sun rise and set?

My clumsy and rather dictatorial response to this was, 'These are super questions Michelle, but I think you should try and come up with some answers.' Undeterred by my less-than-constructive response, she produced the following piece a week later:

Why do we have to drink water? I think it's because it makes our throats feel moisturised. . . . How is sand formed? It might be by the sun when it is hot in the desert but I'm not sure. How does the sun rise and set? I an not sure but it might be because the earth is moving round so that the speed is making it rise and set. Why is there so much crime and violence? It might be because they haven't got a job and they haven't got anything to do.

Michelle, and other children whose Think Book entries have followed this pattern, illustrate how thinking can take place while a piece of writing is being produced. At first Michelle demonstrates that she is puzzled about many natural phenomena. But, by writing about these puzzles, she begins to come up with tentative explanations.

A few children who belong to this group actually manage to adopt the question and answer approach right from the beginning.

> *Who do other people speak different languages in the world. . . are they born like it? And I don't get it that the world's going round but you cannot feel it and why are other people dark brown and we are white, is it because their mother is black and they're born black. Why is it if you let your cat out he knows his way home. Any why is it if the earth stopped why would we float, is it we were born with the earth?*
>
> Joanne 9

I spent two terms with this second and third year class. By the end of the session the children who had attempted this explorative writing – asking questions and attempting answers – were regularly producing pieces of writing such as the following two examples.

> *How do we grow bigger and bigger? I think it is something inside us that pushes us upwards. How did babies get inside ladies tummies because they don't come out as thin as pins? I reckon babies are 53 centimetres in ladies tummies and they don't grow any bigger until they come out.*
>
> Justin 9

> *I don't understand why black people are black and white people are white. I think it might be because when we were cave men that some of them lived in hot parts of the world and others lived in cold parts but I thought the world was cold then, so why are some people different colours to other people?*
>
> Alan 10

The children who attempt this type of writing and thinking, and succeed relatively quickly, would not necessarily be classified as the most able members of the class. Neither are they always the sort of children who have had a lot of preparation for this type of activity. Right from the start, it seems, some children have more inquiring minds than others. Further observations lead me to suggest that those who I once thought would quickly respond to this work do not always do so. In several instances it has been the quiet, almost withdrawn, children who have produced the most interesting and successful Think Books.

I would make a rough guess that between a third and a half of the class develop Think Books containing the type of explorative writing illustrated above. A significant number, however, concern themselves with a different type of writing. These children are certainly thinking, but their thoughts are focused on people's behaviour and their own relationships with friends, parents and teachers. The following piece, written by Mark (aged 9) demonstrates this:

> *I think that Joanne and I will get married in the future because we have loved each other for years and she has kissed me before and I have kissed her as well. And I have given her lots of presents like a little shell with a little shell mouse on top of it and I have given her love letters and Jo writes me love letters as well. That is why I think we will get married.*

My response to this was, 'Thank you for telling me Mark, I appreciate this. Does Joanne get upset when you get told off like you did earlier this week?' I wrote this because I was genuinely touched by his comments and pleased that he felt he could share his feelings with me. I was also curious about Joanne's feelings when Mark was criticised for some of his less acceptable behaviour. Interestingly, he did not respond to my questions the following week. Perhaps, in his eyes, I was being over-curious, or perhaps he simply had nothing further to say on the matter.

The first piece Louise (10) wrote this term was about a classmate.

> *Sometimes when I'm working Rachael gets on my nerves. She bites her nails and makes funny faces at me. She keeps saying that she's got make up. I think she's a show off. She picks her nose and eats it.*

Her next two entries were about aeroplanes and UFOs but her latest was back on the subject of friends.

> *I wonder why everybody has to make friends and break friends because when I came to Donna she is always shouting at Maria and Maria is shouting at her and they keep breaking friends because Andrea keeps wanting to make Maria break friends with Donna. So I just go and play with Tina while they are shouting at each other. Then here comes Donna and says I'm going off with Tina.*

Not all the writing in this category is concerned with peer groups. Other children worry about their parents or their families, as this piece illustrates:

> *I wonder why my brother always has his own way. My mum and dad always seem to agree with him. Whenever he wants a programme*

*on he always gets it. I am always getting told off for something my
brother has done.*

Ann 10

My response was, 'Thanks Ann, do you think your brother gets
his own way because he's the youngest? Or, perhaps, because he's
a boy?' Some children are more than willing to carry on a dialogue
with me in their Think Books. The following week, Ann replied:

> *I don't think it could be because he is the youngest because I have
> an even younger sister who is younger than he is. I think he gets
> all his own way because he was spoilt when he was younger. . .*

In attempting to categorise the types of subject matter in this
way, I do not mean to suggest that children stick exclusively to any
one kind – for example writing only about people or always producing 'explorative' writing. They do dodge about, but usually settle,
after a few weeks, for one type of entry.

A further significant group of children tend to spend most of
their time writing about school, teachers and school work. Gillian's
(9) first engry was:

> *The thing what's going on inside my head is that the school is like
> a prison.*

Alison (10) recently wrote:

> *I like it in Mr Bicknell's class. He is very nice but I'm scared of
> him, when he shouts it makes me shiver. I like Mr Bicknell because
> he let's us do lots of art and reading. I don't like Mr Bicknell when
> he gets angry like my Dad.*

Paul's (9) entry was concerned with his response to the work that
we had undertaken after finding the pellets of a tawny owl on a
window sill.

> *I think that owl pellets are interesting to take apart because you
> find bones that have come from mice and little birds. It coughs up
> the pellet into little balls of fur and that has all the interesting bones
> and jaw bones in the pellets. Some pellets have 50–60 bones in and
> the owl who coughed up that pellet must have had a feast.*

Yet another group of children started their Think Books by writing about their dreams. Although at the outset I had said that they could undertake this type of writing, I was not very happy about it. I felt that some children would use this as a chance to write about invented dreams or, at best, describe fairly recent dreams but go no further. My fears were realised in a few cases, but on the whole I need not have worried. It seems that most children need a safety valve, giving them something – anything – to write about when they can think of nothing else, and dreams seem to provide this. Very few children continue to write solely about dreams for longer than four weeks. Moreover, accounts of dreams often enabled me to ask open-ended questions in order to stimulate children to write their thoughts about other matters.

The sort of open-ended questioning that might arise can perhaps be guessed at from the following piece by Darren (9).

> *On Saturday I went to a place called NALGO. It had a Space Invader. I thought it was good. My highest is 5000, my dad's highest is 2000. When I came home I had another dream, it was horrible. It was about my dad and me. We was walking home from the pub and we saw a man and he was coming closer to my dad and me. He took me away then I woke up when my Mum brought my breakfast up.*

These then, are the main types of subject matter that the children concern themselves with, and I have yet to find a child who, after a term, cannot be involved in one of the various types of writing and thinking. For some children, the Think Books are much more than just another demand made upon their time each week. To them Think Books serve a real need. These children rightly exploit my original intentions and use their writing to fulfil a purpose of their own.

Ann, for example, is a worrier. She enjoys the chance to share her worries through writing:

> *At night I don't seem able to get to sleep. I seem to be worrying about something but I don't know what. I seem to want to know it but it just won't come.*

Likewise Donna (10), who writes:

> *I have been thinking about this, there is said to be grass fleas on some parts of (the) hills, it is swarming. I think that is what might*

have bit me yesterday. And the lady that has asked me to be her bridesmaid is covered from the top of her legs to her feet with the same spots as I had on my leg yesterday. She went to the doctor's and he said it was dog fleas. But she's had her dog for seven years and he has never had fleas and my mum has bites on her. I think that her dog has been running about and they have jumped off him and then bit my future second cousin then jumped back off. This has been worrying me.

Other children exploit the concept of Think Books in different directions. Apart from using it for explorative writing, Gareth occasionally likes to show off his sense of humour.

It is amazing to think that one million germs can fit on a pin-head! (but that is not really surprising because germs are microscopic!).

Another nine-year-old, Paul, invariably likes to talk about his model making or *Lego* constructions.

I think that Lego is like your own world because you can build anything you want to build with Lego.

Warrick needs to write about his family, and Alan demonstrates, weekly, his love of technical and scientific matters – he recently told me, via his Think Book, how a compressor works! These children have adapted my original intentions to centre on their particular interests or concerns, giving them a chance to share a problem or worry with a sympathetic adult.

(From *Think Books* by Steve Bicknell, a Cherwell Learning about Learning booklet)

[handwritten: what if chickens could drive. eggs wanted to race?]

What if? – some starting points for thinking and writing

What if . . . plants started to walk?
you were turned into a frog?
people discovered the secret of eternal life?
the oceans all dried up?
no-one needed to go to sleep?
you were really given three wishes?
there was another Ice Age?
you were allowed to run the school?
the world runs out of oil and petrol?
you won a prize of £1000?
you were given control over TV programmes?
you discover your best friend is a thief?

What do you think would happen and why?

Children can make up their own 'What ifs', creating a situation or problem to explore through discussion and writing.

Further Reading

Bicknell S. *Think Books* (a Cherwell Learning about Learning project)

Wilkinson A.M., Barnsley G., Hanna P. and Swan M. *Assessing Language Development* (Oxford University Press, 1980)

Wilkinson A.M. *Quality of Writing* (Open University Press, 1986)

Schools Curriculum Development Committee, *About Writing* (The SCDC National Writing Project Newsletter)

5 The Heart of Mathematics

'The ability to solve problems is at the heart of mathematics'
(*Mathematics Counts*, the Cockcroft Report, para 249)

Probably the most famous section of the *Cockcroft Report*[1] (published in 1982) is paragraph 243. In it, the report suggests that mathematics teaching at all levels should include opportunities for:

- exposition by the teacher
- discussion between teacher and pupils and between pupils themselves
- appropriate practical work
- consolidation and practice of fundamental skills and routines
- problem solving, including the application of mathematics to everyday situations
- investigational work

The *Cockcroft Report* emphasised the need to apply mathematics realistically and with a practical approach; it stressed the importance of discussion and understanding. The Report has been widely welcomed as a clear and progressive statement of the task of mathematical teaching, but its recommendations are not new. Nearly 20 years ago the Plowden Report recommended that teachers should devise their own schemes of work and teach maths from the basis of children's interests and personal experiences, encouraging them to make their own discoveries about concepts and relationships.

The extracts from the *Cockcroft Report* and *Mathematics 5–16*[2] in this section show the close relationship that exists between problem-solving and investigational work. Mathematicians themselves are not in agreement as to the distinction between problems and investigations.[3] A problem that can be solved mathematically will entail some form of investigation. Likewise, investigations will produce their own problem-solving situations.

What paragraph 243 of the Cockcroft Report does not do is to distinguish between mathematical *activities* and learning *processes*. Solving mathematical problems and investigating puzzles are activities which occur both inside and outside the classroom. They are the raw material to which the processes of teaching and learning apply. Investigation can be thought of as a process which includes discussion and practical work. Problem solving is an activity which provides a context for all the important teaching and learning processes of mathematics – exposition, discussion, practical work, practice of skills and investigations. Leone Burton's article *Problems and puzzles* (page 80) explores further the processes involved in real problem-solving activities.

The Cockcroft Report was about the building of confidence – of children, of teachers and of the public – in the teaching of mathematics. The recent focusing of public attention on standards in education has created pressure for a 'back to the basics' movement, which could lead to a limited view of mathematics and a narrow style of teaching. We need to get across the idea that problem solving is very much part of the 'basics' of mathematics. 'Basic skills' should be seen as the ability to apply techniques to solving problems in real and novel situations, not as tricks to enable children to get the right answers in a work-book.

In her case study *The canoe problem* (page 88) Janet Duffin shows how a problem can be tackled in a variety of ways, by a variety of people (including children, teachers and parents), with positive and unexpected results. It is often easier to understand solutions worked out by others than to discover a solution for oneself (the *Cockcroft Report* para 229). The positive attitudes of teachers can have a profound influence on pupils' approach to mathematics – encouraging such strategies as making up rules, adapting rules, discussing the merits of different approaches, trying different ways of achieving a solution . . . All these can lead to a growth of confidence and a sense of real achievement.

The teaching of mathematics is a demanding task. Most schools choose to use one of the published mathematics schemes to provide structure, continuity and balance. However, it is vital to broaden any given scheme to include the interests and understanding of particular children, and to add the breadth and depth that problem-solving challenges can bring. As Cockcroft points out, one of the difficulties of mathematics teaching is the great variation in attainment rate between children – which may amount to a 'seven years difference' (para 342) in particular topics at a particular age. One way that Marion Bird copes with this varying range of abilities is to introduce a 'starter' to the whole class. She invites the children to work at a given problem for a short time, asking them to jot down any questions which occur to them about what they are doing, then calling upon them to pool their ideas. In her case study *Secret messages* (page 92) Marion Bird describes one such 'starter' and the work which followed.

In the final section there are some suggested starting-points for problem solving and investigation work. In mathematical teaching there are no hard and fast rules or fail-safe methods that will ensure success. The best results are achieved when a teacher is able to present problem-solving ideas in his/her own way. This may involve sharing a personal, real-life problem – how to tile the kitchen, how much material to buy for curtains, which particular brand is the best buy . . . bringing mathematics alive in a way that no textbook or workcard can. It will also involve encouraging children to raise questions and suggest problems themselves and allowing them to develop mathematical ideas in their own way. The aim is to create a new relationship between people and mathematics, one in which mathematics is seen to be a servant rather than a master.

The ability to solve problems . . .

Problem solving

249 The ability to solve problems is at the heart of mathematics. Mathematics is only 'useful' to the extent to which it can be applied to a particular situation and it is the ability to apply mathematics to a variety of situations to which we give the name 'problem solving'. However, the solution of a mathematical problem cannot begin until the problem has been translated into the appropriate mathematical terms. This first and essential step presents very great difficulties to many pupils – a fact which is often too little appreciated. At each stage of the mathematics course the teacher needs to help pupils to understand how to apply the concepts and skills which are being learned and how to make use of them to solve problems. These problems should relate both to the application of mathematics to everyday situations within the pupils' experience, and also to situations which are unfamiliar. For many pupils this will require a great deal of discussion and oral work before even very simple problems can be tackled in written form.

Using mathematics to solve problems

321 All children need experience of applying the mathematics they are learning both to familiar everyday situations and also to the solution of problems which are not exact repetitions of exercises which have already been practised. When young children first come to school, much of their mathematics is 'doing'. They explore the mathematical situations which they encounter – perhaps sorting objects into different categories or fitting shapes together – and come to their own conclusions. At this stage their mathematical thinking may reach a high level of independence. As they grow older this independent thinking needs to continue; it should not give way to a method of learning which is based wholly on the assimilation of received mathematical knowledge and whose test of truth is "this is the way I was told to do it".

322 Mathematical explorations and investigations are of value even when they are not directed specifically to the learning of new concepts. Children should therefore be encouraged, for example, to work out the best way of arranging the seating for the audience at

the school concert or to compare the cost of various packet sizes and brands of food for the classroom pets. The extent to which children are enabled to work in this way will depend a great deal on the teacher's own awareness of the ways in which mathematics can be used in the classroom and in everyday life.

323 The development of general strategies directed towards problem solving and investigations can start during the primary years. Children should therefore be given opportunity to become familiar with the processes which can be used in work of this kind. One of these is to *make a graphical or diagrammatic representation* of the situation which is being investigated; for example, if two dice are being thrown, the scores obtained can be recorded graphically. There may be a *pattern in the results* which are being obtained which can lead to the *making of a conjecture* to forecast later results; for example, 2 points on a circle can be joined by one line, 3 points can be joined in pairs by 3 lines, 4 points by 6 lines and so on. Efforts can then be made to *discover whether, and explain why, the conjecture is or is not correct.* It is sometimes appropriate to *set up an experiment,* for example to discover the length of a seconds pendulum, or to employ the strategy of *looking at a simpler related problem*; an example of this latter strategy is that the number of squares (of any size) on a full-sized chessboard may be too many to count, but a 2×2 and a 3×3 board are more manageable, and a pattern begins to emerge. It is necessary to *develop persistence in exploring a problem,* for example the number of different shapes which can be made from a given number of squares of the same size, and the ability to *record the possibilities* which have been tried. Finally, it is important to develop the *ability to work with others* in the discussion of possible approaches and to *be able to communicate progress* which has been made by means of words, diagrams and symbols.

324 Not a great deal is yet known about the ways in which these processes develop nor are suitable materials for teachers readily available. There is need for more study of children's spontaneous problem-solving activities and of the extent to which strategies and processes for problem solving can be taught.

Present knowledge suggests that, if children are not enabled to tackle problems which are at the right level for them to achieve success as the result of concentrated effort, their problem-solving abilities do not develop satisfactorily.

From *Mathematics Counts* Report of the Cockcroft Committee (HMSO, 1982) p. 73, 94–5.

Problem solving

4.11 There are often unpleasant connotations in the general usage of the word 'problem' and, to some extent, this can carry over into mathematics lessons. But if problem solving is an essential part of mathematical activity throughout the years 5 to 16 and pupils acquire a confidence in their own abilities through tackling tasks appropriate to them, some of the apprehension often expressed by many pupils should diminish. In fact, many children entering school can already solve simple problems – having five sweets and eating three they can recognise that they have two left, although, understandably, few can do the corresponding manipulation (5 – 3). There are various sources of suitable problems: textbooks, reference books, professional journals, games and puzzles, other subjects in the curriculum, adult life and employment. But a classroom where a range of activities is taking place and in which pupils express interests and ask questions can also provide on-the-spot problems. Teachers need to exploit these situations because there is greater motivation to solve problems which have been posed by the pupils themselves. Problems should be chosen with a range of possible outcomes: some problems have a unique solution; some have no solution; others would have a solution if more information were available; many will have several solutions and the merit of each may need to be assessed. The process of starting with a real problem, abstracting and solving a corresponding mathematical problem and then checking its solutions in the practical situation is often called mathematical modelling. It is worth stressing to pupils that, in real life, mathematical solutions to problems have often to be judged by criteria of a non-mathematical nature, some of which may be political, moral or social. For example, the most direct route for a proposed new stretch of motorway might be unacceptable as it would cut across a heavily built-up area.

Problem solving and investigational work will often involve some practical element.

For example, most pupils would find it easier to obtain the number of cubes in this diagram (Figure 5.1) by doing it practically rather than performing a calculation on paper.

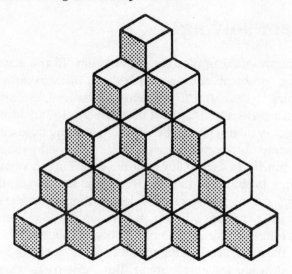

Figure 5.1

Investigative work

4.12 The various approaches considered in this chapter need not be isolated from each other but may all be part of the same activity. In particular, clear distinctions do not exist between problem solving and investigative work. Nevertheless in broad terms it is useful to think of problem solving as being a convergent activity where the pupils have to reach a solution to a defined problem, whereas investigative work should be seen as a more divergent activity. In an investigative approach pupils are encouraged to think of alternative strategies, to consider what would happen if a particular line of action were pursued, or to see whether certain changes would make any difference to the outcome. In fact, it might be through an investigative approach to a problem that a solution emerged; for example, if the problem is to find the most economical way to package bars of chocolate of a certain shape it would be necessary to investigate various possibilities before coming to a decision.

4.13 Of course, practical work, problem solving and investigative activities are time consuming and some schools will be concerned that their introduction will result in unsatisfactory coverage of the content of the mathematics curriculum. A useful analysis might be made by means of a grid such as Figure 5.2 in which these approaches are directly related to content. This highlights at least two features:

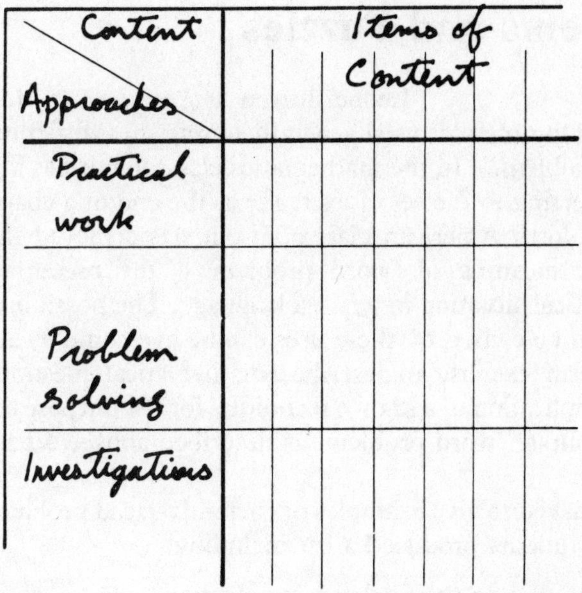

Content Approaches	Items of Content				
Practical work					
Problem solving					
Investigations					

Figure 5.2

by reading across the grid the strength of the impact of particular approaches and by reading down the grid the depth of coverage of particular items of content are revealed. As a result the teachers will see more clearly where the strengths and weaknesses are and what needs to be done to ensure breadth and balance in terms of both content and classroom approaches.

(From *Mathematics from 5 to 16* (HMSO, 1985) para 249)

Problems and Puzzles

Leone Burton *with the help of Mark Burton*

The word 'problem' is used generally to refer to a difficulty – 'What is your problem?'. In the mathematics classroom it has a particular usage referring to the set of exercises at the end of a chapter in the text. In North American classrooms, it has achieved the further particular meaning of 'word problem' – the presentation of a mathematical situation in written language. The possible confusion which can be caused by these uses can be overcome by agreeing to use the term 'exercise' to describe a mathematical question demanding the application of a known technique for the purpose of practice, and the phrase 'word problem' as described above. What, then, is a problem?

When asked to give examples of currently-faced problems, a class of adult students produced a list including:

● how to vote in the forthcoming election
● what to serve at a dinner party
● how to pass the forthcoming examination

Dealing with such problems, which can range from the trivial to the life-threatening, demands such procedures as:

● collecting, classifying, analysing and using information
● searching for relationships
● making and testing hypotheses
● discriminating between objective and subjective information (between needs and wants)

For example, the problem of how to vote could be dealt with by a careful sifting of party manifestos compared with whatever evidence is available of past records; it could be dealt with by a recognition of a subjective preference, preferring the look of candidate X to candidate Y; a value stand could be taken and compared to the value stand of each candidate; or some combination of all of these could be used.

Thinking about how such problems are overcome leads to the identification of a number of factors:

1   A problem is frequently a problem because it is ill-defined. Once the nature of the problem is identified, the method or methods for dealing with it are often clear.

2 Problems rarely have a single solution, indeed problems rarely have a final solution in that they are then "wrapped up" and concluded. More usually problems are open-search in the sense that the method chosen to deal with them is "best fit" rather than exact and relies upon an amalgam of objective and subjective information or even chance. What is then obtained is not a "solution" but a personal resolution of the problem, which the individual judges not as right or wrong but as adequate.

3 Each problem resolution opens up another field of problems.

4 Problems belong to people, they are real and involving to the individual. They present a challenge which the individual acknowledges.

Now consider a puzzle, perhaps a maze, or a crossword, or something like the following:

Use three continuous lines to join up four dots in the shape of a square.

Try it.

If the solution to that puzzle is obvious, try this one:

Replace the letters by numbers to make

```
 HOCUS
+POCUS
PRESTO
```

Or, perhaps:

Work out how many squares there are on an 8×8 chessboard.

Whether or not progress can be made with the chosen puzzle, notice some features of the activity.

1 The puzzle was given to you – it was not 'your own'. In order to do it, you must not reject it but must make it your own. As a consequence, your attitudes to mathematical puzzles and the climate within which the puzzle is received are both relevant to acceptance.

Motivation – creative curiosity

2 The puzzle has a solution which is known to the setter and unknown to the doer. Your problem then is to ease out that solution to the puzzle from somewhere.

Search behaviour

3   The puzzle and its solution are in a known context and the rules for exploring it are established. Otherwise, you cannot even begin. Identifying the *type* of puzzle, or the type of appropriate procedure then becomes a first move. For example, if you were offered a computer puzzle and you knew nothing of computers you would reject the puzzle on the rational grounds that the type of puzzle was such that the context was unknown to you.

Paradigm defined

4   Puzzles often have a 'trick' in them and once you have seen the nature of that trick you are well on the way to solving them. For example, the trick in the puzzle asking how many squares on a chessboard is that you usually think of a chessboard as being made up of unit squares. Now, if a hint is given by suggesting that there are squares of other sizes on a chessboard, can you go ahead and solve this puzzle?

Tricks and hints

Examine some of these differences between problems and puzzles.

Problems	*Puzzles*
Real and involving	Artificial and given
Open search resolutions	Single solutions
Ill-defined and often unconnected to known paradigms.	Well-defined and related to a known paradigm.
Extend indefinitely, either in the range of possible methods of attack or in their development into new areas of investigation	Conclude with the satisfactory solution (answer)

There is one major difference which has not been discussed. Problems are usually serious and demanding on a cognitive level. The satisfactory resolution of a problem frequently provokes new learning or a new rearrangement of old learning in the problem solver. Dealing with problems involves creating a learning environment and the energy generated and consumed ensures that the learning is retained. This would suggest that becoming more efficient at coping with problems would give positive pay-off in terms of life style. Further, the link between problem solving and learning suggests that this experience can valuably be gained in the classroom.

Puzzles, on the other hand, are diversionary and, as long as they do not create too much tension and frustration, they are 'fun'. There is not necessarily any new learning required in their solution – a shift in perception is frequently all that is necessary – and they do not have application or relevance to the world of the puzzler.

Puzzles and problems in the learning and teaching of mathematics

Many educationists who write in the fields of learning and teaching propose problem solving as the ultimate aim in mathematics. If current curricula in mathematics and most frequently observed classroom practice are considered, problem activities in the sense in which they have been discussed are not likely to feature. Much more consistent with general practice is the set of criteria listed under puzzles.

Artificial and given: much of the mathematics which pupils are required to perform falls into this category *from their point of view*. This not only results in poor motivation towards learning but also in a distorted experience of mathematics as being disconnected, unrelated to aspects of their lives which they value, irrelevant despite constant exhortations about utility.

Single solutions: the 'right' answer phenomenon which itself is related to the 'tick' phenomenon, that is, creating conditions where getting ticks is the major motivator.

Well-defined and related to a known paradigm: mathematics as presented in texts is broken down into small and discrete units which are taught and learned in context. Examinations are expected to replicate these conditions and the pupils learn to recognize the context in which they are being asked to work so that they can then apply the appropriate algorithms. Indeed, questions often use the format:

1 prove the following theorem (by memorising?);
2 solve the related "problem" (by application).

Conclude with the satisfactory solution: this is part of the closed nature of the learning. Pupils' motivation is then directed to finishing and questions of elegance of solution, communication of experience, application of learning or extension of enquiring become irrelevant. Thus is generated, by the tricks and hints department, a view of mathematics as being somewhat arbitrary and full of trickery designed to catch out the unwary. This generates a style of learning which is dependent upon filling gaps in understanding by appealing for hints.

Are problems in the classroom desirable and possible?

Mathematicians view their subject as a searching/finding/proving/ searching one. Each journey around the search/find/prove track results in a fragment of mathematical knowledge being established and a new set of tracks being revealed. So mathematics is both a body of established, recognised content and a process by which exploration and establishing takes place.

> There is mathematics to know
> and mathematics to do.

To be involved in mathematics, at whatever level, requires both content and process, otherwise the subject is being experienced in an unbalanced way.

The very procedures which are part of the search behaviour required to pursue mathematics are those which are necessary to deal with problems in general. Earlier, four were listed:

- collecting, classifying, analysing and using information
- searching for relationships
- making and testing hypotheses
- discriminating between objective and subjective information.

To these could be added:

- using particular examples to give a 'feel' for the problem (specialising)
- working systematically
- choosing a method by which to communicate with others the results of the search
- using verification techniques to 'test' out the results
- deriving a statement about the perceived pattern of results (generalising)

These are some of the procedures which are necessary to deal with problems and which are specifically mathematical as well. If experience of them could be made available to pupils in the classroom it would appear to be most desirable from a mathematical and a general standpoint.

To make such experience possible requires a shift from a content dominated view of mathematics to a content/process view. The purpose of a process lesson in mathematics is to emphasise for pupils the legitimate experience of problem solving procedures while simultaneously challenging them to concentrate upon the learning of new mathematical content. The mathematical content is thus subordinated to the mathematical processes. This inverts 'normal' classroom procedure, which tends to legitimate facts and algorithms in mathematics and negate the meaningfulness of the experience of deriving mathematics. Attention can thus be focused on the problem solving process and its constituent procedures. Pupils can begin to develop problem solving awareness at the level of methodology, and also at the personal level as they confront their own feelings of competence and incompetence. They can use techniques which are helpful in overcoming the rigidities induced by negative feelings.

Once the shift from content to process has taken place, the fact that puzzles are enjoyable and that many of the problem solving procedures can be experienced through the medium of a puzzle can be used in the classroom if:

1 out of the puzzle arises a problem – out of context, open to definition and requiring more than just a perceptual shift;
2 there is open house on methods of tackling and on results;
3 pupils are expected to generate new questions where this is feasible;
4 pupils are asked to communicate their work to tell others what they have done;
5 the focus of attention of both teacher and pupils is on search behaviour.

Example
A spatial puzzle which can meet the above criteria is:

> *A milk crate holds 24 bottles in a rectangular array, four rows and six columns. Can you put 18 bottles of milk in the crate so that each row and each column of the crate has an even number of bottles in it?*

This is a puzzle as long as the requirement is to find one arrangement of bottles satisfying the constraints. One pupil turned it into a problem by asking the question 'Is that arrangement unique?' and, if not, 'How many possible arrangements can be found?'. Further, 'Can these arrangements be grouped in any way to say that some are the same as others?'. Finally, a game was invented using all the previous work.

The report below was the result of an extended piece of work done by two children, Mark and Nohoko, in a classroom offering time for the children to spend on problem solving as one aspect of their mathematical experience. The classroom is organized in such a way as to provide a problem corner, in which information relating to problem solving is displayed. A problem a week is offered but the previous weeks' problems are not withdrawn so that, at any one time, groups of children can be working on extensions of previous problems, or choosing to work on the current week's problem. The most striking feature of the work of the children is the encouragement given to them to extend their work by asking questions which acknowledge change and interpretation. For example, in the work shown below, at one stage, the teacher had a discussion with the two children on symmetrical arrangements. She wished to exclude arrangements which could be obtained by a symmetry. At that stage, the two children did not wish to exclude such arrangements. They consequently sorted their arrangements labelling the group in which no symmetries were to be found as 'Miss Osborne's types' (the teacher) and the remaining group of arrangements resulting from a symmetry as their additional arrangements. In the report as presented here, they themselves have excluded the symmetrical arrangements because of the logic of their own reasoning. The teacher gave the children the space and time to arrive at that position themselves.

Puzzles and problem

The thesis being advanced is that puzzle behaviour by teacher and pupils is not productive. However, the content of the puzzles does not have to be jettisoned. If the teacher is aware of the puzzle/problem distinction and its rationale, the emphasis will be changed from seeking a right answer to open search behaviour, from single solution to variation, comparison and evaluation of methods and resolutions, from meeting external requirements to becoming aware of one's own and consequently of others (different) thinking processes. Out of this environment springs motivation to learn mathematics. The key to making such a shift lies in the questions and expectations of teachers and pupils – the desire and interest to explore and understand. Both teaching and learning then become problem solving activities.

From *For the Learning of Mathematics 1*, 2 (November 1980) FLM Publishing Association, Montreal, Quebec, Canada

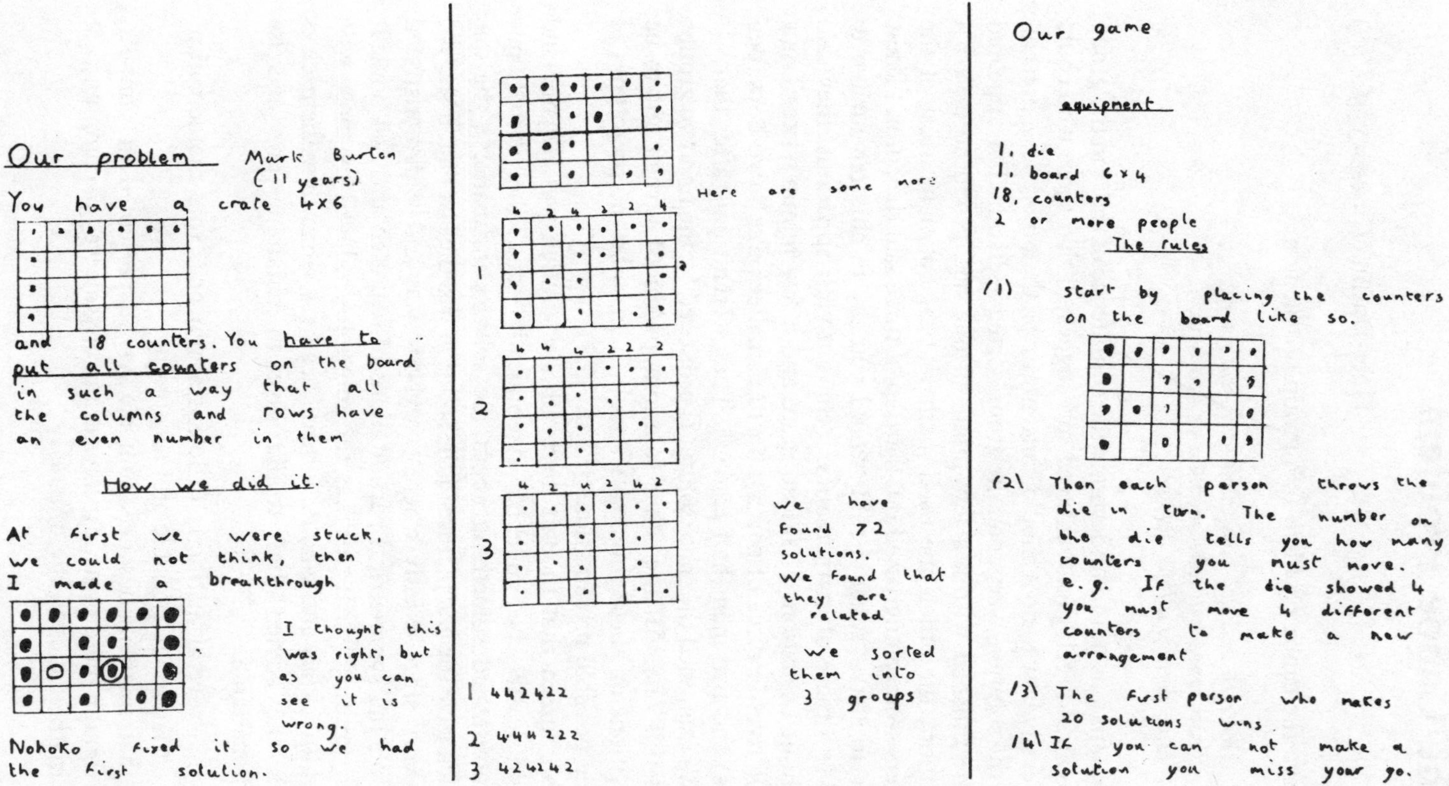

Our game

equipment
1. die
1. board 6 x 4
18. counters
2 or more people
      The rules

(1) Start by placing the counters on the board like so.

(2) Then each person throws the die in turn. The number on the die tells you how many counters you must move. e.g. If the die showed 4 you must move 4 different counters to make a new arrangement

(3) The first person who makes 20 solutions wins.

(4) If you can not make a solution you miss your go.

Here are some more

1

2

3

1 442422
2 444222
3 424142

we have found 72 solutions. We found that they are related

we sorted them into 3 groups

Our problem   Mark Burton (11 years)
crate 4 x 6

You have a and 18 counters. You have to put all counters on the board in such a way that all the columns and rows have an even number in them

How we did it.

At first we were stuck, we could not think, then I made a breakthrough

I thought this was right, but as you can see it is wrong.

Nohoko fixed it so we had the first solution.

Figure 5.3

The Canoe Problem

Janet Duffin (*University of Hull*)

I gave the canoe problem to a group of teachers

> *Two men and two boys want to cross a river.*
> *Their canoe will take one man or two boys.*
> *How do they all get across?*

I was anxious not to undermine the confidence of those in the group who already felt disadvantaged so I suggested that those who could see easily how to do it should concentrate on their method of presenting the solution. Very soon the group sorted itself out. Two appeared to be finished within a few minutes; one had produced a verbal solution, the other one used mathematical notation. Most of the others seemed engrossed but a group of three said they didn't know how to start. 'What' I said 'would you say to children unable to tackle a piece of mathematics?' 'Get out your apparatus' they said without hesitation. I said no more and a few minutes later I saw their river (a piece of paper), boat (a smaller piece), two boys (pen tops) and two men (half pencils). They weren't long after that.

We examined the three solutions produced by the first two groups and this one. All the other solutions produced turned out to be variations on these three so we took them to be the prototypes of three possible presentations (Figure 5.4).

All agreed that though the symbolic solution was elegant (and could easily be checked algebraically) and the verbal one demonstrated something about the solver's inclinations, the one which gave the *best* picture of the solution was the last one; it showed at every stage exactly where everybody was and it demonstrated interesting symmetrical permutations of two men and two boys. It was significant that this was the solution produced by those who could not start and who only made headway when they themselves took the advice they would give to children. The exercise demonstrated:

1   that several distinctly different approaches to a mathematical situation are possible and acceptable;
2   that mathematics need not always be presented in symbols, though these provide a concise and elegant way to communicate mathematics to the initiated;

verbal	symbols	pictorial
two boys across	+2b	
one boy back	−1b	
one man across	+1m	
one boy back	−1b	
two boys across	+2b	
one boy back	−1b	
one man across	+1m	
one boy back	−1b	
two boys across	+2b	

△ boy   ○ man

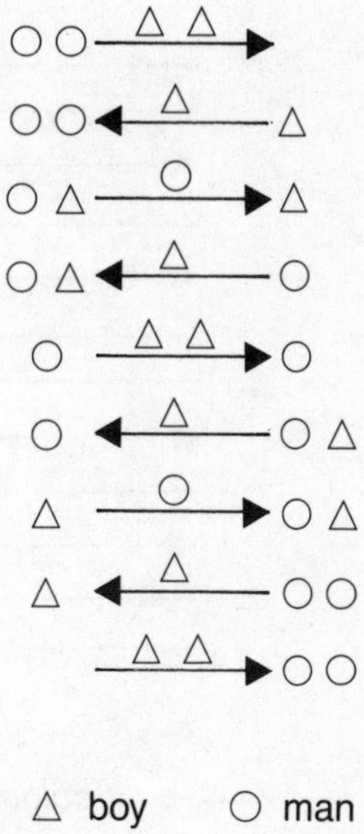

Figure 5.4

3 that the use of equipment does not cease to be a necessary part of the classroom after the primary years;
4 that those seen as 'less able' may sometimes produce a more informative solution than high-fliers.

I have continued to give this problem to teachers, children, parents and students on initial teacher training and I always find that something new comes from each group of people I work with. This leads me to add another important aspect of problem solving to the above list:

5 that there is room for endless variation; we should never assume that all is known about a problem.

Children were the first to introduce colour into a solution. What colour does is to highlight the important fact that once a man has gone across it is wasteful to bring him back so he must never go across if there is no boy there to return with the boat. The first child to produce this solution missed that fact and so the proposed strategy was less economical than was possible although it was not 'wrong' (Figure 5.5).

colour solution   child's colour solution

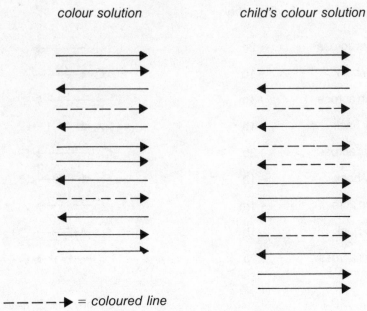

— — — — ➔ = *coloured line*

Figure 5.5

At a later date when I gave this problem to a group of parents one confessed to having difficulty. She said:

'I've got   2 boys across
            1 boy back
            1 man across
            1 boy back   but I don't know what to do next.'

'You have to start again' said another of the parents. The penny dropped and the problem was quickly resolved.

In the ensuing discussion the parents realised that the four lines above constitute a unit which has to be repeated. Someone then pointed out the connection with programming a computer. (We had been looking at some simple *Logo* graphics the previous week.)

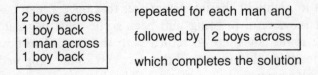

2 boys across	repeated for each man and
1 boy back	
1 man across	followed by 2 boys across
1 boy back	which completes the solution

Figure 5.6

'You can handle any number of men you like as long as you have the two boys' they said, showing an intuitive grasp of the concept and power of a 'loop' and repetition. This observation was interesting, because it showed the way that problem solving can encourage discussion. More importantly it demonstrated how, once an inquiring mind is beginning to emerge, associations and inferences begin to be available to people who formerly would have felt themselves to be totally inept mathematically.

Just before Christmas I had a letter from one of my former students who had been trying this problem in his classroom. They arrived at a symbolic solution (Figure 5.7).

$$C - \text{child} \quad A - \text{adult}$$
$$+2C$$
$$-1C$$
$$+1A$$
$$-1C$$
$$+2C$$

Figure 5.7

Suddenly another child (not particularly bright, according to my student) said 'It's a palindrome'. That is interesting because it shows another aspect that can be added to the original list.

6   that problem solving can help children relate mathematics to other subjects.

Perhaps it is necessary to emphasise that most of these points emerged in the subsequent discussion of the problem. So the final point is

7   that discussion is crucial to mathematical development.

Didn't Cockcroft say that, or something like it?

Secret messages

Marion Bird (*West Sussex Institute of Higher Education*)
When a group of my class of eight- and nine-year-olds came in from break, they were intrigued to find the following written on a piece of paper in the middle of their arrangement of tables:

1) DV   SZEV   YVVM   YZXP   ZY   HXSLLO
   ULI   MVZIOB   GSIVV   DVVPH.
2) PVS   TDIPPM   IBT   POMZ   CFFO   PQFO
   GPS   UXP   ZFBST.
3) WOMCM   BCM   WOSCWA   GOSMYCMZ   SZ
   WOM   GHBPP.

Several said that these must be 'secret messages' and immediately set about trying to decode them. Soon the whole group was involved. Figure 5.8 is Colin's account of how the code could be unravelled:

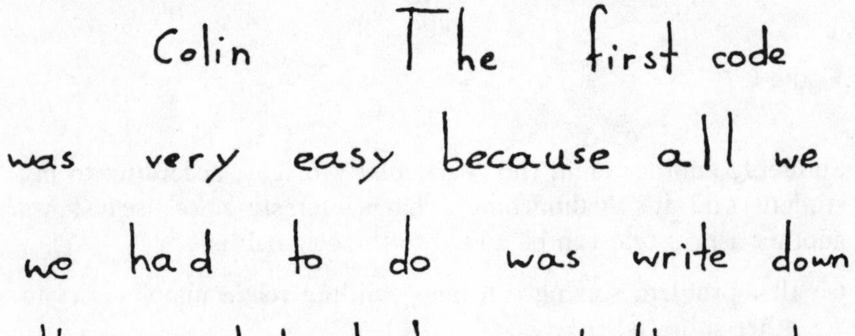

Colin   The first code
was very easy because all we
we had to do was write down
the alphabet and then write
down the alphabet back to
front like this.

A b c d e f g h i j k l m n o p
Z Y X W V U T S R Q P O N M L K
Q r s t u v w x y z
J I H G F E D C B A.

Figure 5.8

Several children tried to sort out the next message in the same way, but they quickly realised that the same method would not do. By the time a few more minutes had passed, however, Kay had worked out what was needed. Part of the continuation of Colin's record is shown in Figure 5.9.

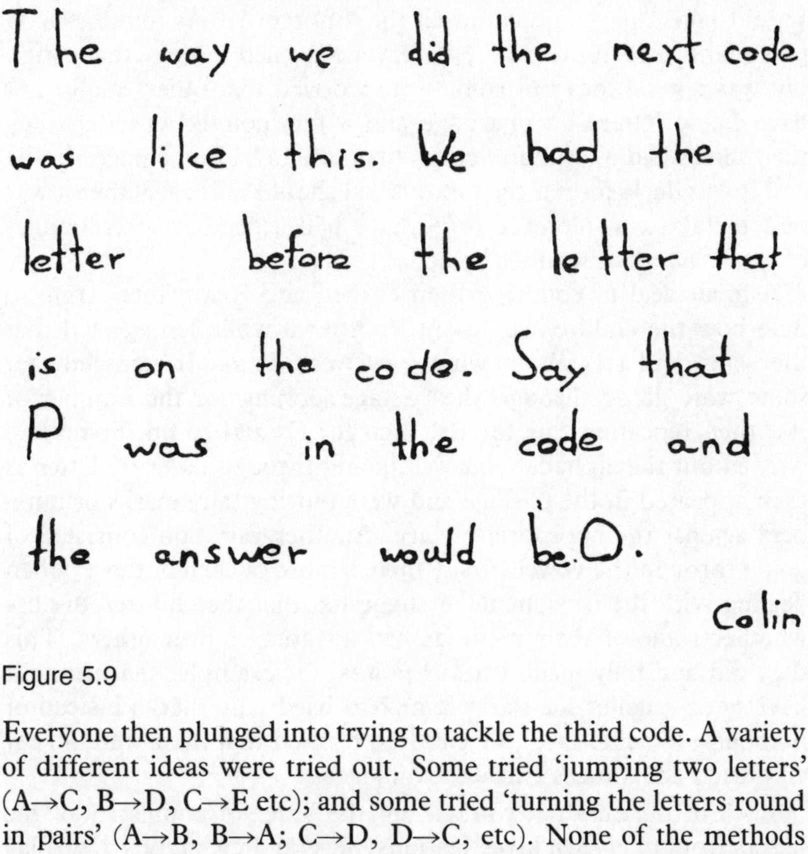

The way we did the next code

was like this. We had the

letter before the letter that

is on the code. Say that

P was in the code and

the answer would be O.

Colin

Figure 5.9

Everyone then plunged into trying to tackle the third code. A variety of different ideas were tried out. Some tried 'jumping two letters' (A→C, B→D, C→E etc); and some tried 'turning the letters round in pairs' (A→B, B→A; C→D, D→C, etc). None of the methods worked. I tentatively suggested that there might not be a pattern in the way the letters had been assigned. Lee said that he thought that it could not be worked out, then, to which Barry replied 'we needn't give up that easily!'.

I asked if it were possible to try approaching the problem from another angle. I thought the children might suggest looking to see if substituting common words like 'the' or 'and' would help at all, but Shaun immediately said that he thought some *letters* were more common than others and that some, like Z and X, were hardly used at all. He thought that we could find out 'more about that' and use it to help us. I asked how we could find out which letters seemed to be used more than others, to which Geraldine said 'we could look in our reading books'.

I invited the group to take out their reading books. Several started calling out letters which they thought were the most popular, but they disagreed with one another and some changed their minds when they looked again. Then Natalie suggested that everyone should take a page and count all the different letters to see exactly how many of each there were. Everyone seemed to agree that counting was a good idea but some were worried that others might not have many letters on one page and a few pointed out that they themselves had a lot more letters than others had on a page. In the end it was decided that each individual should judge whether it was best to take a whole page or perhaps half a page or several pages of his or her own reading book.

A great deal of counting then ensued and it was interesting to note how the children set about it. After a while I suggested that they stop and talk about what they were doing. It emerged that some were going through the passage looking for the number of As, then repeating this for Bs, then for Cs and so on. Some had written out the alphabet and were going through letter by letter as each appeared in the passage and were putting tally marks or numbers against the appropriate place. Another variation consisted of going through the vowels first ('there's more of each of those') then dealing with the consonants. I suggested that the children discuss whether some of their methods had advantages over others. This they did and they made various points, for example, that it might have been quicker for Barry if he had used tally marks instead of numbers. In some cases the children realised that there were no cut and dried advantages and disadvantages.

Each of the children worked out the order of popularity of the letters from their own investigations. Several drew graphs to display the results. Interestingly, some of the children were surprised that the results differed from person to person. Others said that it was 'obvious' that they would differ. By way of explanation, Joanna said that if somebody had a book about a queen then he or she would have lots of qs, whereas other people might not have so many.

I asked how we could use all these apparently different findings to try to decode the message. Peter said that we could use the results of the person who had the most letters, then Shaun suggested putting everyone's results together. The latter idea was met with much enthusiasm by the rest and they wanted to set about it immediately.

I asked how they might collect all the numbers. They settled on drawing out a large grid with the letters of the alphabet along the vertical axis and their initials along the horizontal. Each member of the group then put his or her score for each letter in the appropriate place.

Before long, everyone seemed convinced that E would win overall. Several became interested in which letter would be the second most popular. This resulted in a great deal of reasoning and arguing. The children shared out the task of using calculators to work out the letter totals. Then the group set about putting these in order, starting with the most popular. Natalie put the letters from the original third message in order of frequency too. This gave

M,   C, O, W,   S,   B, G, H, P, Z,   A, Y

Several children then started to match up this list of letters with what they called the joint 'popularity of letters' list, giving:

$$M \rightarrow E$$

$$\left.\begin{array}{c} C \\ \text{or } O \\ \text{or } W \end{array}\right\} \rightarrow \begin{array}{c} O \\ \text{or } A \\ \text{or } T \end{array}$$

$$S \rightarrow R$$

$$B \rightarrow L \text{ or}$$
$$G \rightarrow D \text{ or}$$
$$H \rightarrow H \text{ or}$$
$$P \rightarrow W \text{ or}$$
$$Z \rightarrow G$$

$$A \rightarrow C$$

$$Y \rightarrow V$$

Some children were rather annoyed that the two bunches of letters did not provide 'answers' straight away. What they did not then realise was that the M→E, S→R, A→C, and Y→V pairings could not be relied upon either. Several started to substitute the appropriate letters from these pairings in the message, giving:

```
WOMCM    BCM    WOSCWA    GOSHYCMZ    SZ
 E  E     E        R  C      R  V  E    R
WOM    GHBPP.
 E
```

They became supicious that something was wrong when they realised that there was no two-letter word beginning with R. Several then said that they thought it was not possible to match the letters up exactly. I talked with them about how their 'letter popularity' findings might not give them exact answers but could perhaps be used to give them some idea of which letters were more appropriate than others as substitutes for particular letters in the message.

Looking back at the letters inserted under the message, Shaun said he thought the E might be right because the second word or the last but one word could be THE. He suggested that they rubbed out all the other letters they had put in (R, C, V), but left E and tried T for B and H for C to make BCM become THE. However, this meant that the first word would end with EHE which seemed unlikely. So Shaun suggested still leaving the Es but rubbing out the rest again and substituting T for W and H for O to make WOM become THE. This gave:

```
WOMCM    BCM    WOSCWA    GOSHYCMZ    SZ
THE E      E      TH T        H   E
WOM    GHBPP.
THE
```

That looked much more promising! Natalie suggested that the first word could be THERE or THESE. When those were both tried out, the use of the R looked most fruitful, because the second word could then be ARE. Substituting R for C and A for B throughout gave:

```
WOMCM    BCM    WOSCWA    GOSHYCMZ    SZ
THERE    ARE    TH RT        H   RE
WOM GHBPP.
THE   A
```

Lee suggested that SZ could be ON or IN as S and Z had been used several times and I, N and O were high up the list in the popularity chart. Trying out O for S meant that WOSCWA became THORT, which did not make sense, but I for S seemed fine because, as Martin shrieked out, the third word could be THIRTY. Then Geraldine guessed the message: 'THERE ARE THIRTY CHIL-

DREN IN THE CLASS'. We checked that this did not lead to any occurrences of the same letters from the encoded message ending up at different letters in the decoded one, which it did not. There were squeals of delight that the message had been unravelled!

I asked the children to think back over how they had used the letter popularity chart they had made. They decided that they had not used it much at all but that it could be a lot more helpful if they had longer messages to decode or if there were few words like 'the' or 'there' to help them. I asked them if they thought that a longer message would have all its letters in exactly the same order of popularity as in their chart and they agreed that it probably would not but that their chart should be able to give them 'clues'. They also seemed to realise that if more people had participated in counting the frequency of letters in passages from the reading books, their chart might have ended up rather differently. However, it seemed to be generally felt that these letters at the top were unlikely to move down the chart very much, nor the ones at the bottom to move up very much.

Extensions to the work

1   Some children made up other messages and coded them, then gave them to other members of the group who tried to decode them, this time using a combination of knowledge of popular words, the group's popularity of letters chart and a great deal of reasoning!

2   Geraldine wanted to find out the grand total of all the totals for the letters in the chart. This idea appealed to the rest of the group too.

3   Some of the children had previously been finding out about the Morse Code. I suggested that they now looked to see if there were any connections between the symbols assigned to the letters and the popularity of the letters. They soon realised that popular letters such as E had much shorter symbols associated with them than rarely-used letters such as Z.

I suggested that they might make up their own version of the code, assigning symbols to each letter in their order of popularity list so that the further down the list they went, the longer the symbol. They decided that they would say that a dot takes ½ second and a dash 1 second to send and set about finding all the possible combinations of dots and dashes for given lengths of time. This led to questions such as 'Can I be certain I have found all the combinations?'

For fun, some of the children tried out assigning the list of symbols in the opposite order so that the shorter the symbol, the less popular the letter. They then made up messages and compared the lengths of time it would take to send them in the two versions of their codes.

```
                                                    Barry
   A. B. C.  D. E. F. G. H. I. J. K  L  M N O  P q  R  S  T u v w x y
Z  1  1  1   4  1  4 70 1  8  1 1 0  4  2 0  5  9  2 4 0  2 0 1
0  2  1  1   2  2  1 1 10 1  1 1 1   1  1 1  0  1  1 1 1  6  5 0 1
0  3  2  2   3  2  1 10 1  1 1 1     1  1              1    1  1
   4  3  3   4  2  2     2  2  2     2  2 2  2  2  2  2    2  2
   5  4  4   5  3  3     3  3  3     3  3    3  3  3  3    3  3
   6        6  4  4     4  4  4     4  4    4  4  4  4    4
   7        8  5  5     5  5  5     5  5    5  5         5
   8        9  6  6     6  6  6     6  6    6
   9       10  7  7     7  7  7        7    7
  10·      11     8     8  8  8           8
  11       12              9           9
  12       13             10
           14
           15
           16
           17   E. A. N. S. L.I. W.R.D  U.O.G.C.  F.H.P.Y  B M Z J Q X V
```

Geraldine

Our Argument

Barry and I had an argument about which letter was the second most popular. Barry thought that it would be A because there were seven of them near the top of list but there were three T's all nearer the top than the seven A's, but to solve the argument we decided to add them all up on a calculator and in the end it happened to be that neither of them were second most popular but O was, A was next and T was next. A very popular letter was first, that was E.

Some starting points for problem solving and investigation

Number

Number patterns How many ways can you arrange five dots? What numbers of dots make triangles? Into what patterns could you rearrange the desks in your class? What are the good and bad points of each arrangement?

Number stories If *x* is the answer what is the question? Let *x* be a chosen number. What problems can you pose with *x* as an answer?

✶ *Number sequences* eg 1,3,5,7,9 (Find the missing numbers) Make up your own number sequence puzzle.

Number mazes Fill a grid of squares with numbers. What puzzles, problems, questions, can you create from it eg find the highest/lowest number moving vertically or horizontally through the maze, adding the numbers, in a given number of moves.

✶ *Splitting numbers* Take a stick of cubes eg 10. How many ways can you split it? What patterns do you find? What questions can you pose?

Estimating large numbers Can you estimate the number of grains in a pile of rice? Can you estimate the number of words in a page? Can you think of any ways of counting that would give a more accurate answer?

Finding fractions How many ways can you shade a shape to show a given fraction eg ½ of a 2×4 rectangle? How would you find a fraction of a given shape eg ¼ of a leaf?

Investigating probability What is the probability of tossing heads or tails? Estimate and check the results of a given number of throws. What are the possibilities with two coins? Investigate dice. What questions could you ask yourself?

Number series Starting with 3, add together the digits of the previous two numbers (the Fibonacci series). When does the series start repeating itself? Try adding the digits of the multiplication tables. What number series can you find?

Create your own numerals Design your own numerals (using any base) and make up some number problems.

Measurement

Measure an object Take any shape or object. What mathematical questions could you ask about it?

Routes Find on a road map the shortest route between two marked places. What other problems could you pose with your map?

How heavy Sort out some objects in order of heaviness. Ask some questions about the weight of the objects. Estimate heaviness by looking and feeling, then check weights.

Product analysis Given two or more packs of the same kind of product, which is the best value for money? What other questions could you ask?

Just a minute How could you estimate the passing of a minute if you had no clock? Test the accuracy of solutions.

A time piece Describe how you could make an instrument that could measure the passing of time.

Area and perimeter Make shapes with the largest/smallest perimeters using shapes of a given area.

Measuring a wavy line How could you measure a wavy line, eg the outline of a head, using only a ruler and coin? (Thread is easier!)

Measuring around Take a cylinder eg empty cotton reel, and a long piece of thread. How many times can the thread be wound round the cylinder? Estimate first.

Up and down A frog fell into a well 10 metres deep. Each metre he crawls up, he slips down half a metre. How long does it take the frog to get out of the well if he climbs one metre an hour? (Make up your own frog problem/mathematical story).

Shape

Tesselations Find out what shapes fit together to make patterns. What do these patterns suggest to you? To what uses could they be put? Create your own tesselating shapes.

Symmetry Which numbers and letters are symmetrical? Create your own symmetrical design eg flag, snowflake. . .

Triangles How many triangles can be made on a 3×3 pinboard?

Squares Draw a pattern on a paper square, transfer it to card and cut out the pieces. See if your friend can reassemble the square. Will the shapes make another pattern?

Circles 'Cut the cake'. One straight line drawn across a circle will cut it in two, two lines can divide it into four, three lines into seven.

How many pieces can you get into four straight line 'cuts'? Do you notice a progression?

Nets Can you draw a shape which, if cut out and folded up, will make a box? Use squared paper. How many different shaped nets will fold to make a box?

Co-ordinate shapes Draw an outline shape on graph paper inside co-ordinate lines. Plot co-ordinate points around your picture from your co-ordinate clues.

Dotty puzzles Draw four rows of five dots. Draw as many squares as possible without taking your pencil off the paper, and without retracing or crossing any drawn line. Which strategy produces the best results?

More starting points for mathematical problem solving can be found in Chapter 11: Games for Problem-Solving (p.202) and in the books mentioned in the Bibliography.

Logic

Mathematics is to do with logical outcomes and a child's mathematical experience will include a wide variety of logical puzzles. Children should be given some freedom to choose their own problems, perhaps from a class collection, and to tackle them in their own way – through words, pictures, numbers, manipulation of materials, model-making, movement and drama. Here is an example of a logical puzzle that could be tackled in a variety of ways:

The Hat Problem

There were three prisoners, one of whom was blind. They were offered their freedom if they could succeed in the following game. Their jailer produced three white hats and two red hats and, in the dark, placed a hat on each prisoner. The prisoners were then taken into the light where, except for the blind man, they could see one another. (They could not see the hat on their own head.) The game was for any prisoner to state correctly the colour of the hat he himself was wearing. The jailer asked one of the men who could see if he knew, and the man said 'no'. Then the jailer asked the other man who could also see if he knew, and his answer was 'no'. The blind man at this point correctly stated the colour hat he was wearing, winning the game and freedom for all three.

What colour hat was he wearing, and how did he know?

Summary

The following are some of the effects of problem solving on mathematical learning. It:

- motivates children and generates enthusiasm;
- provides opportunities for creativity;
- builds confidence and independence;
- develops collaborative learning;
- enables children to apply facts and skills already acquired;
- encourages discussion and investigative activity;
- shows mathematics to be useful, meaningful and valuable.

Notes and references

1   *Mathematics Counts* (The Cockcroft Report) (HMSO, 1982)
2   *Mathematics 5–16* (HMSO, 1985)
3   see 'Problems, investigations and confusion' David Wells, in *Mathematics in School*, January 1985

Further reading

Bird M. *Generating Mathematical Activity in the Classroom* (The Mathematics Centre, West Sussex Institute of Higher Education, Bognor Regis, West Sussex PO12 1HR 1983)

Bolt B. *Mathematical Activities* (Cambridge University Press, 1985) *More Mathematical Activities (ibid)*

Burton L. *Thinking Things Through* (Basil Blackwell, 1984)

Brown S. and Walker M. *The Art of Problem Posing* (Franklin Institute Press, 1983)

Charles R. I. *Problem-Solving Experiences in Mathematics* (Addison-Wesley, 1985)

Hollands R. *Lets Solve Problems* (Basil Blackwell, 1986)

Mason J., Burton L. and Stacey K. *Thinking Mathematically* (Addison-Wesley, 1982)

Meyer C. and Sallee T. *Make it Simpler: A Practical Guide to Problem-Solving in Mathematics* (Addison-Wesley)

Whittaker D. *Will Gulliver's Suit Fit? Mathematical Problem Solving with Children* (Cambridge Educational, 1986)

6   The use of computers

'True computer literacy is not just knowing how to make use
of computers and computational ideas. It is knowing when it
is appropriate to do so'.

Seymour Papert '*Mindstorms*' (p155)

What is important about the use of computers in primary education
is not what appears on the screen but what goes on in the child's
mind. The true value lies in the quality of interaction between the
program and the child, between child and child, and between child
and teacher, that computers can inspire. One of the most striking
aspects of the use of computers in the primary classroom is the
amount of discussion that is generated. The quality of children's
talk will differ greatly according to the program being used. Some
programs generate purposeful discussion, enhancing the children's
ability to think clearly, express themselves effectively and come to
achieve joint decision making. The use of computers to stimulate
group and sometimes whole class discussions may prove to be one
of the most important advantages of having computers in primary
schools. In her article '*Thinking Things Out: Solving Problems with
a micro*' (page 105) Anita Straker suggests some programs and ways
of working that will stimulate such discussion.

Even a bad program can have its uses. Recently an infant working
in a group doing a drill-and-practice maths program was overheard
saying 'I don't understand this, let's go and work it out for ourselves.
You can leave it, it won't mind.' Many of us have suffered similar
bouts of 'computer indigestion' – the Menu looks appetising but
the fare turns out to be pretty tasteless. Children are generally more
responsive. They usually enjoy taking time off 'work' to play the
'game' which has been currently loaded, and if the program is brief
enough everyone in a class can have a turn. This is characteristic
of the first stage of computer-use, when the machine is still being
treated as a toy and not as a tool with an integrated role to play in

the primary curriculum. At this stage there are two common com-
plaints:

1 *We've used these programs, can we have some more?*
2 *There are so many programs, how can we select what is best?*

One of the ways forward is to build up a core of content-free
software tools that will encourage open-ended investigation and
problem-solving. Examples of such tools include: a Logo or turtle
graphics package; a word processor; a database (like ANIMAL or
FACTFILE); an adventure game handler/writer; TRAY; a story
writer; a picture generator. All these tools will help to develop the
skills of problem solving, communication and information handling.

At their best, computers should enable you to tackle the problems
that you want to solve in the ways that you want to solve them,
away from the computer. Computers should be there to encourage
independent thought, rather than dependence on a shimmering
screen. One way that this may be achieved is through control technology. In *Problem solving with control technology* (p 113) Carol Wisely
shows how a computer can be used to serve the needs of children
in a problem-solving investigation. She shows how, with the use of
control technology, the computer can be put firmly under the control
and at the service of child and teacher. Control technology is only
just beginning in primary schools; there will be exciting develop-
ments to come, and much need for classroom-based research. Given
the necessary support and the courage to experiment, teachers and
children can become pioneers in this field.

Thinking things out: Solving problems with a micro

Anita Straker

To suggest that problem-solving activities should play an important part in a child's day at school gives the impression that something new is advocated for primary education. Yet as long ago as 1942 William Brownwell offered a number of *Practical suggestions for developing ability in problem solving*[1] which appear as relevant as any which appear today.

Common sense dictates that skill acquisition through repetitive practice is less important than the processes of analysing a situation and devising a means of coping with it. But even where teachers have been committed to the provision of problem-solving activities for children there have been hurdles to overcome. The Cockcroft Committee highlighted these in Paragraph 324:

> Not a great deal is yet known about the ways in which these (problem-solving) processes develop nor are suitable materials for teachers readily available. There is a need for more study of children's spontaneous problem solving activities and of the extent to which strategies and processes for problem solving can be taught.[2]

When the Cockcroft Report was published in 1982 computers were new to the school scene and little mention was made of them. Since then, it has become evident that the school computer can be a powerful medium for exploring problems in all sorts of ways.

A problem exists when either an individual or a group of people wants to achieve something that is not immediately attainable. The problem and its solution will generally have three basic features: some given information which describes the circumstances or the setting for the problem; a sequence of actions or procedures which the problem solver can use to try and reach a solution; and a goal which describes the required outcome.

The process of solving the problem is usually defined with an active verb:

- *Decipher* a passage of coded text;
- *Ascertain* the greatest capacity of an open box made from a rectangle of card by cutting a square out of each corner and folding up the flaps;

- *Detect* the culprit when some goods are stolen from a country house;
- *Identify* a fossil found in the chalk quarry near the school.

In each of these problems the outcome is clear-cut, although the routes taken to arrive at an 'answer' may be very varied. But not all problems have a unique solution. Some may have no solution; some might have a solution if more information were available; some have many possible solutions. In more open-ended investigations children can be encouraged to pursue alternative strategies, to seek evidence to support their conjectures, to compare their different results, and to ask what would happen if, or what would happen if not:

- *Investigate* what happens if you repeatedly apply the rule 'If a number is even divide by two; if it is odd multiply by three and add one';
- *Invent* a dice game that allows a win three times out of four;
- *Design* and then *produce* a repeating wallpaper pattern for a doll's house;
- *Build* a bird table so that you know (without constantly watching) when a bird has landed;
- *Make* an automatic washing machine with spin dryer for doll's clothes;
- *Decide* where to go to buy the best potato crisps;
- *Find out why* several of the shops in the town in 1881 were connected with rope-making;
- *Discover* which factors are important when choosing the strongest conker for a game.

The examples I have listed are very varied, but what they all have in common is that each of them has been tackled by primary school children, and in every case the problem-solving process was aided by making use of the school's computer. Some of these problems would never have been attempted if the micro had not been available; in other cases the investigation would not have been so thorough, because the amount of data involved would have been too cumbersome to manage.

How do teachers make a start when problem solving like this is introduced into the classroom? Cockcroft described a lack of suitable materials, so where can teachers find problems suitable for classroom investigation? Some obvious sources are magazines like *The Problem*

Solver[3], books like *Science, Models and Toys*[4], or TV broadcasts like *Mind Stretchers*, all of which provide good starting points. The software now available for British primary schools includes a variety of programs which contain specific problems. There are puzzles like *Raybox, Colony* or *Mallory;* adventure games like *Merlin's Castle, Little Red Riding Hood*, or *L;* simple simulations like *Bees, Viking England* or *Fletcher's Castle*.

Problem posing is an important adjunct to problem solving. One way to stimulate children to ask questions is to make collections and to think of things to ask about them, to do to them or with them. Menus, maps, travel brochures, advertisements, newspaper headlines and so on, might all suggest a problem to be explored. So might collections of pebbles, fabrics, metals, seeds, woods, or powders. Historical information from parish registers, census records, or old newspaper reports, or present day data like weather statistics, football results, train times, tables of heights and weights, all offer good starting points for questioning. Constructional materials such as card, dowel rod, wheels, string and wire, or Lego and Meccano, can act as another stimulus. These resources need only be coupled with suggestions to build, assemble, plan, produce, create, discover, compare, come to a decision about . . . and an investigation has begun.

If the lines of enquiry come from the children themselves, so much the better. The HMI document *Mathematics 5 to 16* puts this very clearly.

> A classroom where a range of activities is taking place and in which pupils express interests and ask questions can also provide on-the-spot problems. Teachers need to exploit these situations because there is greater motivation to solve problems which have been posed by the pupils themselves.[13]

Problem solving is like cooking: it is something that you learn about and become more skilled in by actually doing. Yet all too often in the past the only experiences children had to draw upon were those involved in completing work-sheets where the key words, the research strategies, and even the resources to be consulted were already identified and suggested to them. 'Use your atlas to find out . . . and then complete the following paragraph.'

With software like a database it has become feasible for children to investigate thoroughly their own questions about anything from the flight of parachutes to opinions about a school record library.

With *Logo* they can explore the world of turtle geometry. If a control package like *Controller* is available they can use the micro to control a windmill with rotating sails, a model of Big Ben, a tiger trap, or any other device which they themselves have decided to design and make.

A wide range of children's problem-posing activities can be supported by general purpose software tools: a database; a graph-drawing package; a word processor; a picture-making program; the programming language *Logo*; a control package. By using these tools to find answers to their own questions children start to develop very real problem-solving skills: learning to identify the problem, to plan a strategy, to check and refine the solution. At the same time they begin to appreciate the importance of questions like:

- What do I want to find out or to do?
- What information or material do I need?
- Where can I get it from?
- How appropriate is it?
- How shall I collect it?
- How shall I organise it?
- How can I use it to answer my questions?
- What results of my investigation should I record?
- How and to whom should I present these?
- How should I use the outcomes? Who else might use them and why?

One of the most interesting conversations I have ever had with third-year juniors was with a group who were engaged in the problem of inventing a monster (as part of a computer activity). The children had reached a point of the program where some information about a monster (in this case, Werewolf) was provided, and they were asked to consider whether or not the monster was real or imaginary. Their first reaction was that Werewolf was real 'because we've seen it on the television'. The planned lesson was abandoned. Instead a long discussion took place about the kind of evidence presented in different TV programmes, with the children for the first time questioning the validity of photographs, the selection of material, and the possible vested interests of television producers or advertisers.

Some teachers might feel reluctant to work in this kind of unforeseen way because it is difficult to anticipate the reactions of the children or the directions which they might wish to follow. The same is true when problem solving is first introduced into the classroom. Teachers may feel that they will not necessarily know what to do if the children get stuck. One of the secrets lies in good planning and organisation. It is often easier for teachers to make plans if they have themselves worked the problem through beforehand. They can then consider the possible routes the children might take, assess which materials or information might be needed and which skills will be involved, and plan accordingly. I do not, of course, intend to suggest that the children should be expected to come up with the teacher's solution. Thinking through a problem in advance is simply one of the ways in which the necessary organisation of the classroom environment can be anticipated.

Perhaps one of the most important things to do is to allow sufficient time for the whole problem-solving process to take place. Time is needed for the problem to be understood, for the discussion of difficulties, for mulling things over and making several attempts at a solution. More than anything else, time is required for children to be thorough and for work of a high standard to be achieved.

It can also be helpful to use a strategy of sympathetic questioning so that children are encouraged to approach a problem systematically. In the initial stages of identifying the problem and clarifying its important aspects it is possible to help children by asking questions like:

- What does the problem ask you?
- What does the problem tell you?
- What are the conditions which must be obeyed?
- Is there enough information? Could you get any more?
- Is there too much information? Which bit is the most important?
- Could you write down the problem in a different way?
- Would it help to draw a diagram to represent the problem?

At the stage when children are attempting to attack the problem teachers can recommend that they draw on their previous experience, use intuition or even employ trial and error. Strategies which can be suggested if a group of children is short of ideas can include:

- think of any similar problem;
- try a particular or special case;
- break the problem down into smaller parts;
- control the variables one at a time;
- work backwards;
- use trial and error;
- eliminate possibilities.

A brainstorming session may help at this stage, with ideas being noted on a large sheet of paper. Once the suggestions start to flow, it is important that no-one in the group intervenes, or criticises any of the ideas, however far-fetched. The session continues until nothing new is being put forward. The feasibility of the ideas can then be discussed, and a short-list prepared for further and more detailed consideration.

A tentative choice for a way of proceeding will be made by the children, tried, rejected or modified, and a route to the solution will gradually evolve. As it does, children can again be helped by using prompts like:

- Is all the information being used?
- Could the information be organised in a different way?
- Are there any patterns?
- Are you following this rule or that condition?
- Do you already know something which would help here?

If the children's plan is sound then it needs to be carried out carefully. Children need to be encouraged to check the steps they have taken. At this stage the teacher can ask:

- Is the result sensible?
- Have you solved each part of the problem?
- Have you satisfied all the initial conditions?
- Are there any other possible solutions?
- Are things in the right order?
- How can you be sure?

Finally, children can be urged to reflect on their experiences through questions like:

- Is the result what you expected?
- Which was the crucial step or discovery?
- Could the solution be shorter, more efficient, or more elegant?
- Would the outcome be different if . . . was altered?
- What other problems can you solve now?

In suggesting these prompts I do not intend to give the impression that a primary teacher should constantly oversee or dominate the problem-solving approaches of children. They are intended as a resource to be used when children have come to a halt, when they need help in becoming more systematic, or when they need to extend their repertoire of problem-solving strategies. If the questions were ever to be seen as a checklist, then teachers might as well solve all the problems themselves and announce the solutions to the children.

When children are solving problems it is worth stressing to them that in real life solutions have often to be judged by criteria of a social, economic or aesthetic nature, unrelated to the practicalities of the problem. For example, one group of children may want to observe the feeding habits of birds without keeping a constant look-out. To solve the problem, they could construct a tilting bird-table which rings a warning bell in the classroom when a bird has landed, but the sound might be quite unacceptable to the rest of the class.

In the past, we have frequently constrained the development of information-handling and problem-solving skills by guiding young children through tasks, by identifying problems before children encounter them, and even by supplying the 'best' solution. Yet if children are to become autonomous learners and good problem solvers we must help them to be responsible for decisions about who they work with, how they work, how they think, how they present their results, and even for suggesting the question to be answered or the problem to be investigated.

Some primary schools have found it easier to achieve these aims by making use of the micro in the classroom, rather than by using traditional resources. Good software is not only a powerful stimulus and a substantial tool for problem solving. It also assists teachers to change their role from being providers of what children do and learn to being a resource to be used by children. If teachers are prepared to try this change of role, even for only part of the week, it can allow them, perhaps for the first time, to observe children and to listen to their discussions. This is not intended to imply that an heuristic approach to learning means that children are left to their own devices. The role of the teacher is to help children to refine the problems which are suggested, to ask questions at the appropriate moment, to challenge children to justify their arguments, and to encourage them to reflect on what has been achieved.

> In developing problem solving skills, teachers have the important task of helping pupils to tackle problems analytically and to adopt logical procedures in solving them. At the same time pupils must be allowed to make mistakes and to follow false scents in what is essentially an exploratory process; and the teacher has to resist the temptation to give the 'right' answer, or to over-direct the pupil, otherwise the skill is not developed or practised.[8]

In the classroom, as well as in the adult world, many problems (and their eventual solutions) can appear to be simple or even trivial. Yet the intervening process between posing the problem and arriving at the solution may be very complex. It is the process of reaching a solution, combining choice and decision making with creative thinking, which is the essence of learning.

During the last three years every British primary school has acquired at least one micro. Some primary schools have two or three. One that I know has sixteen. Numerous introductory training courses have taken place, and many primary teachers are using a computer to enliven the existing work of the school. Yet in only a few schools is the computer, a substantial resource for problem solving, making an innovative contribution to the curriculum.

The other day I was asked by someone whether or not it would matter very much if all the computers in our primary schools disappeared overnight. I am not entirely sure of the answer, though I should like to think that it would be 'Yes'. But if the response to the question is to be positive, then British primary schools should aim to use their school computer for what it does best: supporting children who are thinking things out, exploring and investigating, processing information and solving problems. In this way the momentum gained over the last three years might continue.

Problem solving with control technology

Carol Wisely (*Advisory Teacher for Primary Technology,*
London Borough of Richmond)

The meaning of control technology

The human race was the first species on earth to take advantage of the materials of the natural world to significantly adapt the environment. Tools were created to increase our efficiency in controlling this environment and consequently to enable us to exploit it. With the invention of machines and engines we reached the limit of control by human power alone and a new technology of mechanical control came into being. Soon systems that had no regular human input were invented and then we had automatic control. Now, of course, whole systems of machinery and circuitry are controlled by 'pseudo-intelligent' micro-processors, often popularly known as robotics, and it is this phenomenon that we generally mean when we use the term 'Control technology'.

In the classroom this term normally means using the computer and a suitable 'interface' device to control external devices other than a monitor or printer. One common example might be a 'turtle' which can be controlled using the computer and instructed by LOGO commands to draw shapes and patterns on the floor.

The links with problem solving

The technological method is an example of a problem-solving activity, and follows the same pattern as the 'classic' problem-solving process shown in Figure 6.1.

Sometimes the problem will be a 'sideways' diversion from another activity that is going on. A science activity recently threw up the following problem. The children were testing sheets of different types of paper. One of the tests required them to hold the piece of paper horizontally to see how much it curved over. They soon discovered that this was influenced strongly by the way they held the paper. In order to make this a 'fair' test they had to invent a

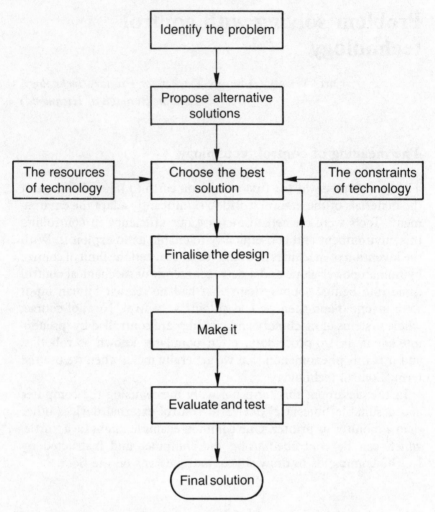

Figure 6.1

device that would hold the paper for them. This they eventually did, using a bulldog clip as an integral part.

On other occasions the activities will arise out of a theme that is being studied. Many of the classic primary school 'topics' have technological content, and children delight in the creation of models, particularly models that work. To them it may seem like play, but it is in play that so much real learning goes on – constructional play, and the making of soap-box go-carts for example. Unfortunately this type of activity is on the decrease as 'bought' toys become more sophisticated and children more competitive in terms of possessions.

Maybe we should increase the amount of time given to constructive play in the classroom.

Quite often children will have their own ideas of what they want to make and what problems they want to solve. Their motivation in these circumstances is far greater than when working on a task they have been given. The beginning of the control technology project in my own classroom was the desire of a group of children to make a lighthouse; this arose out of a science session on bulbs, batteries, and switches.

Another way to include problem-solving activities in technology might be the 'challenge' or 'Great Egg Race' type of situation, where children are given a problem that might be artificially inspired (to a greater or lesser degree), or might have arisen out of thematic work. An example of this might be: 'contrive an interesting journey for a marble' or, more precisely, 'produce a device that allows a marble to fall from a height of 40cm in not less than 10 seconds'.

Introducing the computer

There are many opportunities for technological problem solving in the classroom without involving the computer at all, so why bother to introduce it? To answer this, I think we must go back to the justification for using computers in other areas of the curriculum. They are there to extend, enrich and enhance activities that would be going on anyway. They act as a resource, albeit a very powerful and many-faceted one. The problem-solving activities we provide should be structured in such a way that they encourage children to develop skills as 'technologists' and begin to understand more complex concepts. Using the computer for control technology is an ideal way of doing this.

The 'marble' activity described above, for example, could be extended through use of the computer, into the construction of a timing device that makes use of rolling marbles. Another classic 'egg race' idea is that of building, out of simple materials, the highest tower capable of supporting a small object. This can be extended by insisting that the structure is also able to detect any attempts to remove the object.

Sometimes the computer helps simplify a problem that appears insoluble. That is exactly what happened in my class when the children decided to build a lighthouse. Figures 6.2–6.4 show how they set about it.

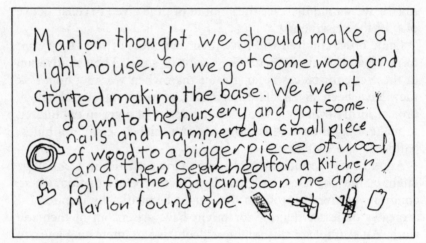

Figure 6.2

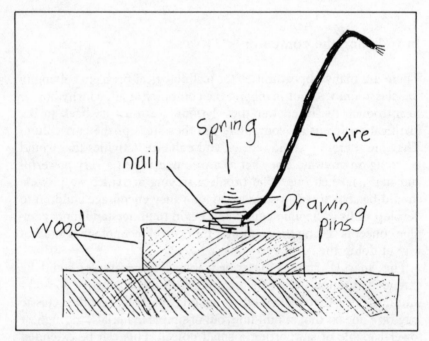

Figure 6.3

Having constructed the lighthouse, they then wanted the light to 'flash'. The light was 'controlled' by a small, external, manually-operated switch of the drawing-pin and paper-clip variety. The chil-

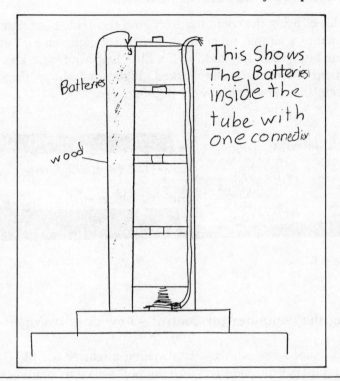

This Shows
The Batteries
inside the
tube with
one connedi·

Batteries

wood

We fixed on a spring and some wire
Beacause a spring is a good contact.
for electricity. We put on the spring and
held it down by drawing pins and we
twisted on the wire and then put
the tube on top. To hold the batteries
in place

Figure 6.4

dren painted a translucent bottle black on one side and inverted it over the top of the lighthouse, the intention being to revolve it and cause the light to 'flash'. (This, of course, is very similar to the way a real lighthouse works.) However, the children had no success in putting this into practice. They became very disheartened and would happily have abandoned the project at this point. Then I introduced the idea of using the computer to control the light. I suggested that they wrote a simple program to switch the light on and off at a regular rate. This they did, with a little help, and were absolutely delighted when it actually worked. Figure 6.5 shows the simple program that they wrote to get it going.

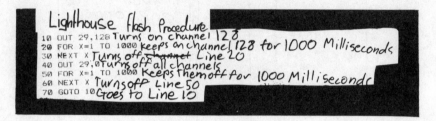

Figure 6.5

Using the computer for control – how does it work?

At this stage a few words of explanation might be useful.

Computers print messages on a monitor screen by sending simple messages that cause the minute individual dots that make up the screen light up or stay dark, ie simple 'on' or 'off' messages. All the internal communication within 'the guts' of the computer is in the form of these simple on or off messages. These are signified mathematically by the digits 1 (on) or 0 (off). The 'machine language' that the circuitry understands is based on units of eight of these digits or BITS (BInary digiT) that make up what is called a *byte*. With the use of a suitable interface device the computer can send out numbers that control a set of eight switches. For example, the decimal number 10 converts into the following Binary form:

0   0   0   0   1   0   1   0

which would switch on the corresponding switches in a row of eight.

The computer can also 'read' the settings of a set of eight switches and convert that into a decimal value. The common interface devices used in control technology take the form of an 'input/output' box with eight sockets for output – to which motors, bulbs, buzzers and so on can be connected, and eight input sockets – to which varying types of switches can be connected.

Some sort of Control language is needed to program the computer. My children used BASIC for the project described above. However, this involves the children understanding the Binary number system (no bad thing, perhaps!), and some of the commands are clumsy. A better example might be to use CONTROL extensions for LOGO, or a LOGO-type Control language such as *Control it* (further details are given at the end of this article). Both of these use much more straightforward commands such as 'Switch on', 'Switch off' and 'Read' and refer to the switches by labels (0 to 7) rather than their Binary equivalent.

(This may seem somewhat confusing, but don't worry if you haven't understood it. The children picked it up far quicker than I did!)

Outline of the project

Once the children had written their program, I left them to get on with it. They were well used to computers and had experienced very sophisticated software. Yet their delight knew no bounds when they first hooked up the equipment to the lighthouse, typed in a simple command, the light came on, typed in another and off it went again. It is amazing that such a simple thing should have such a great effect; this proves once again that children need to be the active participant in any interaction with the computer.

Having finished the lighthouse the children became very interested in the input/output box and the varying switches it came with. The device we were using is a simple and robust box called *Control It*, made by Deltronics.[9] It has an integral power source, 6v or 12v, so that it can control motors, and it comes with the following input devices:

- a push-button switch
- a pressure mat – 'on' when trodden upon
- a light-dependent switch – 'on' when light shines on it
- a magnetic reed switch – 'on' when a magnet is brought near it
- a tilt switch – 'on' when moved out of the horizontal

Two children decided to construct a set of traffic lights (this was suggested by the arrangement of red, orange and green LEDs on the box – a somewhat artificial inspiration I fear!). They began working out a procedure to control them, at this 'prototype' stage simply switching the lights on the box on and off. At this point I gave them a different control language (BITS) that had the simpler LOGO – like commands mentioned earlier. They took to it very quickly and much preferred it to BASIC. Figures 6.6 and 6.7 show two of the procedures they wrote in this language.

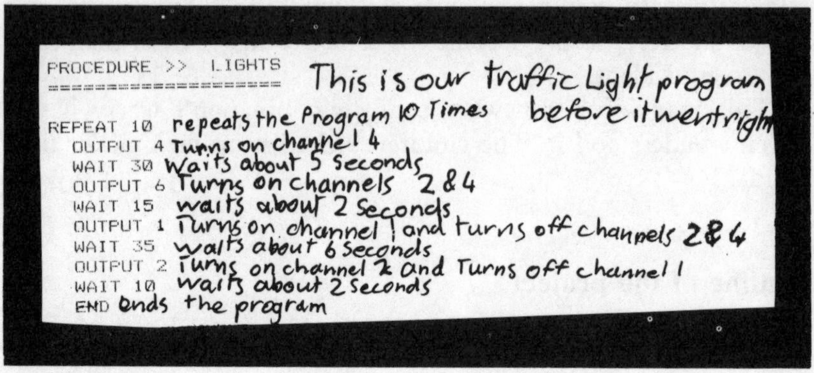

Figure 6.6

Figure 6.7

The children constructed a large model of the traffic lights and wired it into the box. They wanted to turn it into a Pelican crossing and so connected a push-button switch via the input side of the control box. They took the whole process very seriously, even going out of school with a stopwatch to find out the exact timings of our local crossing. Figure 6.8 shows their final procedure (in BASIC).

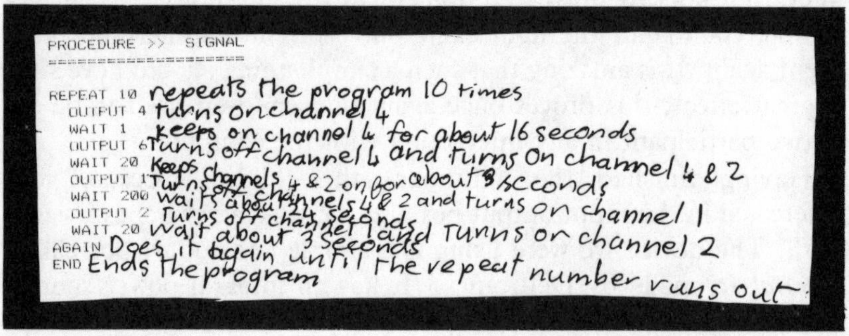

Once the children had discovered how to use the control box they started to play with the input devices. Their favourite was the pres-

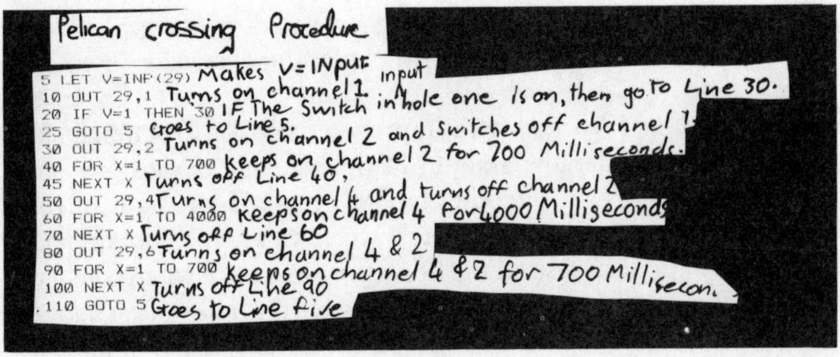

Pelican crossing Procedure

5 LET V=INP(29) Makes V=INPut input
10 OUT 29,1 Turns on channel 1.
20 IF V=1 THEN 30 IF The Switch in hole one is on, then go to Line 30.
25 GOTO 5 Goes to Line 5.
30 OUT 29,2 Turns on channel 2 and switches off channel 1.
40 FOR X=1 TO 700 keeps on channel 2 for 700 Milliseconds.
45 NEXT X Turns off Line 40,
50 OUT 29,4 Turns on channel 4 and turns off channel 2
60 FOR X=1 TO 4000 Keeps on channel 4 for 4000 Milliseconds
70 NEXT X Turns off Line 60
80 OUT 29,6 Turns on channel 4 & 2
90 FOR X=1 TO 700 Keeps on channel 4 & 2 for 700 Milliseccon.
100 NEXT X Turns off Line 90
110 GOTO 5 Goes to Line five

Figure 6.8

sure pad (as used in a burglar alarm mat). They connected it up and wrote a procedure that rang a bell every time someone stepped on the pad. Some suggested ways of using it, for example to count the number of people entering and leaving the room. However, classroom design presented a problem here, as the computer could not be set up near the door. They abandoned the idea of counting and returned to a simple alarm system, wiring the mat to a battery-operated door chime. Every time anyone entered the room they were greeted by an electronic version of *The Yellow Rose of Texas*. This led on to a variety of projects as various parts of the classroom were 'alarmed' in some way – there followed an interesting week! Following this, the class began to experiment with motors, using a control language. Motors can be turned on and off and reversed for specific periods of time; there is an enormous range of possibilities.

Conclusions

Clearly, control technology has great potential for problem-solving work. Any model-making activity tends to be problematic, as the ways in which materials are to be put together are explored; this is even more likely when models that work are being created. Control technology facilitates all the 'design – make – test' processes and encourages children to develop a whole range of practical and visualisation skills. The creation of procedures in the chosen control language is a perfect way to develop the skills of logical, abstract reasoning and there is the added benefit of clear feedback as to the success of these procedures. The 'debugging' process is important, and the concept of a 'right' or 'wrong' answer does not apply. Hence the children feel much happier to explore and develop their own ideas.

The children I worked with improved their constructional skills and spent a considerable amount of time solving design problems, 'trouble shooting', and making modifications in the light of these experiences. They observed the real world in order to obtain necessary information, they used the library as a resource when constructing their lighthouse, they worked cooperatively (as so often happens when the micro is involved) and so much discussion went on at every stage that it was easy to see how their language skills might improve through this type of activity.

I would recommend, however, that any teacher who wishes to introduce control technology first makes sure that the children have had some experience of technological activity. It is quite easy to devise home-made pressure pads and tilt switches, and to construct automatic control systems without using the computer. The children gain an enormous amount from this 'Heath Robinson' approach and it pays off when they use the 'new' technology and specialised equipment. Such experimentation also gives them a far greater insight into the way these devices work and dispels the mysterious 'black box' image.

Having said all this, I hope it will not seem too off-putting. Control technology is exciting – and actually demands little computer time as most of the time is spent constructing the models. Anybody who uses Logo with their children will find that using a control language improves the children's skills in the turtle graphics application of Logo enormously – perhaps as a result of the experiences afforded by the practical activities. In 1959 the Crowther Report pointed out:

> From infancy, girls and boys investigate the material world. Their interest is not wholly scientific but arises from a desire to control or use the things around them.

The new technology of micro-computing has given us, as teachers, the opportunity to create a fertile environment for these investigations.

Notes and references

1 *Practical Suggestions for Developing Ability in Problem Solving* W A Brownwell. The Psychology of Learning, Chicago: Part II of the Forty-first Yearbook (National Society for the Study of Education, 1942)
2 *Mathematics Counts* Report of the Committee chaired by W H Cockcroft (HMSO, 1982)
3 *The Problem Solver* David Wells (Rain Publications, 8 Carmarthen Road, Westbury-on-Trym, Bristol)
4 *Science, Models and Toys* Science 5 to 13 (Macdonald Educational, 1974)
5 RAYBOX, BEES, COLONY, MERLIN and MALLORY; *Posing and Solving Problems with your Micro* MEP Primary Project (to be distributed through LEA advisers, 1985/6). L (Association of Teachers of Mathematics, Kings Chambers, Queen Street, Derby. 1984). FLETCHER'S CASTLE, VIKING ENGLAND (Fernleaf, 31 Old Road West, Gravesend. 1983/4). LITTLE RED RIDING HOOD (Selective Software, 64 Brooks Road, Street, Somerset. 1985)
6 *Mathematics from 5 to 16* HMI Curriculum Matters 3 (HMSO, 1985)
7 CONTROLLER. *Posing and solving problems using control technology.* MEP Primary Project (to be distributed through LEA advisers, 1985/6)
8 *The curriculum from 5 to 16* Curriculum Matters 2 (HMSO, 1985)
9 The Deltronics Input/Output box is available as part of a kit called *Control It* which includes various switches and also the necessary software. Information regarding the kit is available from: Resource, Educational Development Centre, Kingfisher First School, Coventry Grove, Doncaster DN22 4PY

Further reading

Govier H. *Problems and Investigations in the Primary School using the Microcomputer as a Resource* (IT Centre, Davidson Road, Croydon, 1985)
Papert S. *Mindstorms* (Harvester Press, 1980)
Usborne Publishing produce a number of computer books for children. They include:

Expanding your Micro J. Tatchell and L. Howarth; *Experiments with your Computer* (various authors); *How to Make Computer-Controlled Robots* and *How to Make Computer Model Controllers* by Tony Potter; *Practical Things to do with a Microcomputer* J. Tatchell, N. Cutler and G. Waters.

7 Science and technology (CDT)

> 'Teach your pupil to observe the phenomena of nature: you will soon rouse his curiosity, but if you would have it grow do not be in too great a hurry to satisfy this curiosity. Put the problems before him and let him solve them himself. . . Let him not be taught science, let him discover it.'
>
> Jean-Jacques Rousseau 1763

For many years science in primary schools invariably took the form of nature study, with the 'nature table' as the focus in the classroom. Curriculum development in the 1970s was aimed at broadening the scope of science teaching to include elements of physical science. Rather than teach science as a body of scientific knowledge the emphasis was on ways of learning how to be a scientist. However by 1978 the HMI Report on Primary Education in England said that although science was attempted in the majority of classes, it was only seriously developed in one class in ten – and was often limited to nature study. Since then, problem-solving activities have been increasingly recognised as important for the intellectual development of children, and there has been growing awareness of the need to prepare children for an increasingly technological society. So to science has been added a new element in the primary curriculum – craft, design and technology.

How does science differ from CDT? One way to distinguish them is to say that science is often concerned with the question 'Why?' (the principles behind the working of things) whereas technology is more concerned with 'How?' questions (how principles can be applied). Craft, design and technology is the process of designing and making things. For many children one of the earliest CDT experiences is building sandcastles, in which simple tools (bucket and spade) are used to manipulate material (sand) to produce an intended outcome (sandcastle).

One of the dangers with CDT, as with science or art, is that it may become subject bound. The various activities involved in designing and making are most effective when taught as problem-solving processes across the whole curriculum. Designing and making, according to the Equal Opportunities Commission

> helps to develop in people such qualities as imagination, inventiveness, resourcefulness and flexibility. Industry and commerce need people with such qualities but people as individuals also need these qualities in order that they may be able to challenge and change their own roles in life if they so wish.[1]

The process of designing and making involves recognising the nature of the problem, identifying possible solutions and then testing them by constructing them and evaluating the outcome. The process can be seen in terms of a flexible design loop that includes a broad range of creative activity (Figure 7.1).

Sue Dale Tunnicliffe has put the problem-solving approach to science into a simpler four-step process which she calls the PTDR approach.[2]

Problem	The problem is given to the children, who discuss and express it in their own terms.
Think	The children think of solutions and draw up a plan of action.
Do	The equipment is collected and experimental work begins. (If it doesn't achieve the results, it is 'back to the drawing board'.)
Report	The group discuss results and their way of reporting (which may be written, taped, drawn, acted out etc.)

In her article *What's the Problem?* Sue Tunnicliffe develops these ideas further and shows how problem-solving challenges can be related to the teaching of science.

The close relationship that exists between science and technology is shown in Keith Geary's contribution *Science through Technology*, in which scientific understanding is developed through a technological problem-solving activity – the building of a stone monument (how did they move those stones?). Ways of introducing this investigation, and of recording the work done, are suggested. It is left

A design loop

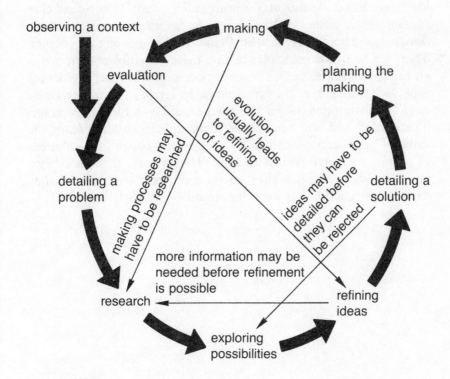

observing a context

making

evaluation

planning the
making

*evolution
usually leads
to refining
of ideas*

*making processes may
have to be researched*

*ideas may have to be
detailed before
they can
be rejected*

detailing a
problem

detailing a
solution

more information may be
needed before refinement
is possible

research

refining
ideas

exploring
possibilities

Figure 7.1

to the teacher, and child, to adapt and use the material in their own ways. Much of our knowledge is at an intuitive level, through our problem-solving activities we can make this knowledge explicit. Experience leads to concept formation. Along the way we also learn a lot about the properties of materials, about the forces that can act on and through materials, and about the cooperation that is needed to make an engineering enterprise successful.

One of the reassuring features of designing and making is that there is no established body of knowledge that the teacher or the child needs to learn or apply. The knowledge needed to find answers to a particular problem can be built up as the investigation proceeds. The *Case study on castles* (page 147) shows how purposeful enquiry through a problem-solving approach can lead to unexpected results – and provide a lot of fun for teacher and child in the process.

'More emphasis than at present should be placed on work in three dimensions and some of this might be of a simple technological kind aimed at designing and making things work' (*The School Curriculum* 1981). Some starting points for problem solving through design and technology will be found at the end of this chapter. There are scientific principles behind these activities as there are in all human activities (as the teacher once said when her child's leg was stuck 'Remember the principle of the lever!'). These principles need to be brought out by the teacher, often at the review stage. The teacher will also need to be there to help children learn the value of perseverence, and to be open to the possibilities inherent in things. As Lewis Mumford said: 'However far modern science and technics have fallen short of their inherent possibilities, they have taught mankind at least one lesson: Nothing is impossible.'

What's the problem? Science with a problem approach

Sue Dale Tunnicliffe (*Advisory Teacher, Primary Science and Technology, London Borough of Richmond upon Thames*)

Problem solving in primary science work has two main aspects. First there is the *challenge* type of problem. Here the teacher introduces the problem to the children and initially there is no child input. In designing a solution to the teacher-originated problem the students experience fundamental science facts. They may encounter a *real* problem in carrying out the experiment involved in solving the challenge. Real problem solving may also be encountered in work originated by the children, for example in topic work or extension science work.

Talking for understanding

I started tackling science experimental work through a problem-based approach when I felt that children needed:

- to discuss the nature of the work so that they understood the situation in their own terms and knew what was expected of them and what possibilities for experimental activities there were;
- to be encouraged to use their existing reservoir of knowledge and experiences in solving the problem;
- to take a far greater part in assuming responsibility for the organisation of their work.

I wanted to get away from the 'recipe' science approach of giving the child a work card or telling the group what activity was to be followed. To tell the children what equipment they need and what to do with it once they have it will neither generate a great deal of enthusiasm nor give the children opportunities for taking decisions and for independent thought. Children's participation – in discussing the nature of the work and how the situation might be approached, and calling upon the stock of relevant experience they have already acquired – is essential for developing the decision-making patterns required in working life. I wanted the children to impose their personalities on the work, rather than the other way around.

Of course, it is important that children learn to follow instructions and work within defined parameters. It also requires a teacher confident in class management and scientific method and content to follow a problem-solving approach and abandon the instructional one.

The problem approach

The problem is described using visual aids (where relevant and available) to help focus the children's attention. Then the teacher initiates discussion of the problem, involving the whole class. Gradually the children understand the nature of the problem; the first ones to do so explaining it to their peers in their own terms.

What is already known?

Through talking, the children recall existing knowledge, facts and techniques which might be relevant to the problem and its possible solution. A child's past experiences should always be valued – they are part of the ongoing building process of education, and vital to the development of each individual's personality. Even where the experiences are not directly related to science or maths, they may have much to offer. Children might, for example, come from an agricultural background in another country and have very relevant experience to contribute. After all, science experiences are essentially a part of living.

Selecting the line of action: which solution?

Next, each group is asked to sift through all their information and decide what they think is useful in formulating a possible solution. They usually come up with many ideas and need to discuss these and decide which they can realistically investigate. Then they rank the solutions (giving reasons) to choose which one to try first.

Trying the solution

The group (or an elected scribe) formally write down the solution they want to try and their prediction of the outcome. I like to use flow charts at this stage, to encourage clarity of thought and brevity of recording. The children list the equipment they need and work out where they can obtain it (within the limits of the science room/ school). I ask them to:

1   plan how they will set it up;
2   decide who will fetch each piece of equipment;
3   decide who will set up each piece of equipment;
4   allocate the manpower resources of the group for the experimental tasks.

A natural leader usually emerges and proceeds to organise the others.

Part of the planning process is to decide what kind of results are being looked for and how they can most efficiently be recorded as the experiment is happening. I stress that it doesn't matter if modifications to the equipment, the experimental method or the recording process have to be made as the work progresses. Flexibility and adaptation are the order of the day. I also think children need 'permission' to be able to change their minds as they carry on with the work, without fear of being reprimanded.

Evaluation

When the work has been completed the group draws up conclusions about what they have discovered and how the work could be extended. This evaluation is very important; the children decide how they could have improved the experiment, and why such a course of action might have been more effective. Throughout, the enthusiasm of the pupils is noticeable. For many, the problem-solving approach is highly motivating.

Summary

The problem-solving approach in science work generally follows these stages:
   Definition: the nature of the problem is stated
   Interpretation: children discuss the problem and formulate it in their own terms

Review: they recall existing knowledge which may be relevant to the problem

Formulation of possible solutions: groups put forward various ideas, with their reasons for choosing them

Ranking of solutions: they put their solutions in order, starting with the one they intend to try first

Selection: groups consider controlling factors such as equipment, time etc and select a proposal

Planning they plan the experiment (equipment, manpower resources, sequence of actions, method of reading and recording results)

Prediction: groups suggest what they think might happen (with reasons)

Experiment: they conduct the experiment

Monitoring: they modify the method/recording in the light of practical experience. (If necessary, they may redesign the experiment and start again.)

Results: groups share and interpret the results. Has the problem been solved or do they need to experiment further?

Solution: they announce their problem-solving strategy

Evaluation: children discuss how the work could be improved. Did they find out what they anticipated? Would an alternative solution have been effective? What did they need to change?

Reporting: groups decide on the form their report should take – written, verbal, visual – and present it.

Approaching science in this way means that children become positively involved. They use skills of management which are not called for in conventional, prepared experimental work. It is much more the students' science than the teacher's, although by determining the nature of the problem set the teacher does guide the conceptual and skills learning involved – fostering both content and process skills.

Here are some examples of the problems or challenges that can be put to children, involving science work rather than the constructional problem solving usually associated with technology.

Cargoes

Problem:
What shape will carry the most cargo (marbles or dice cubes) while still floating? (The mass of material you can use is constant.)

Solution:
Try making different shapes – always using the same mass – and see at what amount of loading they sink.

Prediction:
What do you know about objects in water? What is the effect of the water on the object with regard to measured mass? What feature do objects which float have in common? Can you apply this to your shapes and predict which type of shape will float best and carry most cargo?

   Do you know of any shapes which seem to float more easily than others? Do some people float more easily than others? Do the easier floaters have a common feature?

Method:
What kind of equipment will you use? What would be the easiest material to use to make different shapes? How are you going to make sure that each shape is made from the same amount or area of material? What shape will you begin with? How will you record which shapes you try out?

Results:
How will you indicate which shapes hold which amount of cargo?

shape	amount of cargo	volume/area used

Conclusion:
Which shape did hold the most cargo? As all the shapes were made from the same amount of material (either in mass or area) what is the difference between the shapes?

Friction

Problem:
How could you make it a) easier, b) more difficult, to move the same block of wood the same distance?

Knowledge:
Slopes make work easier, as do levers and pulleys. Might the surface over which you move the block have an effect on the energy required to move it? How can you measure the effort required? (Forcemeters or gramme masses).

Equipment:
Blocks (with a hook in one side) or Dienes thousands blocks with string attached; yoghurt pot to catch masses; small masses (which will fit into yoghurt pots) or brass masses on a hook support; ruler; timer; different surfaces (eg sandpaper, cloth, paper towels, plastic, corrugated card, foil, desk top – also differences created by wetting surface with water or detergent); forcemeter.

Method:
Set up apparatus (the block to be used in the test with masses attached, or forcemeter if block is of sufficient mass). What test distance will you use? Should it be the same for all the tests? Why?

Test the block over each surface. Some children prefer to wrap the surface around the block and then run the test each time on a desk top, covering the measured distance.

Masses could gradually be loaded on top of the block to investigate the effects of increasing the load on movability over the surface.

Results:
The results can be entered on a table on which the prediction has previously been written. If masses have been increased, the results could be presented in graph form.

surface	prediction	force required to just move load

Conclusion:
Which surface was it easiest to move the load across? Were some surfaces with similarities 'easy'? Is there an explanation?

Evaluation:
Did we solve the problem? Could we have done this a more efficient way? Could we improve the method? What could we go on to investigate?

Adapted from an article in *Teaching Science*, Spring 1986

Science through technology

Keith Geary (*Senior Lecturer in Primary Science,*
Roehampton Institute)

Historically, the solution of technological problems has triggered the development of scientific ideas within the community of scientists. In the same way, an interest in practical, technological problem-solving activities conducted in the classroom can, on a small scale, develop scientific understanding in children.

Of course, total understanding of a scientific principle will not be generated by a *single* problem-solving activity. Several related activities will probably be needed before a glimmer of understanding appears. It helps if the teacher has some knowledge of the principles, as a basis for discussion, but even without such understanding the teacher should be able to put children in the way of learning, simply by presenting them with the problem to solve practically.

The problem of moving large slabs of rock and then mounting them vertically in the ground, as tackled by our ancestors, can be presented on a small scale for practical solution by the children in the following way.

Classroom activity
Start the project by describing to the children the problem of moving a large slab of rock over several kilometres and then erecting it vertically in the ground. A piece of wood about 60cm by 8cm by 3cm could be used to represent the stone monument that has to be moved and erected.

Ask the children to imagine themselves as matchstick-sized people who have to move the 'stone' a distance of 10km (represented by a distance of 10m) and then erect it in a hole in the ground. They can only use matchstick-sized forces (say the strength of a little finger), some rope (sewing cotton), some logs (twigs or pencils) and some spoons or twigs as digging tools. It is important to let the children do the job practically rather than just imagine they are doing it.

When they have exhausted their enthusiasm, or have completed the task, the children should be encouraged to discuss the ideas they have used, before looking at the ones suggested in these notes.

The suggestions here are not complete; there are other ways in which the problem could be solved and some children may think of original ideas that you, the teacher, have not considered. The children should be encouraged to work them out in practical detail and to explain them to the rest of the class. The next great engineer is at school somewhere today – and he or she may be in *your* class!

So far as existing knowledge is concerned, concept statements relating to each activity are included in the notes. But remember, the concepts will not be developed as a result of a single activity like this. You will have to devise other activities based on the same concepts.

In the past, people who have completed great engineering projects, like erecting stone monuments, have sometimes told the story of their achievements in the form of wall decorations with pictures and words. Some children might like to make a wall picture telling the story of their achievements in the same way.

How did they move the stones?

In many parts of the world our ancestors have put up huge stone monuments. These massive lumps of rock, sometimes weighing 40 tonnes and 30 metres in length, were often moved several kilometres before they were lifted into the positions where they have stood for thousands of years.

The Stelae of Ethiopia, and Stonehenge in England are just two examples of rock monuments set up by ancient engineers in many parts of the world.

In order to accomplish these great feats of engineering people had to devise appropriate technologies (ways they could do it). As a result, they developed an understanding of scientific principles which are just as useful to us nowadays as they were to people then.

Would *you* know how to move the stones across the land?
Would *you* know how to lift them into position?
Perhaps they tried to move the stones from place to place by *pushing* them.
The word *push* is the name we give to a special kind of **force**.
A force is something that makes things move.

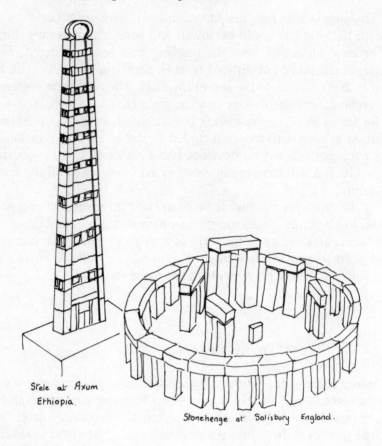

Stele at Axum Ethiopia.

Stonehenge at Salisbury England.

Figure 7.2

But one man pushing could not move the stone by himself, he would need help.

I can't move it

Figure 7.3

Perhaps 100 men all pushing together could move the stone. But that would be difficult to do because there would not be enough room for all 100 men to push on the stone at the same time.

Forces can be added together.

Things like wood can transmit (pass on) *forces to other things they are touching.*

Perhaps someone thought of the idea of using a log of wood that several people could hold and use to push against the stone at the same time.

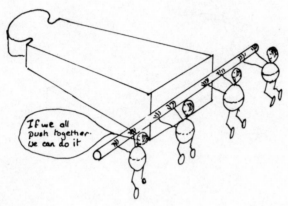

Figure 7.4

The log would add all their separate pushes together and produce one big push against the stone.

But perhaps the log broke!

Forces can bend and break things like wood.

And if the log did break they would have had to think of a different idea.

What idea would *you* suggest?

Figure 7.5

Perhaps they tried to move the stones from place to place by pulling them.

The word *pull* is the name we give to a special kind of **force**.

A force is something that makes things move.

Push and pull are the names of forces.

But one man pulling could not move the stone by himself, he would need help.

Figure 7.6

Perhaps 100 men all pulling together could move the stone. But that would be difficult to do because there would not be enough room for all the 100 men to pull on the stone at the same time.

So perhaps someone thought of the idea of using rope wrapped round the stone so that several people could hold the rope and all pull together. The rope would add all their *pulls* together and produce one big pull on the stone.

Forces can be added together.

Things like rope can transmit (pass on) *pulls to other things they are attached to.*

Things like rope cannot transmit pushes.

But perhaps the rope snapped!

Forces can stretch and break things.

And if the rope did break they would have had to think of a different idea.

What idea would *you* suggest?

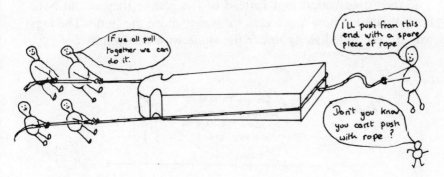

Figure 7.7

The trouble with moving a big slab of stone over the ground is that it is not just hard to move because it is big. It is also hard to move because it presses down into the ground and cannot slide along easily. When you push it, it seems as if the stone is pushing back against you.

There is a force called friction which makes it difficult for things to slide over each other.

Forces can stop things moving as well as making them move.

Some forces make things move and other forces stop things moving.

Perhaps someone thought of the idea of letting the stone slide along over smooth pieces of wood.

Smooth surfaces make friction forces become smaller.

And perhaps they thought of rubbing grease onto the wood to make it easier for the stone to slide over.

Oil and grease can make friction forces become smaller.

Figure 7.8

If they used round logs instead of flat planks they would have been amazed at how much easier it was to move the stone. The logs would have rolled along under the stone without sliding.

Figure 7.9

When things roll there is no sliding friction force to stop them moving.
Perhaps someone thought they might be able to roll the stone into place.

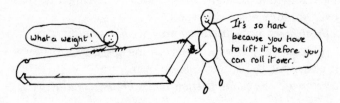

Figure 7.10

When you roll some objects it is difficult to move them because, in order to make them roll, you have to lift one side against the *pull* of gravity.
The pull of gravity is a force.
Do *you* know the name we use for the *force* that is the *pull* of gravity?
Perhaps someone thought of adding discs or circles of wood at each end of the stone to make it easier to move.

Figure 7.11

What do *you* think is wrong with the way the second one has been made?

Perhaps someone thought of using a pulley wheel.

A pulley is a wheel round which a rope can pass. It changes the direction of the *pull*.

A pulley can change the direction in which a force acts.

Perhaps someone wondered if there was another way of using the pulley wheel. Should the pulley wheel be on the tree or on the stone that was being moved?

A pulley can be used to change the size of a force as well as the direction in which it acts.

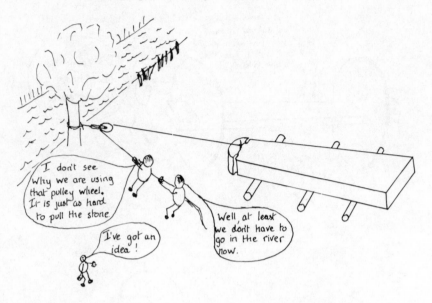

Figure 7.12

Do *you* think it would make any difference if the pulley wheel was tied to the tree or to the stone? How would you find out?

Figure 7.13

When they finally reached the place where they wanted the stone to be they had to solve another problem.

Figure 7.14

How would they lift the stone into position?

Perhaps someone thought of building a mound of earth to slide · the stone up and raise it above the hole.

A slope can be used to raise something more easily than lifting it.

Figure 7.15

But it would take a long time to build the mound of earth and afterwards they would have the job of taking the earth away again.

So perhaps they thought of a different idea.
How would *you* raise the stone into position?
Perhaps someone thought of using a lever.

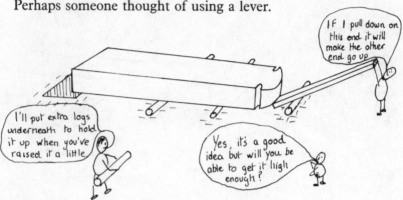

Figure 7.16

A lever can be used to change the direction in which a force acts.

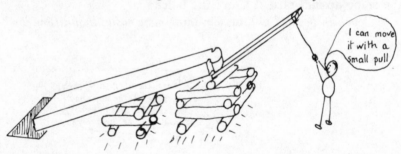

Figure 7.17

A lever can be used to change the size of a force as well as the direction in which it acts.

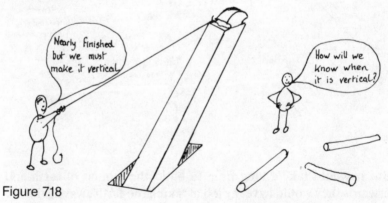

Figure 7.18

A case study: Castles

The starting point for this work was the BBC programme *Watch* on the theme of Castles and Life in a Castle. Following these programmes, the children's interest focused upon a castle's defensive features. It was decided that the main features were:

- strong, high walls
- strong doors or drawbridges
- narrow windows
- location (ie built on high ground to give occupants a clear view of an approaching enemy and to slow attackers down)

A castle was built with these features and then it was decided that it had to be attacked. After a heated discussion the following options were selected:

- knock down the door (battering ram)
- climb over the wall (siege tower)
- undermine the walls (a tunnel dug by sappers)
- throw rocks at or into the castle

Most children preferred the last option (naturally) though some built excellent models of a battering ram and a siege tower. The first attempts at firing a missile simply involved hand-held rulers or plastic Meccano rods. It was fairly difficult to hold the missile on the end of the ruler, so a box was fastened onto the end of a Meccano rod to solve this problem. A competition then developed, and so did arguments about whether it was *fair*. Some children were nearer the castle than others and different sizes and weights of missile were being fired.

Ground rules were agreed to make the competition fair:

- the machine should stand on the floor when fired
- it should be free-standing
- a minimum distance from the castle was established
- a standardised missile (tissue ball) was found

The following stages show the problems encountered in making the seige machines, and how they were resolved:

Mark 1

The previously produced rod and boxes were fastened to a base.

Problem:

Not very stable. The rod fell sideways and the machine would not consistently fire straight ahead.

Mark 2

Two rods were fastened side by side on the base, and joined together at the missile holder (forming a triangle) this made the machine more stable, and it fired straight ahead.

By this time the *Watch* programme had changed its theme to houses. The children had recently watched the wooden frame of a roof being assembled, and triangles were definitely popular.

Problem:

Though the missiles were now thrown straight ahead, they did not go high enough to reach over the castle wall. The missile stayed in the box far too long and needed to be thrown out somehow.

Help given:

What happens to a passenger when a car crashes? The car stops but the passenger keeps on moving.

Mark 3

A bar for the rods or box to crash into was fastened to the base and the missile was thrown out on impact.

Problem:

The missiles would not travel far enough. By this time, too, the Meccano rods were bending, retaining that shape, and not springing forward fast enough.

Mark 4

An elastic band was fastened from the 'crash bar' to the missile box to make up for the lack of spring in the Meccano rods.

Success!
The first missile landed in the castle.

Mark 5

Attempts were made at fitting sights on the machines, for example, lined-up holes to look through.

Help given:
Why do people have two eyes positioned as they are? What happens when you move an object progressively closer to your face?

Why do you look cross-eyed? Both eyes and the object form the corners of a triangle. What happened to your eyes and the triangle as the object moved nearer or farther away?

Two sights were fitted, one at each side of the machine.

Could you use an elastic band on a life-size seige catapult?

Examples of siege catapults were found in books, and attempts were made at making a wooden see-saw with heavy weights at one end.

Problem:
Even though more weights were added, the missile would not travel very far. Someone suggested making one side of the see-saw longer.

Mark 6

An estension was added to the see-saw, with a matchbox to hold the missile.

Success!
The missile travelled the length of the classroom.

Question:
Why did the extension work?

We looked at the distance travelled by each end of the see-saw. The missile end travelled farther than the weighted end. They both started and stopped at the same time. Some children realised that the missile end must be travelling faster than the weighted end, and if the missile was travelling faster when it was thrown from the box, it would travel farther. They wanted to extend the catapult again to check this, but, instead, several matchboxes were mounted along the existing arm. The children successfully predicted which matchbox positions fired missiles the shortest and the farthest distance and they are at present involved in measuring those distances.

From *Designing and Making* (East Midlands and Yorkshire Forum of Advisers in Craft, Design and Technology)

Starting points for investigation

The important concepts to do with technology can be divided into four elements: *materials, energy, structures* and *control*.

1 Materials
Explore the qualities of materials – are they hard/soft; strong/weak; stretch/non-stretch; lightweight/heavy; magnetic/non-magnetic etc.

In what ways can you classify a range of materials? To what uses could they be put? What could *you* make out of them? What tools are needed to work with a particular material?

(Set up a Materials Table and ask the children to collect, identify and arrange different materials. Can they describe a material so that others can guess what it is, without seeing it? Put a mystery material in a Feeling Box for children to handle – what can they say about it?)

2 Energy
Explore the powers needed to work things. How is energy produced and 'stored'? How is it used? What problems does it solve? Can you use it to power a model, or to produce light? Investigate batteries, create a simple electric circuit, power a model with rubber band and clockwork motor. Find out what role energy has to play in any topic that you are studying.

3 Structures
Explore ways of building things. Investigate the load that structures can carry (is it linked to the thickness of materials used?). Build towers out of various materials eg art straws, strips of wood, constructional kits. Study how parts are arranged and joined (triangular shapes are basically stiff, rectangular shapes may need bracing), and what makes them stable. Investigate real structures eg an electricity pylon – and reproduce your own model version.

4 Control
Explore ways in which we can *control* how something works. Investigate a machine eg a bicycle, and see how it is controlled – the use of levers (brakes, handlebars) cranks, gear wheels and a chain. See how electrical control works through switches of various kinds.

Find out how computers can be programmed to control switches and models. In what ways would you like to see machines controlled?

Some problem-solving activities

- Design an underwater house.
- Design a cage that will allow a hamster to get more exercise.
- Design a trap to catch a mouse without hurting it.
- Design a litter bin that would encourage people to put litter in it.
- Design a machine that would help you play a game or sport.
- Design a piece of apparatus for an adventure playground, which could be used in many ways.
- Design a toy for a young child, with at least one moving part.
- Design a machine that would be helpful in the house.
- Design and make a model of a car of the future.
- Design and make a model spaceship out of available materials.
- Make the tallest structure possible out of a newspaper and masking tape.
- Make the strongest bridge that will span a gap eg one metre between two desks, using 5 sheets of A4 paper, Sellotape and scissors. Test what weight it will support.
- Make the longest bridge you can that will support a tin of beans using 4 sheets of card, newspaper, Sellotape and scissors.
- Make a slope down which a marble can travel, using 2 sheets of A4 paper, 2 sheets of A4 card, Sellotape (one metre maximum) and scissors. See how far you can make your marble jump.
- Make a way of rolling a marble down a slope (eg raised desk) as slowly as possible, using card, scissors and Sellotape.
- Make a device for keeping a plant watered, using a plastic bag, plastic cup, straw, Sellotape and scissors.
- Make a 'roller' out of a cylinder eg cotton reel, elastic band, a bearing and a matchstick. Test how far it will roll.
- Make a parachute that will carry a small object to the ground as slowly as possible, from the materials available.
- Make a paper 'aeroplane' that will fly the maximum distance through the air.
- Make a container that will hold and protect an egg, using an A4 sheet of card, scissors and glue.

Remember when comparing designs that every contribution is of value. There is as much to be learnt from deficient and ineffective models as from the most successful.

Notes and references

1   *Equal opportunities in CDT* (Equal Opportunities Commission, 1983)
2   See 'No problem!' in *Junior Education*, August 1986

Further reading

British Association for the Advancement of Science *Ideas for Egg Races and Other Practical Problem-Solving Activities* (1983)

Coventry LEA *An Introduction to CDT in the Primary Curriculum* (1983)

Department of Education and Science, *Craft, Design and Technology in Schools: some successful examples* (HMSO); *CDT – A Curriculum Statement for 11–16+* (HMSO, 1981); *Technology in Schools* (HMSO, 1982); *Science in Primary Schools* (HMSO, 1983)

The East Midlands and Yorkshire Forum of Advisers in Craft, Design and Technology *Designing and Making* (1985)

The Engineering Council and the Standing Conference on School's Science and Technology, *Problem Solving: Science and Technology in Primary Schools*, 1985

Equal Opportunities Commission *We Can Do It Now* (1981)

Johnsey R *Problem-Solving in School Science* (Macdonald Educational, 1986)

Stoker Dr A. (ed) *Problem-Solving in Primary Schools* (a booklet published by Sunderland SATRO)

Williams P and Jinks D. *Design and Technology 5–12* (Falmer Press, 1985)

Science 5–13 (Macdonald Educational, 1972)

Problem Solving in Science and Technology (City of Manchester Education Committee)

8 Clues to the environment

> Mr Polly . . . left the private school at fourteen and by that time his mind . . . was a thorough mess. The nice little curiosities and willingness of a child were in a jumbled and thwarted condition . . . He thought of the present world no longer as a wonderland of experiences, but as geography and history, as the repeating of names that were hard to pronounce, and lists of products and populations, and heights and lengths, and as lists and dates and oh! and Boredom indescribable.
>
> (H G Wells, *The History of Mr Polly*)

Education has come a long way since the days of Mr Polly. The study of human variety and human achievement has traditionally been the concern of history and geography. Later these subject divisions were expanded to include social and environmental studies. More recently the social subjects or 'the humanities' have been included under the banner of 'integrated studies' – known in most schools as Topic or Project work. In 1976 a Schools Council Project Team summed up this area of education as the study of Time, Place and Society. 'Is it possible' they ask 'to talk of someone being educated if he has no conception of the past, no awareness of the world around him, and no understanding of the workings of human society?' (p22)[1]

Another aspect of being an educated person is the ability and desire to play an active part in society. One way to encourage this is to promote a problem-solving approach to the study of Time, Place and Society, to build up skills and concepts through first-hand experiences, helping children to seek and make sense of clues to their environment.

The present is in a continuous process of change. Children can come to an understanding of this key concept of change by becoming involved in its processes – studying the differences between 'then' and 'now' when investigating the past; between one place and another; and between ways of adapting to different environments and different societies.

In her article, Sue Millar shows how, in seeking '*Clues to the past in the environment*', a problem-solving approach can enrich and provide a focus for social and environmental studies. The case studies *Litter* and a *Conservation project in Newcastle* show ways in which problem solving can be directed to local environmental issues.

Clues to the past in the environment

Sue Millar (*Lecturer in Heritage Management,
Birmingham University, Ironbridge Gorge Museum*)

What have the contents of a dustbin in common with Hampton Court? What does Teddington High Street share with a country lane in Surrey? They all provide clues to people in the past. Exactly how and why I shall explore later.

Clues to the past are all around us wherever we live. Our heritage of city streets, country villages, churches, castles, historic houses and gardens, archaeological sites and landscape provides rich resources for a study of the past in the environment.[2] But this increasingly available, readily accessible and varied raw material of remains from the past only provides clues when we have a problem to solve. Once we have begun an investigation then these sources – buildings (exteriors and interiors), street furniture, ruins and estates – provide the excitement and immediacy of 'the real thing' and of being in touch with the past, literally in some cases. These sources offer first-hand evidence of a type that cannot be found in documents and pictures. They give us clues to the past, if only we can read and understand them.

Two issues are raised here. First, problem solving by its very nature creates a dilemma for historians. Historians ask questions about people's past lives to which there are a few right answers and few solutions. Problem solving, however, introduces the idea of investigation and the necessity of asking questions and seeking, if not finding, answers. This is very much the realm of the historian. We may never know why Stonehenge was built, but it does not stop any of us, at any age, tackling the problem. Yet this inevitable degree of uncertainty may be one reason why problem-solving techniques are generally less readily applied to history, in relation to the environment, than to other areas of the primary school curriculum. Second, reading a three-dimensional object, large or small, whether it is a historic house, a Wedgwood vase, or a Roman ruin is different from reading two-dimensional material such as old letters, official documents, paintings or photographs. Regrettably, teachers are not given training in how to do this. Broadly speaking, however, the skills needed to examine the historic environment are the same as those required to study any environmental situation in the countryside or town, whether the problem is rare flowers on an overused river bank or traffic congestion in the local shopping centre. Such skills are already familiar to many teachers. It is merely a question of transferring them to the historic environment and using the right ones to investigate a particular problem.

In what follows, I explore the range of skills that can be used in relation to the historic environment and, through a series of case studies, show how they can be put into practice in the primary school. During this discussion it will become clear that a historical focus on the environment adds an extra dimension to environmental studies, social studies, history courses and topic work. In fact, work on the historic environment is acquiring status in its own right under the label 'Heritage Education'.[2]

What then are the skills needed for Heritage Education? What are the skills needed for problem solving in the historic environment? They are skills involving visual awareness – looking and recording; tactile experience – touching and feeling; oral abilities – listening, story telling and role play; numeracy expertise – handling chronology, measuring and estimating; and spatial awareness – using maps and diagrams, and also dance and movement. Important as these technical skills are, in themselves they are empty of purpose without the exercise of imagination in the form of an empathetic response to the past. According to the HMI report *History in the Primary and Secondary Years*, 'Historical empathy is the ability to enter into some informed appreciation of the predicaments or points of view of other people in the past.'[3] Put more simply, it is the ability to put yourself in someone else's shoes and wear your own at the same time – looking at the situation from both the inside and the outside – a difficult but not impossible task.

Posing problems about the past in the environment invites pupils to act as detectives. Using the skills outlined above, they search for clues, organise, analyse and interpret evidence and seek a solution. A classroom exercise developed by the Schools Council Project, *Time, Place and Society: 8–13*[4] asks children to examine the contents of a dustbin as clues to learning about the family who threw the objects away. I have tried this exercise with children, students and teachers (see Figures 8.1 and 8.2). The response to the question: 'What kind of family threw away this rubbish?' varied enormously. On the one hand it included the somewhat obvious deduction: 'One man, who has a dog, and has been doing some decorating and watching television'; on the other hand it included less obvious possibilities: 'A family away on holiday who used the wallpaper for packing and ate junk food' or 'A family whose freezer has broken

THE DUSTBIN

Have you ever thought how much your
'dustbin man' could find out about your
family if he took a careful look at the
contents of your dustbin

I've made a list of the contents of my
dustbin.
In it were:

Chicken bones   1 tin of pineapples
5 tins of Lassie   3 tins of baked
   Meaty Chunks   beans
1 tin of carrots   5 cigarette packets
2 tins of evapo-   1 *T.V. Times*
   rated milk   3 eggshells
1 tin of peas   Bits of wallpaper

*What could you learn about my family
from these clues?*

Figure 8.1

down.' The question of social class was raised by adult groups and
alluded to by the children. Amidst laughter, imagination ran wild
on occasions, but what was immediately apparent to adults and
children alike was that there are gaps in the evidence. There are
things we do not know as well as things we do. The next question
followed automatically, 'How can we find out more about the family?' In discussion it was agreed we could look at their house or

TABLE OF OBJECTIVES

Skills			Personal Qualities
Intellectual	Social	Physical	Interest, Attitudes, Values
1 The ability to find information from a variety of sources, in a variety of ways. 2 The ability to communicate findings through an appropriate medium. 3 The ability to interpret pictures, charts, graphs, maps, etc. 4 The ability to evaluate information. 5 The ability to organise information through concepts and generalisations. 6 The ability to formulate and test hypotheses and generalisations.	1 The ability to participate within small groups. 2 An awareness of significant groups within the community and the wider society. 3 A developing understanding of how individuals relate to such groups. 4 A willingness to consider participating constructively in the activities associated with these groups. 5 The ability to exercise empathy (i.e. the capacity to imagine accurately what it might be like to be someone else).	1 The ability to manipulate equipment. 2 The ability to manipulate equipment to find and communicate information. 3 The ability to explore the expressive powers of the human body to communicate ideas and feelings communicate ideas and feelings. 4 The ability to plan and execute expressive activities to communicate ideas and feelings.	1 The fostering of curiosity through the encouragement of questions. 2 The fostering of a wariness of over-commitment to one framework of explanation and the possible distortion of facts and the omission of evidence. 3 The fostering of a willingness to explore personal attitudes and values to relate these to other people's. 4 The encouraging of an openness to the possibility of change in attitudes and values. 5 The encouragement of worthwhile and developing interests in human affairs.

Figure 8.2

flat; interview them, or read their correspondence and accounts, if they would let us; and make a comparative study of their dustbin with those of other families in the street. In other words, in order to be more accurate in solving the initial problem, we need to use corroborative evidence. Further clues need to be found and followed through. The contents of the dustbin in themselves are not sufficient evidence on which to base an informed opinion as to the kind of family who threw away the rubbish.

On the surface a switch from the classroom and the contents of a dustbin to Hampton Court Palace in the leafy outer London suburb of Richmond-upon-Thames might seem extreme. But Hampton Court Palace, just like the dustbin, provides source material from the past, although of a completely different character and quality, in a completely different context and from more distant times. Hampton Court is vast, so it is important to select the problem that pupils are to solve extremely carefully. It might be, 'What was it like to live in Hampton Court Palace at the time of Henry VIII?' or, on a smaller scale, 'What were the kitchens like at Hampton Court at the time of Henry VIII?' or the problem could be less directly relevant to the mainstream history of the palace and more directly relevant to the needs of the visiting children.

I used the gardens of Hampton Court Palace for an experiment with six-year-old pupils from St Mary and St Peters School, Teddington. We visited the grounds of Hampton Court in March, at the end of the Spring Term, with two problems to solve: 'What different kinds of shapes can you find in the gardens and what different kinds of spring flowers can you see growing in the gardens?' The palace itself was incidental. A term's work on shape and watching spring bulbs grow led up to the visit. There were no worksheets. We walked around in groups looking at everything and talking about what we saw. We went round the maze – a soluble problem. We sang, had a great deal of fun, ate our packed lunches and returned to school.

The paintings done by each child the next day revealed the success of the project. The pupils recognised and understood the relationship between the shapes they had been using in mathematics and the topiary pyramid-shaped trees in the formal gardens. The maze captured their imaginations. They got lost in it and at the same time were able to experience its shape and design. Flowers were the right colours. As a whole the paintings done by the class had an immediacy that those done before the visit lacked. The teacher and I had asked questions that could be solved in a historic environment and that were appropriate for young children. We encouraged them to use visual and oral skills and experience the space created by the maze and formal gardens. We introduced a unique part of our national heritage to local children, many of whom had never seen Hampton Court before. It was a broadening, enjoyable experience, relevant to what the children were learning in the classroom and relevant to gaining a deeper understanding of historic gardens. Hopefully those children will return with more problems and more questions as they grow older.

Hampton Court has a special place in England's heritage and history. It is impressive at a glance and is England's second most popular tourist attraction after the Tower of London. Teddington High Street, also in the borough of Richmond-upon-Thames, is a stark contrast. With small shops, restaurants, and cars parked illegally on both sides of the road, it would not merit a second glance on a quick drive through. It is ordinary. But it offers a chance for older primary school pupils to investigate the roots of a small suburban community and find out how it has changed through time.

The problem I set students training to be primary school teachers was 'Why is Teddington High Street as it is now?' We needed a starting point like the contents of the dustbin. We decided to begin with one house in the street, one example of change.[5] The house at the corner of Vicarage Road and the High Street dates from the early 19th century. Since then it has had three shops built on to the front, an estate agents, an electrical store and an off-licence (see Figure 8.3). The side view, as well as the front view above the shops, shows that the house was once a large, elegant, white building in the classical style (see Figure 8.4). Students recorded this information with cameras and tape-recorders (always preferred to drawing and note-taking). But when was the building altered? The people in the estate agents are unsure, around the beginning of the present century, they think. The library has the bill of sale confirming that this house was the vicarage and was sold in 1881 (see Figure 8.5). An early photograph, also in the library, shows that before it was sold, the house was used as a post office. From these additional clues the students got some idea of how the building had changed over the past hundred years or so, but they still had not found out *why* it had changed.

At this stage we returned to the High Street. I wanted the students to be confident in making deductions from what they had observed and recorded, with minimal additional information. We looked again and, in general terms, we worked out that a large house with over three acres of land was not needed by the busy, densely-populated and prosperous commuter community of Teddington today, whereas shops like an estate agents, an electrical stores and an off-licence are essential. From the simple additional clues that we had found we worked out that this must have been the case for about a hundred years. Therefore Teddington must have been a growing, thriving community for at least that length of time. Of course, it is possible to continue with the investigation and look at maps – which will tell us that the railway came to Teddington in 1863 and thus encouraged its growth – but this is not necessary. The street provides the strongest, most dynamic and most approachable record for pupils of all abilities of primary school age. It provides a record of change and continuity in the lives of people in the community. Understanding how and why Teddington High Street is as it is now, is a soluble problem for older primary school children.

The two examples I have given so far illustrate what can be done in an urban setting with clear directions by the teacher. The next

Figure 8.3

Figure 8.4

TEDDINGTON, MIDDLESEX.

PARTICULARS

OF A VALUABLE

Freehold Building Property,

. . . . Eligibly situate in the . , ...

HIGH STREET, TEDDINGTON,

And within Five Minutes' Walk of the Railway Station, comprising

THE VICARAGE HOUSE:

Being a Comfortable Residence with Front and Rear Gardens and Outbuildings; also

VALUABLE BUILDING LAND,

The whole containing about

3 ACRES AND 15 PERCHES,

Including the Site of proposed Road, having Frontages to the High Street, and admirably adapted for

VILLA RESIDENCES AND SHOP PROPERTY.

The Land is bounded by Properties belonging to — HUMPHREYS, Esq., E. WALTON, Esq., Mr. KEEN'S TRUSTEES, W. TAYLOR, Esq., and Land occupied by Mr. TRUEFIT.

POSSESSION OF THE WHOLE ON COMPLETION OF THE PURCHASES.

FOR SALE BY AUCTION, BY

MESSRS. DRIVER & CO.,

AT THE AUCTION MART,-TOKENHOUSE YARD, LOTHBURY, LONDON,

On TUESDAY, the 25th day of JANUARY, 1881,

At TWO O'CLOCK precisely, unless an acceptable offer be previously made by Private Contract. The Property will first be offered as a whole in ONE LOT, but if not sold then the same will be offered in Lots.

Particulars, with Plan, may be obtained at the Clarence Hotel, Teddington; the King's Head, Twickenham; the Greyhound, Richmond; at the Mart and Estate Exchange, Tokenhouse Yard, Lothbury; of
MESSRS. LEE, BOLTON, & LEE, Solicitors, 2, The Sanctuary, Westminster; of
MESSRS. CLUTTON, Surveyors and Land Agents, 9, Whitehall Place; and of
MESSRS. DRIVER & CO., Surveyors, Land Agents, and Auctioneers, 4, Whitehall, London.

Figure 8.5

two examples illustrate what can be done in a rural setting and show the possibilities that arise when the children themselves take over to some extent. During an art and environment project, at Brockham Green School (near Betchworth, Surrey) the children began telling the art teacher tales of the headless horseman on the old Coach Road. She decided that this legend presented its own problem and needed investigation. The pupils visited the road and explored the local folk tale through art. They carried out research and made a shadow puppet theatre, acted the legend and created their own pictures. The mystery added excitement to the exploration; the problem, almost deliberately, remained unsolved. With a solution the magic and glimmer of truth would disappear.

During a week's summer school at the Weald and Downland Museum, near Chichester, West Sussex, local children worked on problem solving in a quite different manner. Led by the education officer at the museum, they participated in an exercise to find out what it was like to live and work as charcoal burners in the Sussex Weald. They constructed a camp, built ovens, beds and huts, cooked their own food on open fires and made charcoal. Through their experience, and the activities they became involved in, they solved the problem of how a charcoal burner's family lived. It was role play of a very real kind. Above all the local children learnt what vast quantities of wood were needed both for charcoal burning and simply to keep adequate fires burning. With charcoal they made themselves, Nicky and Jamie Carter wrote a guide to a charcoal burner's job – with the simple authority of just having done it (see Figures 8.6 and 8.7).

Each situation that I have described here has taken a different starting point for problem solving using the historic environment. Integrated learning focused on shape and flowers was put into practice in the gardens of Hampton Court. The need to trace 'roots' through local history inspired the project on Teddington High Street. A mysterious legend instigated creative work at Brockham Green School. Finding out about a charcoal burner's livelihood and way of life was the impetus for activity-based learning at the Weald and Downland Museum. The common feature of all these approaches to learning is that they use problem-solving techniques to make active use of our heritage. Why is this important? Learning about our heritage – our historic environment – roots individuals in the place where they live, both locally and nationally. It alerts them to alternative ways of living and so broadens their experience. The use

The Charcoal Burner

The Charcoal burner makes the place to burn the charcoal with wood and earth. he makes it in four stages. He puts earth on it to make it air-tight.

Figure 8.6

What A Charcoal burner Make

A Charcoal burner has to catch his own food and make his own ovens and beds and huts. here is a picture of a charcoal burners bed.

and here is a picture of an oven a charcoal burnar would of met by hinsels

The charcoal burners catch there food and cook it in there ovens and here is a picture of a Rabbit

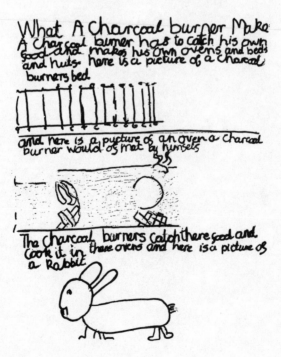

Figure 8.7

of many skills to solve small problems has its immediate objectives, but it also has the underlying intention of training individuals to be aware of their historic environment. The acquisition of problem-solving skills, and a deepened understanding about our heritage, will enable children – as adults – to make judgements about what they would like to see conserved from the historic environment in this fast-changing world. These decisions affect us all and children need to be equipped to participate in the decision-making process as they grow up. Searching for clues to the past in the environment is an important first step.

(Sue Millar was formerly Senior Lecturer in History at St Mary's College, Twickenham).

Case study: Litter (9–11 yrs)

This design problem was an outcome of topic work on 'Litter'. The children had some previous experience of problem-solving and designing.

Introducing the problem

The problem was to design a litter bin which would fit into one of the following environments: the seaside, the town, the countryside. The bin had either to blend in with its surrounding environment or to complement it. It should also encourage people to put their litter into it. To complete the design they had to draw the bin in its environment.

I asked the children to do either a rough design first and then copy it up, or work straight onto best paper. They were also asked to explain in their designs, using either words or diagrams, how the bin encouraged people to use it, how the litter was stored inside the bin and how it could be emptied or even dispose of the litter itself.

The problem was introduced through group discussion and then the children worked individually, discussing their work with me and with other members of the class.

Developing ideas

There were various ideas about encouraging people to put their litter into the bin; some asked for litter when people walked by, some thanked or sang a song to them if they had put their litter in, and others rewarded people with sweets or small gifts.

In discussion some children thought that people should only get one sweet no matter how many pieces of litter they put in; they seemed to view the idea of looking for litter to obtain a reward as 'cheating'. After discussions about this, some designs were changed, the children having decided that it was better to encourage people to look for litter if it improved the environment.

Some designs had the sweets wrapped up in paper and when asked what happened to the paper after the sweet had been eaten, some children thought a second reward should not be given if the person put the sweet paper in the bin. One design had a device which picked up the sweet paper if it was dropped and another had some form of punishment for the people who failed to put their litter in the bin.

Many children did not initially consider how their bins could be emptied or the litter disposed of inside the bin. After this was pointed out some designs were modified to include doors so the litter could be removed. Another design could be rolled over to be emptied. Other designs had the litter stored in bags which could be collected. One or two designs attempted to deal with the litter inside the bins themselves. One had a mechanism for sorting the litter into different types so that it could be recycled; another incorporated the idea of sending the litter along an underground conveyor belt where it was eventually buried. When asked what would happen when no more litter could be buried in that spot, the girl whose design it was suggested that the bin would have to be moved or the route of the conveyor belt altered. The rubbish would be covered over with soil and plants could be grown on it.

Progress

Some children completed their designs with little discussion with me but included ideas which they saw or heard the other children discuss. The problem was worked upon over a period of time, not in a single session, so the children often returned to their design with fresh ideas or modified their ideas after seeing the problems others had encountered. Some of the designs had few changes made to them, the children preferring to stick to their original idea, whilst others had three or four attempts before they were satisfied.

From "*Designing and Making*" (published by The East Midlands and Yorkshire Forum of Advisers in Craft, Design, Technology)

A project in Walkingate infant and primary school

Nancy Elliott (*Senior Primary Inspector, Newcastle upon Tyne*) When a dairy milk factory, adjacent to the school, closed, Newcastle local education authority bought the site to extend the school playground. Using the initial plans for an extension of the cemented playground, the two headteachers involved the pupils, their parents and local residents in decision-making about how the site should be developed. In the end, the LEA, and the city landscape department brought in the British Trust for Conservation Volunteers, who prepared a plan which was approved by the LEA. £16 500 was allocated over two years (1981–83), and the Manpower Services Commission started work on the site with a bulldozer.

The headteacher takes up the story:

'From the time when the final plan was accepted the childen were involved; first in observing and commenting upon the developing landscape. Later forecasting and projecting how things might be. Wellingtons, yellow plastic jackets, spades and barrows were all provided for the children's use. If they were to work on the site, they had to 'look the part', and have tools that they could handle.

The two Manpower Services Commission workers became part of the school: it turned out that they had a natural talent for talking with children.

£1600 worth of trees and shrubs were delivered along with fertiliser, peat and posts. A Saturday Club was created for children; the planting season was limited and every minute mattered. Planting went on six days a week with children of all ages and adults involved. The local comprehensive school sent groups of 14- and 15-year-olds to help and by late March 1982 most of the planting was completed.'

The headteacher noted the following broad headings under which educational benefits were available to the children:

a   Children were engaged in discussion, observation, calculation, recording.
They studied plant growth and care from first-hand experience.

c   They developed appreciation of beauty and the importance of conservation.

d   Various scientific studies were undertaken.

e   Interaction between the children and the community – especially the elderly – became an important social feature of the work.

f   Photography of the stages of development of the work provided a stimulus for written work.

g   Making tape-recorded interviews and writing notes, letters, descriptions, etc., became natural and motivating forms of communication.'

Each class of pupils learned at an appropriate level of sophistication, as problems came to light and were resolved by co-operation and collaboration.

From *Teaching thinking* by Elizabeth Hunter-Grundin (a Schools Council pamphlet, published by the School Curriculum Development Committee, 1985).

Notes and references

1   *Place, Time and Society 8–13* Schools Council Project on History, Geography and Social Science (Schools Council, 1976; SCDC, 1983)

2   The following organisations provide education services and issue a journal free to schools.
    The National Trust, 8 Church Street, Lacock, Nr Chippenham, Wilts SN15 2LB Tel: 024 973 43
    English Heritage, 15/17 Great Marlborough Street, London W1V 1AF Tel: 01 734 6010 (ext. 810)
    The Civic Trust, 17 Carlton House Terrace, London SW1Y 5AW Tel: 01 930 9414

3   The Heritage Education Trust, St Mary's College, Strawberry Hill, Twickenham, Middx TW1 4SX Tel: 01 892 0051 (ext. 202)

4   *History in the Primary and Secondary Years* – an HMI View, DES (HMSO, 1985) p 3

5   'Place, Time and Society, 8–13: The Project's view of the meaning of history today' Frederick Thompson in *Teaching History* No 32, February 1982, Historical Association

6   *Behind the High Street* Kenneth Hudson (Bodley Head, 1982)

Further reading

Place, Time and Society 8–13 Schools Council Project on History, Geography and Social Science (Schools Council 1976, SCDC 1983) useful publications in this series include: *Curriculum planning in History, Geography and Social Science* and *Clues, clues, clues: Detective Work in History* and teachers' guides to other themes.

9 Art, drawing and decision-making

'Creativity is not a special faculty with which some children are endowed and others not. It is a form of intelligence and as such can be developed and trained like any other mode of thinking.'

The Calouste Gulbenkian Report 1982 *The Arts in Schools*

Art is a problem-solving activity. It can be defined as a kind of *visual thinking.* Even a simple picture can present problems which need to be solved. Mark, aged 5, was going to paint a picture of his garden. Carefully he painted a strip of blue sky across the top of his paper, and then a strip of green grass along the bottom. He knew that the sky was up there and the grass was down there. When asked 'What is in the middle Mark?' he frowned, thought for a long moment, and said 'I don't know'. The process of drawing, painting and constructing is a complex one. Anyone who has tried to draw or follow a complicated diagram will know what hard work visual thinking can be.

Art is a way of coming-to-know, through processes of exploration, experiment and discovery. The child assimilates through the senses a vast amount of information. Artistic expression helps in this process of assimilation, in this coming-to-know through sensory experience, by helping to develop perceptual sensitivity. This can be achieved through problem-solving activities involving form, colour, shape and texture. Art can integrate knowledge and skills into the child's own experience. Art also helps in the expression of knowledge for it provides a language for the child's thoughts.

Art requires organisation, the organisation of materials and ideas. In her article *Art as a decision-making process* (page 175) Jenni Hallam shows how this organisation can be a shared undertaking involving teacher and child. Her case-study reveals how a problem-solving approach to art can evolve in practice, and how the children rather than the teacher can become decision makers when responding to an artistic challenge.

Art is a way of learning in which problems can be solved, and relationships worked out. One of the most potent means of achieving this is through the use of drawing. Children often prefer drawing to words as their medium for thinking. The reasons are easy to see. Young children are not always very good at expressing ideas in words but drawing is something that every child can do. Through drawing a child can achieve clarity and ease of expression. Drawings can be extended, altered, modified and changed – the whole problem is before you. Children may be handicapped in terms of verbal expression but they suffer far fewer visual handicaps. Drawing can be the major means of expressing ideas for children who are disadvantaged in other areas. In fact for people of all ages, including the most gifted, drawing and sketching can be powerful tools for thinking and problem solving.

The developmental stages of drawing tie up closely with the whole process of cognitive growth; the well-known *Draw a man test*[1] is a good indicator of mental age. Drawing not only reflects a child's intellectual growth, it can also encourage and stimulate that growth. Every child draws and every child, given the opportunity, loves to paint. Little motivation is necessary for young children, it seems a natural way of learning. A boy was once asked by his teacher what he was going to draw. 'God' he said. 'But nobody knows what God looks like' replied the teacher. The boy began to draw. 'They soon will' he said.

Children seem to have a need to draw, to express their understanding of the environment, and the relationships between objects and people. Every drawing, whether it be by a nursery child or a professional artist, demands a great deal of intellectual involvement – often at the highest levels of absorption and intensity. The teacher's job is to provide the circumstances, the motivation and the materials for this to happen. Joan Jones in her article *Problem solving through cartoon drawing* shows ways in which problem solving through drawing can be a stimulating and enjoyable classroom activity – not least in the opportunities it provides for children to discuss what they have drawn.

The sharing of artistic experiences through discussion and 'showing' can help build self-esteem, and develop an awareness of the creative effort of others – both important aspects of problem-solving through art. It is often the teacher who has the most important role in placing a *value* on what a child has done. Picasso, towards the end of his life, had no doubt about the value of children's art: 'When I was a child' he said 'I could draw like Titian, but it took me all my life to draw like a child'.

Art as a decision-making process

Jenni Hallam

When asking children to write stories or poems we expect *them* to make most of the decisions. We may provide a stimulus, by reading a poem, displaying an object or whatever; we provide the tools needed and a conducive environment in which to work; we remain available to give advice, if required, or help with spelling; but essentially it is the child who structures the piece. The child invents the characters and describes the events; decides what to include and what to reject; where to start and where to end. Most children have very strong feelings about the success or failure of their own work, and may reject a piece as unsuccessful and try again with a new approach. We encourage such independence as part of the 'creative' writing experience.

When the end product is a visual image, the teacher's approach is often very different. Specific instructions are given; and a restricted range of materials, often including templates to make sure the child gets the shape 'right'. The teacher attempts to ensure that all the problems have been solved before the lesson begins. Or they go to the other extreme, presenting the children with no stimuli or structured challenge, just expecting them to paint a picture. Very young children may work happily in such a situation; they are spontaneous and fluent in their use of materials and the sensual pleasure of pushing a wet paintbrush against paper will absorb their interest.

We *should* give children the opportunity to explore materials in this way, but as the child grows older a different, more conscious form of learning can come about through art. Discoveries can be made through thinking, as well as seeing and feeling. To achieve this learning we must provide the child with a problem to be solved and the means with which to go about solving it.

The challenge can take many forms. It may be a visual experience which provides the stimulus – a person dressed up for the children to look at; a bicycle brought into the classroom; a fruit or vegetable cut in half; even the view through the window. A new technique can act as a stimulus in itself, providing the teacher can strike the right balance – giving the child enough information to deal success-fully with the new material, but not giving the solution to every problem. The problem can be a formal one – for example create a design using two squares, a circle and a line, but unlike the mathematical problem, to which there is only one correct solution, the permutations are endless.

The problem itself may present the child with his first decisions, in selecting from various objects to study, or choosing his viewpoint for a drawing. A second set of decisions will occur with the choice of media, paper and working conditions. Within the work itself, the child has a multitude of choices to make, about the positioning of images; the relationship of shapes (with each other, and with the background); how to use materials to create required textural effects; whether to use colour and if so, how. Finally the child makes an analysis of his own results and makes decisions regarding them.

What follows is an example of how this kind of problem-solving approach can evolve in practice. In the Autumn Term, a teacher wanted to introduce some second year children to printing. The class had amassed a collection of shells, stones, driftwood etc from various summer excursions, and the children's obvious interest in these suggested their potential as a stimulus. The collection was displayed so that the items could easily be examined and handled; the starting point for the printing project was close observation of the objects through drawing and painting. The children were provided with magnifying glasses; a choice of media including soft pencils, charcoal, pastels, chalk, wax crayon and paint; and a selection of different shapes, sizes and colours of paper.

Some children chose a single shell or stone to study; others created their own mini-displays of various items; some created imaginary seaside backgrounds, others made a series of drawings exploring different aspects of the chosen object. In the second week the printing techniques and materials were introduced and demonstrated. The children were shown how to roll out the ink, how to make a monoprint, and how to make a printing block using pressprint (polystyrene which can easily be engraved with a pointed tool). Continuing to use the seaside display as a stimulus the children explored the new medium. They came up against problems; for example, the new effect on the results. Some children discovered that their delicate drawings did not come out clearly, others that too much pressure created a clumsy, blurred line.

The teacher did not tell the children that pressprint could be cut to make shapes with which to print, but a child pressing too hard with a pencil accidentally broke his piece of polystyrene in two, and thereby discovered a different way to make his image. Other children quickly discovered that you could make an image of a shell by pressing it into the polystyrene.

As the results began to appear, decisions were made about how they should be used, and what direction should be taken next. In the third and fourth week, collage materials were added to the range of media available. Some children chose to develop their prints into repeating designs, others into pictures. Some kept them as a series of experiments. During the next few weeks the children's work took various directions. Some decided to continue exploring printing, becoming increasingly involved in the techniques and trying out different methods of combining found objects and junk. Others moved into collage work, using their drawings and prints as integral parts of more complex compositions. Some of the children stayed with their original chosen object throughout the whole project, exploring it in a multitude of different ways. Groups of children decided to join together and combine their results in a finished scene.

At the end of six weeks the class had produced an enormous variety of interesting results. The children had very decided views about the relative success and failure of their various experiments and when asked to select the piece of work they felt had been most successful, they were all able to do so unhesitatingly. Following the project, many of the children continued to explore printing techniques at home and bring examples of the results into school.

This term the same class were doing chromatography as part of a colour project in class. The beautiful results inspired the children to create pictures, converting their coloured blots into flowers, butterflies, volcanoes, etc. These children naturally and skilfully incorporated printing techniques into their compositions. Printing has become a part of their creative vocabulary and can now be employed as a means to solve problems of imagery.

Perhaps a note of caution should be introduced here, on the problem of balance. If we provide no structure and no instructions children may be overwhelmed with choice – to the point where they have no real choice to make, as the following quotation from G H Bantock illustrates:

'I once watched a class of infants brought up on free activity methods attempting to make paper hats for a Christmas Party. One child finally evolved a very inadequate copy of a crown he had previously seen. The rest merely copied him. The argument is that the child should be free to choose what sort of hat he wanted, and that in finding out for himself how to achieve his end, valuable educational experience would be gained. The latter notion, pushed to its logical conclusion, would demand the recreation by each generation of the whole of human experience; for if the teacher is not allowed to instruct in the making of hats, why should he be allowed to instruct in anything.'[2]

To ask children to design something without first giving them experience in the techniques involved (in this case cutting card, tissue, silver foil, etc and using them to construct a recognisable three-dimensional form) and without focusing their minds on the nature of the object through discussion, pictures, etc, cannot lead to successful learning. On the other hand, had the teacher provided the complete 'crown making kit', not a great deal would have been learnt either.

We need to set up situations where children can deal confidently with the challenge offered to them. Our role is to provide the initial stimulus and technical knowledge, then to talk with the children on an individual basis, as we would when they are writing a story, hinting, guiding, suggesting, expanding their experience on the basis of their own thoughts and ideas. In this way they will increasingly become the decision makers.

From *Children as decision makers* (London Borough of Croydon, Summer 1985)

Problem solving through cartoon drawing

D Joan Jones

A cartoon can be defined as an amusing drawing, with or without a caption. Quite apart from giving pleasure in its own right, the creation of a cartoon can contribute to the primary child's artistic, personal and linguistic development, as well as providing a stimulus for the growth of problem-solving skills (see Figure 9.1).

It is neither suggested nor envisaged that cartoon drawing should become a timetabled activity. Quite the contrary, for its value lies in its remaining outside established curricular concerns. Not only is cartoon drawing a useful and creative wet playtime activity, being of more positive and educational value than the customary box of dog-eared and tatty comics – it also adapts well to those spare moments when set work has been completed but the remaining lesson time does not permit further extension. Cartoon drawing has the added advantage of being an on-going activity that requires no marking, correcting or close supervision.

The cartoon can be a creative and communicative art form, lending itself not only to the development of drawing skills but also to the extension of the child's language. However, for the purposes of this article, it is the problem-solving aspect which takes precedence. A problem-solving situation is set up by offering a task which requires interpretation through drawing. To complete the work, pupils must pass through the three stages associated with problem solving: the initial state, the intermediate state, and the goal or end state.

The initial state

The initial state in cartoon drawing is concerned with gathering, considering and sifting ideas that will satisfy the demands of the topic and result in the end state, ie the finished cartoon. This initial state is akin to the preparatory stage of the creative act, and lends itself to the brainstorming and synectic approaches used in many problem-solving activities.

Brainstorming
Brief moments between lessons lend themselves admirably to intense sessions of brainstorming, or to quieter synectic considerations –

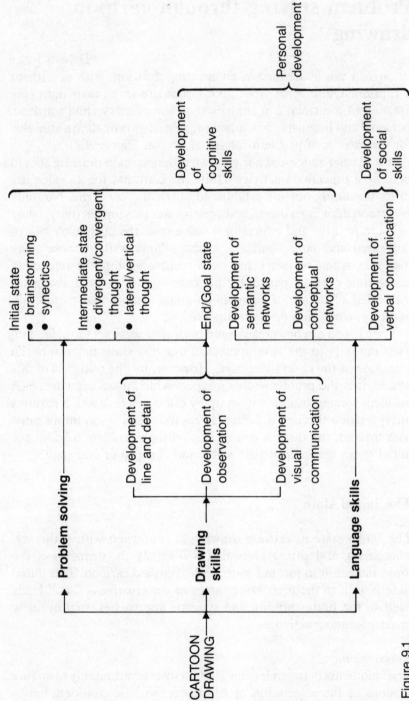

Figure 9.1

whichever proves most appropriate to the topic in hand. Pupils are encouraged to view cartoon drawing as an open-ended task, through which they can express their own interpretation of the title or topic. There are no teacher-imposed criteria. The only demands made are that the final offering be complete, be at a level of presentation compatible with the child's ability, and be handed in on time.

In a brainstorming session pupils' responses to the topic in hand consist of rapidly-offered, uninhibited outpourings associated with the title. No criticism is offered and no judgement made, no suggestion is too wild to be given consideration. The children are then free to order these suggestions and ideas according to their own interpretations.

If cartoon drawing is approached in this way, the more reserved, inhibited and conforming children will begin to relax, and will eventually offer their own associations for peer consideration and amusement. No two people interpret the same situation identically, nor do they have the same experiences, so it is essential that there is no adverse comment from teacher or pupils. Deviation from the norm and unusual associations often inspire the greatest creativity and originality.

Criticism of the *standard* of the presentation is a different matter. If possible, it can be very helpful if all cartoons are displayed somewhere (either mounted or still in the drawing book) for peer approval or criticism. Such comments can be both salutory and satisfying. In these circumstances, there is often no need for the teacher to impose standards.

Synectics

The synectic approach may not provide as lively or as intense a session as brainstorming, but it offers a valuable alternative. Synectics encourages the use of analogy in creativity, whereby the familiar can be made strange and the strange familiar. The two most appropriate forms of synectics for cartoon drawing are the personal analogy – where the pupils are asked to place themselves directly in a situation (eg *Toadstool village, Leave me alone!*) or the fantasy analogy – where the imagination is liberated from normal constraints and boundaries, and allowed free rein (eg *Tree people, The battling bluebell*).

Occasionally, both approaches are appropriate for the same topic. An example is the idea of *Banana boats*. Here, a brainstorming session elicited ideas for a wide variety of boats – rowing boats, gondolas, submarines, yachts, battleships, motor boats. . . Alternatively, the synectic approach gave pupils an opportunity to envisage themselves sailing in a banana boat and to imagine the equipment, crew, weapons etc (see Figure 9.2).

This initial stage serves to stimulate ideas and encourage pupils to recall existing knowledge and information they may not previously have associated with the topic. It generates and uncovers new ideas and associations, activating and extending both the conceptual and semantic networks. At this stage, also, may occur the bizarre links that sometimes lead on to highly original and individual interpretations.

The intermediate state

The intermediate state of a problem-solving activity can be said to coincide with the *incubation* and *inspirational* stages of the creative act. The pupil's thought processes are set in motion during the brainstorming sessions. Then there is a pause before the drawing starts – caused by the onset of the next lesson, break, or home-time – during that space, or incubation period, ideas that have been stimulated may seem to settle and lie dormant. Often, it is during these periods of apparent mental inactivity that ideas form, mingle and reform, to surface later as inspiration. The final, goal state may be visualised at this stage, before drawing starts, but detail may not emerge until the drawing is underway.

Small group discussion and interaction are invaluable during this intermediate stage, for this is the analysing, sorting, synthesising phase for ideas. In other words, it is the *thinking* period.

Convergent and divergent thinking

In school there is often a tendency to set tasks to which there is only one correct solution, ie they require 'thought convergence'. Teachers, it is suggested, emphasise and encourage convergent thinking, neglecting the divergent aspect. Yet the latter often leads to creativity and originality. The non-conforming traits of divergent thinkers may make them apparently less popular with teachers. But such people often create the most original offering, be it cartoon or artefact.

Cartoon drawing is open-ended and has no clearly defined, correct solution; it thus encourages the originality of the divergent thinker,

Banana Boat

Figure 9.2

and helps the teacher offer a positive and acceptable challenge to the non-conformist pupil. So, for example, by comparing and contrasting a problem set in cartoon drawing with one set in mathematics, pupils can come to understand and appreciate the different types of thinking involved, and the value and application of each type.

The ability to think divergently is best assessed through open-ended tasks and objective activities such as cartoon drawing, rather than through contrived, commercially-produced exercises and detached, weekly half-hour lessons.

Lateral thinking

Divergent thought has similarities to de Bono's 'lateral thinking': the suggestion that when vertical and sequential steps fail to solve a problem, a move sideways, or laterally, to view the stalemate from a different angle, may open up a fresh track towards a solution.

Pupils can experience this through cartoon drawing if they are encouraged to view the topic from an angle other than the immediate or the obvious. Does the title *Four eyes*, for instance, necessarily have to refer to people who wear glasses, or to creatures which have four eyes? Do the eyes have to be placed together, or in rows, or even in the head?

In cartoon drawing there is a need and a place for both divergent and convergent thought, for lateral and for vertical thinking. Divergent and lateral thinking may lead to originality, but sequential and convergent thinking are also required to bring those thoughts to completion and to represent them in a finished form (the goal or end state) which can be understood and appreciated by others. The success of a cartoon lies ultimately in its effectiveness as a means of communication.

The goal or end state

The goal, or end state, in this context, is the act of creating the cartoon, which should satisfy and answer the problem set. In some instances, such a solution may indicate a move away from existing or conventional patterns of thought and interpretation, resulting in originality.. This state is a valuable stage in cognitive and personal development. It can encourage fresh confidence and renewed efforts, and stimulate others to further mental activity and artistic endeavour.

Requirements

Requirements for cartoon drawing are minimal – a selection of felt-tip pens and a book of cheap, plain paper are all that is needed. A large (15″×10″) plain exercise book, cut in half, is ideal. It is a good idea to set a time limit – for example, a title or topic can be suggested on a Monday, and the completed cartoon handed in by the following Friday. This approach helps promote self-discipline and self-management – qualities the pupil will need on transfer to secondary school, where he or she will be handling homework schedules and assignments.

Some children, dissatisfied with their initial attempts, will waste several pages on false starts, so it is wise to restrict them to one page for each cartoon. This disciplines the impulsive child, and forces some measure of initial planning on all. Setting a weekly cartoon helps maintain the children's interest, and the opportunity to start afresh gives new hope to those whose previous effort had proved a disaster or a disappointment.

Some suggestions

The elehenocatopus!	Banana boat
Tree people	Banana split
Leave me alone!	Wot a Wally!

Clowns	Boot lorry
Toadstool house	Witch doctor
Silly sausage	The kettle family
Globe trotter	Tea-pot house
Football fan	Grass-hopper

The chairman
A pretty ugly mug
Battling bluebell

Notes and references

1   *Children's drawings as measures of intellectual maturity* D.B. Harris (Harcourt, Brace, Jovanovich, 1963)
2   *Freedom and Authority in Education* G.H. Bantock

Further reading

Arnheim R. *Visual Thinking* (Berkeley, 1971)
de Bono E. *The Dog Exercising Machine* (Jonathan Cape, 1970); *Children Solve Problems* (Jonathan Cape, 1970)
The Calouste Gulbenkian Report, *The Arts in Schools* (1982)
Harris D.B. *Children's Drawings as Measures of Intellectual Maturity* (Harcourt, Brace, Jovanovich, 1963)
Lowenfield V. and Brittain W.L. *Creative and Mental Growth* (Macmillan, 1982)
Schools Council, *Art and Craft Education Project 8–13* (Van Nostrand Reinhold, 1974)

10 Moral problems

'Man has created new worlds – of language, of music, of poetry,
of science; and the most important of these is the world of the
moral demands, for equality, for freedom, and for helping the
weak'.

Karl Popper

Moral education does not feature on the timetable as a subject. Most
teachers regard it as happening all the time, through all the activities
of the school. Special attention may be paid to moral questions
during assembly, in religious education lessons and at times when
the teacher needs to encourage good behaviour. Responsibility for
moral education runs across the whole curriculum, for there is no
dimension of education or of life where moral concerns are irrelevant.

Throughout their school lives, children need opportunities to
formulate their own ideas about moral questions and conflicts of
interest. As they get older they also need to face the problems which
confront each individual in a complex modern society. The growth
of moral understanding is a slow process, but a vital one for individual development and for social survival. The constitution of
UNESCO expresses it thus 'Since wars begin in the minds of men,
it is in the minds of men that the defence of peace must be constructed'. If we expect children to grow up with the ability to make
reasoned judgements on moral questions, and to face the problems
of an uncertain future, we must give them the experiences and
training that will help them to acquire it. Perhaps 'peace studies'
should begin in the reception class.

Young children are full of questions about the world. Given the
opportunity to express themselves they respond well to the universal
stimulus – 'What do you think?' Here a group of infants discuss
the question of whether animals should be killed or not:

    Child: I don't think animals should be killed.
    Teacher: Why not?

Child: Animals have done nothing to us, why should we kill them?
Teacher: Sometimes animals are killed because people want to eat them, like cows or rabbits.
Child: We shouldn't kill cows – they give us milk and that's good for you.
Child: If we kill animals we shouldn't eat them. You wouldn't want to get eaten would you?
Child: It's not fair to kill animals to eat them. There are plenty of other things to eat.
Teacher: Some animals are killed and eaten because they taste nice.
Child: That's not fair.
Child: Sometimes you have to kill animals when they are very ill.
Child: Or if it's hurt, in an accident or something.
Teacher: Some wild animals kill people. Should animals be killed if they are dangerous?
Child: Like tigers – they can kill people.
Child: I think we should only kill animals when they have killed six people or more.
Teacher: Should an animal be killed if it only kills one person?
Child: No, because it doesn't know what it is doing.

Children of all ages enjoy discussing such questions and sharing thoughts, experiences and anecdotes. The job of the teacher includes posing questions, keeping the discussion moving, helping children to understand the problem and to express their own thinking, and showing the value of thinking co-operatively – that you discover more by thinking with others.

There is, however, an important distinction between getting children to discuss openly what they think about moral questions, and teaching them to be 'good' (if that is possible). Some regard religious education as concerned with 'helping children to lead a good life' and transmitting moral values.

Religious education

Religious education is essentially about the understanding of religion. This understanding can be developed by exploring the moral dimension within religions – and this in turn may have an influence on the child's own moral development and choice of lifestyle. But although the connection between morality and religion is a close one they should not be confused.

Morality is *inside* religion, in that each religion has its moral code by which believers are required to live. Morality can also be based outside religion. Moral values can be held and justified without appeal to religious authority. The morality of 'common sense' or of social welfare are examples of this. Moral problems face all people, and moral values can be shared by people of different faiths or of no faith.

> 'The overlap of religious with moral education occurs when children are exploring ideas, feelings and actions involved in the ethical teaching of religious traditions and in the moral conflicts that might arise in the life of the believer.'
>
> (Hertfordshire Agreed Syllabus, 1981)

Most of the people who have influenced the history of this country and helped form its laws, have been Christians. Christian values have permeated our culture, affecting the moral outlook of the majority of people. The Christian Church has played a major role in providing education in this country. In Christian schools, moral education is conducted in accordance with the principles of the Christian Church. It is easy, therefore, to give the impression that the only basis for a moral code is the Christian ethic.

Many are now questioning the traditional assumptions of moral education. With the increasing pluralism of our society, many feel that it is no longer appropriate or helpful to teach a moral code that depends on religious belief. In any class today there are likely to be children from a variety of backgrounds and traditions. Even those from a Christian background may not themselves accept it. Moral education should not be concerned with trying to hand on a Christian ethic – although in the context of religious education it will explore many aspects of that ethic. We should aim to free moral education from its dependence on religious education, to help children become morally autonomous, capable of independent thought and self-rule and able to understand the principles of moral judgement that govern their behaviour.

Moral and social education

A boy once wanted to watch a particular TV programme. Three other members of his family wanted to switch to another channel.

They took a vote and switched channels. 'Why', asked the boy, 'is it better for three people to be selfish than one?'

The essence of many moral problems is conflict of interest. The resolution of problems – if it is not achieved by force – must be through the growth of empathy and understanding in personal relationships, the use of reasoning and the application of such principles as fairness and reciprocity (Do unto others . . .). Moral awareness develops through everyday experiences and can be expressed through any activity. Story-time is one such daily activity in which moral experiences can be explored with primary children.[1] A question that can be asked after almost any story is 'What makes people bad?' The theme of what is good and what is bad, and how they come to be, is universal, and so are the problems. The conflict between good and evil is a theme common to all major religions, and *religious stories* provide many opportunities for exploring moral ideas and decisions.

The judgement of Solomon (1 Kings 3) is the story of one such moral problem. Two women came before King Solomon. They brought one baby with them and they both claimed to be its mother. Solomon was asked to decide between them. He said that he could not tell which was the true mother, and ordered a sword so that the baby could be divided in half. One woman agreed to this saying that it was the fairest thing to do, but the second woman was horrified and said she would rather give up her claim to the child. Which was the true mother? Solomon ordered the baby should go to the woman who was prepared to give up the child rather than see it harmed. The sort of questions that might arise from this story include: Do you think Solomon's decision was a wise one? Why? What would you have done in Solomon's place?

Another good source of stories which raise moral questions is the local or national news. One such reported story concerned four small girls who were walking home from their infant school. A car drew up beside them. The man inside the car called the girls and said to them, 'Your father says you are to come with me at once. He sent me to fetch you.' The man held the door open. The girls had always been taught to obey their father. What should they do? Three of the girls got in, but the fourth did not. She ran away. The car drove off. The girl ran – but where should she run to? Not home, that was too far, but to a nearby police station. A call went out, the car was stopped, and the three girls were brought back safely. The girl who raised the alarm was questioned by the police. What made her run off instead of going too? 'I don't know', she said, 'but Mummy and Daddy are always saying "Think!" They say "You've got a mind of your own, use it". So I thought. I thought that if Daddy really wanted us he'd come himself, and I thought that the man only said one Daddy, and we've got three Daddies, all of us I mean. So I ran.'

This news story appears in a book of themes and stories for *assembly*.[2] Although not a time for much pupil discussion the school assembly can often provide a stimulus for follow-up work in the classroom. Stories used in assembly – whether they be religious teaching stories, fables, folktales, true-life or fictional tales – may raise interesting problems and dilemmas which invite further reflection and examination.[3]

Many of these stories gain from dramatisation. Drama is a potent means of bringing situations alive and exploring conflicts. Older children will be able to improvise situation dramas. They need to be given a clear idea as to the situation and characters, with some suggestions as to how the scene might develop. It is best to have only a few characters (2 or 3). The rest of the class may be invited to offer (constructive) comments and discuss alternative endings. For example, in *The lost purse* one character loses a purse, two others find it. What might they do? How might the situation end?

Another challenge children enjoy is dramatising updated versions of traditional stories (such as the parable of the Good Samaritan) or proverbs and moral sayings ('Two wrongs don't make a right', 'Turn the other cheek', 'You can't judge a sausage by its skin' . . .). Successful role play is often a problem-solving exercise in itself!

Of course, children face *real problems* of their own. The teacher can create opportunities for children to present personal problems for discussion in the classroom, by providing a 'problem box' or holding a general forum where particular concerns, like being teased, being left out, feeling that a brother or sister is better liked, parents arguing . . . could be aired. Children could be invited to vote on which particular dilemma they wish to discuss. The teacher, too, might enter into the spirit of enquiry by presenting one or two dilemmas of his or her own.

What do you think?

Among the published materials that might help in stimulating ideas about moral problems is *What do you think?* by David and Christina Milman.[4] This book invites pupils to express opinions on some of the moral questions which children in the middle years of schooling commonly face.

The book quotes the ancient story of *The blind men and the elephant* (adapted from the Pali Canon) to show how when people argue they are often blind to other people's points of view. The story goes that a king had many wise men to advise him, but they were always arguing among themselves about whose advice the king should follow. The king grew tired of their quarrels. So he ordered an elephant and seven blind men to be brought into the palace courtyard. The blind men each felt the elephant in turn. One thought it was a great pot, others a fan, the handle of a plough, a snake, the pillar of a palace, the side of a barn, and a strong rope. The wise men laughed. The king told them that *they* were just like the blind men – blind to other points of view. Only when they could learn to see each other's point of view could they be called 'wise'.

We all see things in different ways. A bucket of water may look like a bucket of water, but as a character in Norton Juster's *The Phantom Tolbooth* remarks, from an ant's point of view it is a vast ocean, from an elephant's it is a cool drink, and to a fish it is home. Ask the children to look at a stone, a stick, a pond – and then to make a list of how many ways they might be seen. Teaching children to de-centre, to look beyond their own egocentric viewpoint, to put themselves into another's shoes, is an essential part of the growth and development of moral consciousness.

In the section entitled *It's not fair!* children are asked to consider various situations represented in cartoon form and to draw their own cartoons to show some of the times when they or someone else has said 'It's not fair!'. They are also invited to act out a family argument which arises from someone saying 'It's not fair!' with everyone giving reasons for their own point of view. Starting from feelings of unfairness in their own lives, children are encouraged to consider wider social concerns – whether it is fair that many people in the world are starving, homeless, unemployed, dying from disease, or not given the chance of education.

In *I don't care!* children are asked to think about the things they care most about, for example, being popular, being clever, their family, having friends, the way they look, their future and so on, and to rate these things in a questionnaire. They are then asked to consider things that other people care very much about – pollution, plants, animals, other people in society – and who they think is in need of special care.

I don't like you explores some of our reasons for liking and disliking people. Charles Lamb wrote, 'I am in plainer words a bundle of prejudices – made up of likings and dislikings'. The section asks, what prejudices do you have? Children are invited to think about different tastes, sounds, sights, places, people, books, games etc, to write lists of 'I like' and 'I dislike' and to give good reasons for their feelings. They are asked to describe a friend and say what it is they particularly like about them, then to say if they know any people they do not like. Can they say why? Do they have good reasons for disliking them? How do they behave towards these people? Are they fair to them? Extracts from several fictional stories are given, which highlight different aspects of prejudice, and pose the questions 'Do you have prejudices?' 'Ask yourself why.' 'How can you get rid of these prejudices?'

They called me a name considers the problem of teasing. It includes an excerpt from *Lord of the Flies* by William Golding in which the fat boy is given the nickname Piggy. Children are asked what they think the fat boy felt like when he was called Piggy. They are then invited to act out the scene in groups, with each taking turns to be Piggy. Have they ever felt left outside of a group? Do they think the saying 'Sticks and stones may break my bones, but words will never hurt me' a true one? Are some unkind names worse than others? Are some people more easily hurt? Through these and other activities children are asked to reflect on the power of words to hurt others.

There's a fight focuses attention on the question of why people argue and fight with each other. Is using violence the right way to solve a problem? How else might people settle their arguments? One question for discussion is whether imaginary violence shown on television helps to cause real violence. Children are asked to do some research and keep a record of the number of violent scenes on the TV programmes they watch – then to consider whether there is too much imaginary violence on television.[5]

I just did what the others did opens with the rhyme:

> Birds of a feather flock together
> And so do pigs and swine;
> Rats and mice do have their choice.
> And so do I have mine.

Children are asked to think back to their first day at a new school, and to describe how they felt and how they got to know people. An extract from *The Country Child* by Alison Uttley shows how easy it is for one child to be frightened by many. This leads on to considering how crowds can behave quite differently from individual people, and the problems of football hooliganism. Have you ever been in a large group that got 'carried away' – perhaps at school or at a party? What did you feel and how did people behave?

That's cruel! explores cruelty to animals and asks, do you have strong feelings about any animals? Incidents of cruelty to animals are reported and children are asked to look out for reports of cruelty to animals in newspapers. Why do you think it happens? People see animals in different ways – as pets, food, sport, pests, as useful or dangerous. Choose an animal you would like as a pet and describe how you would care for it. Discuss whether we should kill animals for food, or hunt them for sport. Is it wrong to kill any living creature?

That's stealing! presents the temptations that are familiar to all children. Has anyone ever stolen anything belonging to you and your family? Describe what happened and how you felt about it. Are there any good reasons for stealing? Children could go on to consider ways of preventing things being stolen, and perhaps to invent their own burglar alarms. They might also explore, through writing or play-acting, the dilemmas that can arise from finding something that is valuable. Is 'finders keepers' really honest?

The following extract, *That's a lie!* shows how the book presents the problem of lying.

> Sometimes it is easy to tell what is true and what is
> untrue.
> Look at (Figure 10.1)
> Which of these statements are true?
> Which are untrue?

That's a lie!

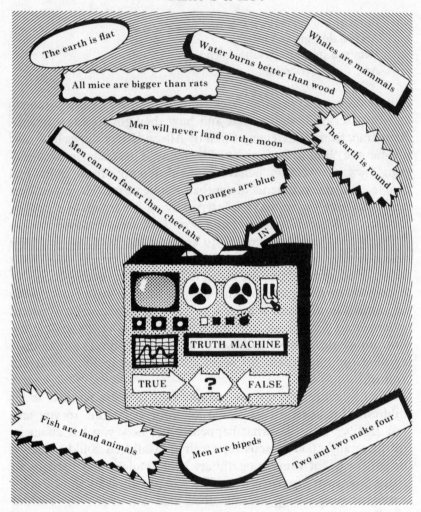

Figure 10.1

Sometimes people know what the truth is but for various reasons deliberately do not tell it – instead they lie.

Read this story:

Once there was a boy who lived in a mountain village. Every day he was sent onto the mountain slopes to look after the sheep as they grazed and to watch out for wolves. He used to get very bored all by himself with no one to talk to.

One day he thought of a way to pass the time. He suddenly

started shouting 'Help! Wolf! Wolf!' at the top of his voice. His trick worked. Nearly everyone in the village left what he was doing and ran out to help him. The only thanks they got was to be laughed at for their trouble. The boy tried his trick two or three times and each time it worked much to his delight.

However one day a wolf actually came out of the woods and the boy cried out in terror 'Help! Wolf! Wolf!' But nobody came. The villagers just said to each other 'Listen to that boy. He's at his tricks again. Just ignore him, the little liar!' So the wolf was able to kill several of the sheep and go on its way without being hindered. The boy was lucky to escape with his life.

> Why did the shepherd boy lie?
> What was the result of his lying?
> Do you think anyone ever believed what he said again?

In the following extract someone tells a lie for quite a different reason.

Read first:

Jesus said to Peter, 'I tell you, tonight before the cock crows you will disown me three times.' Peter said, 'Even if I must die with you I will never disown you.'

(A short time after this Jesus is arrested and taken to the high priest's house where he is put on trial for his life. The priests hate him and anyone who is his friend. Peter, as one of his disciples, is in considerable danger.)

Continue reading:

Meanwhile Peter was sitting outside in the courtyard when a serving-maid accosted him and said, 'You were there too with Jesus the Galilean.' Peter denied it in face of them all. 'I do not know what you mean,' he said. He then went out to the gateway, where another girl, seeing him, said to the people there, 'This fellow was with Jesus of Nazareth.' Once again he denied it, saying with an oath, 'I do not know the man.'

Shortly afterwards the bystanders came up and said to Peter, 'Surely you are another of them; your accent gives you away.' At this he broke into curses and declared with an oath: 'I do not know the man.'

At that moment the cock crew; and Peter remembered how Jesus had said, 'Before the cock crows you will disown me three times.' He went outside and wept bitterly.

from *The New English Bible*

Make sure you understand these words:
disown   accosted   denied
bystander   oath

Why was Peter angry when he was asked by the bystanders if he knew Jesus?
Why did Peter break his promise and lie?
How did Peter feel afterwards?
What do you think you would have done if you had been Peter?
Is lying always wrong?
Before you make up your mind read the following extract:

(The master's book has been torn. Tom knows that his friend Rebecca Thatcher was responsible. The master is determined to discover the culprit and punish him, or her, severely.)

'Who tore this book?'
There was not a sound. One could have heard a pin drop. The stillness continued; the master searched face after face for signs of guilt.
'Benjamin Rogers, did you tear this book?'
A denial. Another pause.
'Joseph Harper, did you?'
Another denial. Tom's uneasiness grew more and more intense under the slow torture of these proceedings. The master scanned the ranks of boys, considered a while, then turned to the girls:
'Amy Lawrence?'
A shake of the head.
'Gracie Miller?'
The same sign.
'Susan Harper, did you do this?'
Another negative. The next girl was Becky Thatcher. Tom was trembling from head to foot with excitement, and a sense of the hopelessness of the situation.
'Rebecca Thatcher' – (Tom glanced at her face; it was white with terror) – 'did you tear – no, look me in the face'– (her hands rose in appeal) – 'did you tear this book?'
A thought shot like lightning through Tom's brain. He sprang to his feet and shouted:
'I done it!'

from *The Adventures of Tom Sawyer* by Mark Twain

Why did Tom lie?
Was he wrong to tell a lie?
What do you think of Tom?

There are many different kinds of lie. This poem is called 'What kind of a liar are you?'

Read the poem carefully:

What kind of a liar are you?

a   People lie because they don't remember clear what they saw.

b   People lie because they can't help making a story better
than it was the way it happened.

c   People tell 'white lies' so as to be decent to others.

d   People lie in a pinch, hating to do it, but lying on because
it might be worse.

e   And people lie just to be liars for a crooked personal gain.
What sort of a liar are you?
Which of these liars are you?[6]

Carl Sandburg

What is a white lie?
Which line describes Peter's lie?
Which line describes Tom's lie?
Is there a line which describes the shepherd boy's lie?
Can you think of your own examples for lines b, d
and e?

Do you think some kinds of lies are worse than others?
Have you ever told a lie?
Can you remember why?
Has anyone ever lied to you? How did you feel about
it?
Write a story or poem about a 'lie'.

From *What do you think?* by David and Christina Milman (Blackie, 1977)

It's against the rules introduces children to the important concept of rules. They are invited to look at and think about the various signs they see around them in their daily lives (see Figure 10.2). From this they go on to consider whether there is a special sign they would like to put up at home or school (designing and drawing their own version of it) What rules should we have in school – rules for children *and* rules for teachers? Could a school run without rules? If not, which rules are the most important? This could lead on to research into the rules of the major religions, or to pupils compiling their own list of rules for living a good life.

The moral problems presented here can be adapted for children of all ages, and presented in many different ways. Visual stimuli – pictures, posters and photographs – can provide starting points for

Figure 10.2

discussion, as can extracts from children's literature. Follow up activities can include writing acting, further research and tape recording. The aim is to help children grow in their understanding of moral problems, and in the ability to make reasoned moral choices, to help them towards a better understanding of themselves and of others. As Alice said 'Everything's got a moral, if only you can find it' (*Alice in Wonderland*)

Moral development

The power of moral judgement develops through a number of stages; from the egocentric lawlessness of early childhood (*anomy*), through rule by fear of punishment or hope of reward (*heteronomy*), rule by a sense of social convention and reciprocity (*socionomy*) and finally a personally developed value system or self-rule (*autonomy*). This can be seen as the process of *decentring* in thinking, of seeing things from another's point of view. As with other forms of thinking there is a spiral of development whereby a person may operate on different levels in different situations.

The following model is a guide as to the different levels on which moral development may operate:

Moral Model
   Attitudes/judgements about self/others and events.
M1 Judging self/others by physical characteristics or conseqences, eg 'She was ugly, so she was bad', 'He broke fifteen cups – naughty.' Judging events by pain-pleasure to the self, eg 'It was a bad day, I hurt my hand'. 'It was a good birthday. I got lots of presents.' 'A bad accident – the fence was smashed up.' Principle of self-gratification – *anomy*.
M2 Judging self/others and events in terms of punishments/ rewards. 'I won't do that, Mummy will hit me.' 'I'll tell Daddy on you and he will beat you up.' 'If I do the dishes, Mummy will give me a new bat.' Events judged as rewards/ punishments, eg 'I must have been naughty last night, the fridge hit me.' *Heteronomy*.
M3 Judging self/others according to the status quo. Mother, father, teacher, policeman good by right of status; the wicked witch, the evil step-father bad by right of convention, eg 'I hated the Jerries, I used to call them stupid idiots'. Reciprocity restricted to the child's immediate circle, eg 'I won't do that – it will upset mummy'. Social approval/disapproval internalised in terms of whether behaviour upsets others or not. Stereotypic thinking. Events judged in terms of effects on other *people*. 'It was a bad accident. All the passengers were badly hurt.' *Socionomy* (internal)
M4 Judging self/others in terms of conventional norms/rules, eg 'It's wrong to steal. It is against the law.' Conformist orientation. Rules are applied literally on the principle of equity or fairness. 'It's not fair. We all did it, so John

should be punished the same as us. We all broke the rule.'
Socionomy (external).

M5 Judging self/others in terms of intention or motive, regardless of status or power, eg 'She didn't mean to drop those plates, so she shouldn't be punished'. 'Teacher was wrong, because she punished all of us instead of finding out who did it.'

M6 Judging self/others in terms of abstract concepts such as a universal respect for the individual rather than in terms of conventional norms of right/wrong conducts. The morality of individual conscience. Rules seen as arbitrary and changeable. *Autonomy.*

M7 Judgement of self/others in terms of a personally developed value *system.*[7]

From *Assessing Language Development* by A. Wilkinson, G. Barnsley, P. Hanna and M. Swan (OUP, 1980)

Piaget said 'Morality is the logic of action'.[8] How we behave is not necessarily related to the judgements we make in deliberately constructed moral dilemmas. The expectations of others – social, parent, peer – have an important bearing on the child's moral judgements and actions, but so do the expectations of teachers and of the school – they too have an important part to play in helping children face up to the moral problems of life.

Notes and references

1   See *Stories for thinking* (on page 42)
2   *Together today* Robert Fisher (Bell and Hyman, 1981)
3   See also the story sections in *Together with Infants* Robert Fisher (Bell and Hyman, 1982) and *The Assembly Year* Robert Fisher (Collins, 1985)
4   *What do you think?* D and C Milman (Blackie, 1977)
5   Recent studies suggest that young people between 5 and 14 years spend an average 23 hours a week watching television – about the same length of time as they spend in the classroom. See *Popular TV and Schoolchildren*, report of a group of teachers (DES April 1983)
6   *What kind of liar are you?* from THE PEOPLE, YES by Carl Sandburg, copyright 1936 by Harcourt Brace Jovanovich, Inc.;

renewed 1964 by Carl Sandburg. Reprinted by permission of the publisher.

7   *Assessing Language Development* A. Wilkinson, G. Barnsley, P. Hanna, M. Swan (OUP, 1980)

8   *The Moral Judgement of the Child* J. Piaget (Routledge and Kegan Paul, 1932)

Further reading

Many of the Agreed Syllabuses discuss the relationship between religious education and moral problems eg Hertfordshire Agreed Syllabus for Religious Education (1981).

See also: Schools Council *Discovering an Approach* (The Schools Council Project on RE in Primary Schools 1973)

11 Games for problem solving

'Avoid compulsion and let early education be a manner of amusement. Young children learn by games; compulsory education
cannot remain in the soul.'

Plato

Play is the central activity of childhood and it comes in a myriad
of forms. At its best, play provides children with activity, enjoyment,
co-operation, discussion, investigation and problem solving. In play
children experience 'the joy of being the cause' (Susan Isaacs).[1]
Through play children can learn things that they would not learn
in any other way. The historian Huizinga argues that all of human
culture derives from our capacity to play.[2]

The essence of games is a sense of involvement in the activity for
its own sake. Games can help children to practise skills and to
develop concepts and strategies. At its most mundane, play may
become a succession of repetitive and mindless routines. Perhaps
as a result of this, in primary schools games playing has largely
been seen as an infant or spare-time activity. It is the job of the
teacher to see that educational play has a purpose and structure –
that it is not merely 'filling-in' time. 'Without the help of a teacher
setting the environment and providing suggestions, children reach
stalemate and their play becomes intellectually aimless.'[3]

In his article *Games – a rationale for their use in the teaching of
mathematics in school* (page 204), Paul Ernest argues that the introduction of games can have many advantages for children of all ages.
He cites research studies which underline the benefits of games
playing in the teaching of mathematics. The same rationale for
games playing can be applied to all aspects of the primary cur-

riculum. What justifies the use of games in the maths lesson can justify it in other lessons, and the benefit of games playing is not restricted to purely mathematical ends. What is important is that wherever games-playing is introduced into the primary curriculum it can be justified on educational grounds, and that its purposive nature as a problem-solving activity is recognised by both teacher and pupil.

Problem-solving games (page 213) presents a personal approach to games playing and offers a collection of games that can be used in the primary classroom as a basis for investigation and for developing problem-solving skills and strategies.

Games: a rationale for their use in the teaching of mathematics in school

Paul Ernest

Why use games in the mathematics classroom? Can games help children to learn mathematics, or are they just a form of entertainment or 'time-filler'?

Many teachers bring out games, puzzles and recreations around Christmas time, or at the end of the Summer term. These activities help to create a light hearted and 'fun' atmosphere in the classroom which pupils and teachers enjoy. But pupils will often say 'that was fun and I enjoyed it, but it wasn't real mathematics'. Are they right? Are games just an enjoyable interlude or can games be used to actually teach mathematics?

Games have many advantages

We have all experienced the enthusiasm generated by games such as Chess, Cards, Darts, Monopoly, Scrabble and so on, by playing ourselves or by watching others play. Games generate enthusiasm, excitement, total involvement and enjoyment.

This is the first and most striking advantage of introducing games into the mathematics classroom. Pupils become strongly motivated, they immerse themselves in the activity, and over a period of time should enhance their attitude towards the subject. In addition to being motivating in themselves, games also add variety to the overall mathematics curriculum, by bringing another varied approach into the teaching of the subject.

The celebrated paragraph 243 of the Cockcroft Report[4] stressed that children need to discuss mathematics, as well as learning it in other ways. When groups of children play mathematical games they need to talk over moves and discuss the correctness of answers and different strategies. Thus mathematical games encourage discussion between groups of children and also between pupil and teacher.

In recognition of the importance of discussion to the learning of mathematics, the new GCSE mathematics examinations[5] will include oral assessment. Thus it is vitally important that any means of encouraging this neglected area of mathematics learning, such as games, is used to help prepare our students.

The recent publication *Mathematics From 5 to 16*[6] stresses co-operative working as one of the aims of teaching mathematics. Children playing a mathematical game as a team quickly learn that they need to co-operate to play effectively. Even children competing against each other are co-operating in playing the game. Thus introducing games into the mathematics classroom can be a way of encouraging co-operation. Through attaining this aim we also encourage discussion.

The success of all mathematics teaching depends, to a large extent, on the active involvement of the learner. Children learn mathematics by doing and by making the concepts and skills of mathematics their own. Playing games demands involvement. Children cannot play games passively, they must be actively involved, the more so if they want to win. Thus games encourage the active involvement of children, making them more receptive to learning, and of course increasing their motivation.

Active involvement not only enhances learning; according to some psychologists it is essential for learning to take place at all. For this reason psychologists including Piaget, Bruner and Dienes suggest that games have a very important part to play in learning, particularly in the learning of mathematics.

Of these three, Zoltan P. Dienes goes furthest by suggesting that all mathematics teaching should begin with games. Although Dienes may be overstating his case, he is a man well worth listening to. Dienes has not only carried out an extensive programme of classroom research, he has also developed some of the best apparatus available for teaching mathematics, including multi-base arithmetic blocks, algebraical experience materials, logic blocks and the number balance. Thus teaching mathematics through games is not only psychologically sound, it is also psychologically desirable.

Games teach mathematics effectively

We teach mathematics so that our pupils will attain mathematical objectives. Of course we also have more general aims such as giving enjoyment, encouraging co-operation, discussion and so on. Leaving these aside, the major purpose of teaching mathematics is the attainment of objectives. This section focuses on three types of objective, and on the use of games in attaining them. These objectives concern helping children to:

- *gain new concepts and develop them;*
- *practice and reinforce skills;*
- *develop problem solving strategies.*

Each of these objectives is considered in turn, but in an order which reflects the frequency with which games are used to attain them.

1　The reinforcement and practice of skills

Much of mathematics teaching revolves around giving children practice in newly acquired skills, or in reinforcing and further developing skills. Games provide a way of taking the drudgery out of the practice of skills, and indeed of making the practice more effective.

A team of American researchers, Bright, Harvey and Wheeler, have carried out over a dozen studies of the use of games to teach mathematics.[7] Two of the studies[8] involved the use of games to reinforce basic multiplication and division facts (with single digit factors) among 14 classes of 9, 10 and 11-year-olds in 1976 and among 10 classes of 10- and 11-year-olds in 1977.

The classes played the games for 15 minutes daily for a total of 7 days. Gains in test performances showed that the games treatment was an effective way to retrain and reinforce children's skills with basic number facts. A study[9] by the same team concerned the use of games to develop further the skill of ordering common fractions. The study showed that the games treatment was effective.

2　The acquisition and development of concepts

One of the main objectives of mathematics teaching is to aid children in acquiring new concepts. A further objective is to assist children in developing and extending their concepts. Mathematical games can be an effective way of attaining both of these objectives. The following studies illustrate this.

The American team of Bright, Harvey and Wheeler carried out two studies,[10,11] with 11-year-old and 13-year-old pupils. The studies concerned the concepts of fairness and unfairness with regard to probability. The pupils played 8 pairs of games one of which is fair and the other unfair, in that one of two players is favoured.

The pupils were tested with 14 items like those shown in Figure 11.1, both before and after the game playing. Some pupils were also given the results of a computer simulation of playing the test games for 50 trials. These pupils showed appreciable gains in their test scores, which the others did not, in both studies. The games helped the pupils acquire the probabilistic concepts of fairness and unfairness, which they could successfully apply in a situation if sufficient information was given.

Edith Biggs carried out a research project[12] teaching both slow learning and able pupils from 7 to 13 years old in twelve London schools (six first schools, six middle schools) over a period of two terms. Games, especially dice games, made up a large part of the teaching programme for all the pupils, except for the older, more able, pupils. Although games were included, the teaching programme for these pupils concentrated more on problem solving and investigatory work.

The following set of problems ask you to choose the game which gives you the best chance of winning. If the chances are the same you are to identify that it doesn't make any difference.

Which game gives you the best chance of winning or doesn't it make any difference?

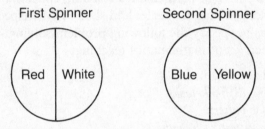

First Spinner   Second Spinner

Red | White   Blue | Yellow

A. Game 1 You spin the first spinner once and you win if you get red.
B. Game 2 You spin both spinners once and you win if you get white and yellow, or white and blue.
C. It doesn't make any difference.

The following boxes contain black and white marbles. To play this game you pick a marble from one of the two boxes. *You win if you choose a black marble.*

If you can play this game only once, do you have a better chance of winning if you pick from Box A or Box B, or doesn't it make any difference?

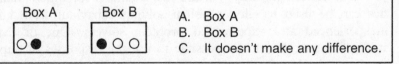

Box A   Box B   A. Box A
                              B. Box B
                              C. It doesn't make any difference.

Fig. 11.1 Sample Test Items for Fair/Unfair Games

With the slow learners Dr Biggs used games first as a diagnostic tool and then for teaching purposes. She reports that most of these children acquired the concepts of place value and an understanding of the four number operations. The children began by showing a prejudice against games, saying that they were not 'proper maths'. During the experiment the children slowly changed their attitudes and began to enjoy the work. As reported there were substantial gains in the conceptual understanding of number.

Dr Biggs' study does not have the same careful experimental design of some of those reported above. Thus the real conceptual gains of the children cannot be attributed solely to the inclusion of games in the programme. It is rather that games played a central part in an effective teaching programme.

3   The development of problem-solving strategies

In addition to gaining and improving skills and understanding, an important objective of mathematics teaching concerns the acquisition of problem-solving strategies and skills. HM Inspectorate have gone so far as to specify the following problem-solving strategies as distinct objectives of mathematics teaching.

- *trial and error methods*
- *simplifying difficult tasks*
- *looking for pattern*
- *making and testing hypotheses*
- *proving and disproving*

Mathematical games can foster the development of most, if not all, of these strategies and higher-level skills, as the following studies illustrate.

Edith Biggs used games in a teaching experiment with more able children aged 7 to 13 years. Dr Biggs observed not only that these children's conceptual understanding deepened, but that their problem-solving abilities grew. Thus this study suggests that the inclusion of games in a teaching programme can aid the development of problem-solving strategies, certainly among more able pupils.

Two American studies[13, 14] found that a game involving mathematics can be used to elicit problem solving behaviour from both inexperienced and experienced problem solvers. One of these studies[16] found that it was possible to use the responses of pupils to games to classify them into groups according to the problem solving strategies they used. Thus these two studies suggest that games can be used both to diagnose the problem-solving strategies employed by students and to encourage the acquisition and development of problem-solving strategies among students.

The Shell Centre has produced a multi-media package[15] which shows (on video) children and teachers learning problem solving strategies through playing '*Pirates*' and other games. Although this is not a research study, it is an illuminating and accessible example of the use of games in developing problem-solving strategies. In conjunction with the studies reported above it serves to illustrate the vital role that games have to play in the fostering of problem solving.

4   The motivational effect of games

The evidence reviewed above indicates that including mathematical games in mathematics teaching aids the achievement of a full range of mathematical objectives. It is quite likely that this success is related to the positive effect of games on motivation and attitudes reported in some of the studies. This hypothesis is confirmed by the result of a study[16] involving nine classes of first- and second-year secondary pupils taught by two teachers in an inner-city school in Detroit.

The experimental programme lasted for two terms. The classes had games included in their mathematics curriculum either both terms, or the first or second term only, or in neither term. In summary, the results of the study were as follows. The absentee rates in the non-games classes were at least twice as high as in the games classes, irrespective of which teacher taught the classes or whether the pupils had played mathematical games the previous term. In the games classes the absentee rates for pupils never reached 20%. In the non-games classes the absentee rates exceeded 20% before half term, and approached 35% to 40% by the end of the term.

The study was designed to minimise the effect of factors other than the influence of the games. The findings confirm, therefore, that games have a strong motivational effect, and this is particularly striking in an inner city, and presumably demotivated, context.

Games should be included in the mathematics curriculum

The evidence reviewed above, which is only a sample of the evidence available, suggests that games are an effective way of teaching mathematics, both in terms of attaining mathematical objectives and in terms of motivating students to learn.

The evidence strongly suggests that if games are to contribute to the effective teaching of mathematics they must be fully incorporated into the mathematics curriculum. During the teaching of a specific topic, or directed at a particular objective, games should be:

1   selected on the basis of the desired objectives;
2   incorporated into the teaching programme.

Used in this way mathematical games have a vital part to play in aiding pupils' achievement and success in mathematics.

From *Mathematics in School* January 1986

Problem-solving games

The last period on Friday in my top junior class was set aside for games and hobbies. It was 'free time' for those who had finished their work and their weekly work diaries, a time for bringing out the collection of class games as well as games and hobby activities children brought from home. For me it was a time to catch up on marking, and other sins of omission, as well as a time to study the informal interaction of the children and to share in their leisure activities. Out would come the chess and draughts, *Mastermind*, *Dungeons and Dragons*, *Scrabble* and small electronic gadgets with flashing lights. A knitting circle would form in one corner (invariably girls, alas). An isolated reader would curl up in the reading corner with the lastest 'can't-put-it-down'. Most were absorbed in a variety of games of their own choosing. All of this provided many illuminating insights into the behaviour and responses of individual children.

What was surprising was the way the children could be divided into roughly two groups according to their games playing. One group contained children who played with some degree of thought and planning, showing evidence of analysis and seeking winning strategies. The other contained those who, in chess-playing terms, were 'wood-pushers', who would play their games in a random and arbitrary way, trusting in the odd lucky break. Members of this second group, the 'wood-pushers', were no less keen on winning. It was just that their approach to a game like *Mastermind*, with its logically-determined outcomes, would be quite haphazard. Nor did they seem to understand that those who solved the *Mastermind* challenge, or won the game of chess, were doing so because of certain repeatable strategies. Instead, they depended on unconscious strategies of random response – wait for a lucky break; if a move fails once try it again later in case it works this time; if you cannot decide what to move repeat a losing move as it might be the best option. Not surprisingly, many of these games-playing strategies were reflected in the children's approach to school work and to other learning situations.

For such children, success was seen as a matter of being 'good' at something (and this was determined by some fixed law of natural providence) or a matter of waiting for a stroke of luck – effortless victory or the 'pot of gold' syndrome. How can we get the message through to these 10 and 11-year-old children that not all of life's games are games of chance? That they can, through thought and planning, gain some control over the raw material of their lives? That successful outcomes are as much a matter of skills and strategies as they are to do with the blind hand of fate? Games playing provides an opportunity for helping children explore these issues and giving them some concept of *strategy*. As well as enjoying playing the games and handling materials, children can be encouraged to record what happens and to devise ways of playing the games with pencil and paper.

Here is a selection of games used with children as a stimulus for investigation and problem-solving.

Matchstick games

Take the last
A very simple game which young children enjoy. It can be played with matchsticks or any large collection of small objects – counters, buttons, beads, coins, dried beans or peas – as long as each pair of players has a large number.

• Put the matches in a single pile on the table.
• Decide on the maximum number that can be taken at any one go – say, up to ten.
• Each player takes it in turn to take matches from the pile, up to this maximum number.
• The player who takes the last match is the winner.

Children can pair off and play a few times for fun. Then get them to consider the strategy. *Is there a way of winning each time? What happens if you work backwards from the problem? Work out strategies for games in which different numbers of matches are taken. Try reversing the game so that the player who takes the last match is the loser, and investigate winning strategies for this.*

Poison
Another simple game, played with matches, counters, blocks – or on paper – which can stimulate the posing of problems.

I   I   I   I   I   I   I   I   I   I

Two players have ten sticks or blocks between them. They alternately take one or two from the pile until there are none left. The player who takes the last stick (the 'poison' one) loses. *Can you work out* strategies so that you always win? What happens if you begin with fewer sticks, or more sticks? Does it matter if you play first or second?

When this game has been played several times using concrete materials, then squared paper can be used in a representational form of the game. Following this, it could be played using abstract numbers. Extend the game by posing questions such as *If you are playing Poison and you have 8 sticks left, how many will you take to ensure that you win? What happens if you can choose to take 1, 2 or 3 sticks each time?*

NIM (the Marienbad game)
A more sophisticated matchstick game – made famous when it appeared in the classic French film *Last Year in Marienbad*. Its name comes from the German *nimmt* (to take). The game is usually played by two and begins with this formation:

```
        O                           |
      O O O           OR          | | |
    O O O O O                   | | | | |
  O O O O O O O               | | | | | | |
```

- Players take turns to pick up one or more matches from any one row.
- The loser is the one who picks up the last matchstick. (Alternatively, the game can be played so that the person picking up the last match (or the last pile) is the winner.)

Children can work out their own variations of the game – varying the number of piles or the number of matches; allowing a chosen number of matches to be taken from each pile; allowing piles to be split in two. Children can use this as a basis to investigate, experiment and create their own games, sharing them with others and exploring winning strategies.

Tactix
Another game in which matches are taken away.

- Matches (or counters) are laid out to make a square or rectangle, for example:

```
| | | |
| | | |
| | | |
| | | |
```

- Players take it in turn to take as many matches as they like from any row or column.
- They may work vertically or horizontally, but the matches *must be next to each other*. (For example in this arrangement:

| | |

only the first two matches could be taken, because there is a gap in the row.)
- The loser is the one who picks up the last match.

Children should be encouraged to discover a simple strategy of playing whereby they never lose. Variations include making the person picking up the last match (or matches) the winner, varying the number of matches, the number of rows, and so on.

Kayles

– –

Again players can take two matches only if they are next to each other.

- Place any number of matches, or counters (up to 20) end to end in a long line.
- Players take turns to take one match – or two, if they are beside each other.
- The winner – or loser – is the one who takes the last match.

Children can seek for themselves the winning strategy, and use it as a springboard to create their own problem-solving games, with the simplest materials.

Pencil and paper/Board games

Tick-tack-toe
Noughts and Crosses should be familiar to all children.

There are only three possible first moves (can children work this out?) and 12 positions after the second player has moved. *Should*

the first player always win? (An OHP transparency might help illustrate the possible strategies.) Once they understand the winning strategy a child cannot be beaten at noughts and crosses – and so loses interest. However, children can have a lot of stimulating fun inventing and investigating their own variations of this game. *Try different arrangements of squares and other shapes. Can you invent a three-dimensional noughts and crosses game? How would that affect the best strategy for winning?*

Achi

This is an African version of *Tick-tack-toe* played on a board of this design:

- Two players have four counters each.
- They take turns to place their counters on the board.
- When all are in position, players take turns to move a counter to a vacant point.
- The winner is the first one with three counters in a row.

What are the best moves and strategies for winning? Could you design, make and decorate your own version of this game?

Go

Getting a number of pieces or shapes into a row is also the basis for Japan's national game *Go*. This is a simplified version.

Players choose different symbols (eg noughts and crosses) and play on squared paper. The object of the game is to make a row of five – vertically, horizontally or diagonally – and to block your opponent's attempts to do the same. Players take turns to draw their symbol in a square, and the first to make a line of five is the winner.

Connect 4

Another variant, where players aim to get a line of four shapes or counters. Commercially-produced sets are available, as well as computer programs based on this game, which again can stimulate a lot of discussion on strategy, tactics and logical outcomes.

Avoid 3

In this variation on *Tick-tack-toe* – the object is *not* to get three in a row. This game can be played with pawns, counters or draughts on a chessboard, pegs on a pegboard, or pencil and squared paper. Players take turns to add a piece to the board. A player loses the game when he plays a piece to make a line of three. (The game can never involve more than 17 moves because the largest number of pieces which can be placed on an 8 × 8 board without having three in a line is 16.)

Work out strategies that will help you to win. Can you make up your own game using counters and a chessboard?

A simpler version is to place eight draughts or counters on the board so that no two are in line vertically, horizontally or diagonally. (For more ideas see *100 other Games to Play on a Chessboard* by Stephen and Addison, published by Peter Owen).

Nine Men's Morris

This is one of the oldest board games. Boards like the one below have been found carved on a roofing slab from an Egyptian temple (c 1400 BC) and on a stone from a Bronze Age burial site in Ireland.

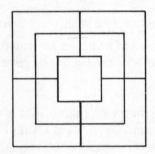

Two players (black and white) each have nine counters which they can place at any of the 24 points on the board.

- In part one, players alternately place their men on the board. In part two, players take turns to move a piece to an adjacent vacant point. The object is to form a 'mill' or row of three – each time this is done a player may remove one of the opponent's pieces.
- The winner is the player who can block all his opponent's men or reduce their number to two.

Three Men's Morris

A simpler version, played on a board with nine points. Players have four counters each and the aim is to get three men in a line.

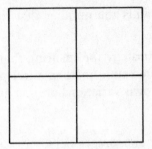

In the cathedrals of Norwich, Canterbury, Gloucester and Salisbury and in Westminster Abbey there are boards cut into the cloister seats, perhaps to relieve the tedium of long services!

Number games

The fifteen game

1	2	3	4	5	6	7	8	9

A simple yet very rewarding number game, played in pairs.

- The game starts with a row of nine squares or cards, labelled one to nine.
- The two players annex one square or card per go.
- The winner is the first player to occupy three squares which add up to 15.

The twenty five game

This uses a set of cards or squares numbered 2–15. Players take turns to pick up numbers, and the first to have numbers which add up to 25 is the winner.

Up to 100

Another simple and exciting number game for two players.

- The first player writes any number from 1 to 10 on a piece of paper.

- The next player writes a second number from 1 to 10, and adds the two together.
- Players go on doing this, taking it in turns to add a number to the total.
- The player who adds the number that makes the total 100 is the winner.

There is a simple strategy for ensuring that one player will win, which involves an interesting mathematical progression. Children can also invent their own variations on this game.

Countdown

A number game that encourages perseverance in problem solving. Begin with nine counters marked from 1 to 9, and three columns:

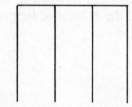

Shuffle the counters face down and place three in each column. Then turn them number side up, ready to play. The aim of the game is to get all nine numbers in a single column in countdown order (ie 9-8-7-6-5-4-3-2-1) with 9 at the top and 1 at the bottom.

- Players move one counter at a time from the bottom of one column to the bottom of another. A counter can only be moved under a *lower* number.
- When a column is empty any counter can be placed at the head of it, as the rule about being under a larger counter cannot apply.
- It may help children to know that there is a way out of every position no matter how stuck you seem! Encourage them to work out variations of the game and investigate how it can be extended.

Count out

One of many number games better played with a calculator; the rules can be amended and adapted in various ways.

- Two to four players key a 3-digit number into their calculators.
- Players take turn to ask their neighbours for a number (from 0–9).

- If the player asked has that digit in his calculator total, he must declare it (eg a 5 in the total of 150 would be five tens or 50) and deduct this from his total.
- The player who correctly identifies the number adds it to his total.
- Players take turns until one player has won all the points, and the others are left with nought.

(Writing the original numbers down before the game helps to prevent arguments afterwards!)

Top secret
A child thinks of a number between 0 and 1000.

- The rest of the class or group have ten questions to find the number.
- All that the child with the number can answer is 'Yes' or 'No'.

(With younger children a limit of 100 may be best, or up to 100 000 with older children).

What strategies will guarantee that the number can be found in under ten guesses? Adapt the game to find a mystery animal, or any object – investigate the strategies for finding the answer with the smallest number of questions.

Puzzles

Tangram puzzles
Tangrams were originally Chinese puzzles; it is because they are so intriguing that they have remained popular so long. Here is how the seven pieces of a tangram fit together:

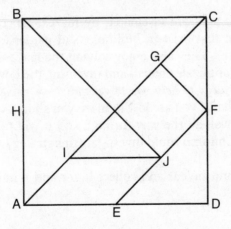

A tangram can be made very simply by folding (but remember, card tangrams will only work if folded and cut accurately).

- Start by folding a square piece of paper diagonally.
- Open it out, then bring in one corner to the centre.
- Fold to give the line EF (see diagram).
- Now fold in an adjacent corner to give the line FG.
- Unfold the square, then fold in half along the line FH.
- Fold AD to meet FH, giving the line IJ.

Present the tangram to the children in the form of a square. Let them take it apart and try to put it together again. Next, ask them to try to form a triangle; then a rectangle. Then let them design their own shapes.

How many different designs can you make, using all the pieces without any overlaps? Draw round them and give the outline to your neighbour to try to recreate the shape.

Can you invent your own tangram? Design a tangram puzzle of your own, dividing a square into several shapes, cutting them out of card, assembling patterns, and creating problems for others to solve.

(Pull-apart tangrams are available from The Mathematical Association, 259 London Road, Leicester LE2 3BE. The Association also produces a colourful poster on tangrams.)

Mazes

Children of all ages are fascinated by mazes, especially *real* walk-through mazes that exist in buildings and gardens (is there a real maze near you?). They also enjoy solving the maze-designs that are found in popular puzzle books – and inventing their own designs.

Is there a strategy to help you to get through a maze? For example people think that if you are lost in maze you should follow the right (or left) hand wall all the way through and it will take you back to the entrance. Children could investigate this strategy, using different mazes.

Children could invent and collect letter and number mazes, for example:

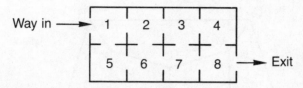

Way in ——→ 1   2   3   4

5   6   7   8 ——→ Exit

What questions does finding a route through this maze pose? What could the numbers represent? Try inventing other versions – and make up a story to go with the maze.

Design your own maze or collect and display different mazes. Create your own three-dimensional maze. There is an interesting penitential maze inscribed on the floor as you enter Ely Cathedral. Where could you have a maze in your school? What would be its design? How would you create it?

Map games

Street maps are a kind of maze. At some time we all have to face the problem of getting from A to B with a map as our only guide. Children can also enjoy the challenge of maps – finding routes, working out the shortest distances between places and planning the best itineraries for real or imaginary journeys.

Children also enjoy inventing their own maps of imaginary places – such as treasure maps and other problem-solving puzzles – with clues to follow. Real treasure hunts around the school or neighbourhood can also be as source of pleasure and challenge.

Many commercial board games are based on maps – finding a winning route and avoiding hazards and pitfalls in order to reach the goal of the game. Children can devise and create their own board games, adapting designs, posing and solving problems along the way.

Strategy games

Hamilton's game (1857)
This game is named after Sir William Hamilton and dates from 1857. In the game, the 20 vertices of a regular dodecahedron are denoted by letters representing towns. The problem is to visit every town only once and return to the starting point. A possible solution is A B C D E F G H J K L M N O P Q R S T U. *What other solutions are there?*

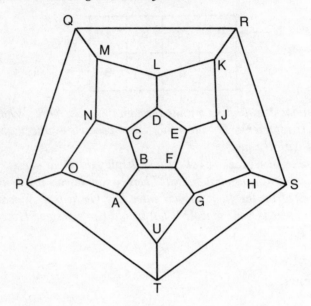

Ko no

Ko no is played by children in China and India. It is one of a number of strategy games which rely on blocking one's opponents. One player has counters at A and B, the other at X and Y. Moves must be to the vacant space, and a player loses when he is blocked. This simple game presents some surprising problem-solving challenges for young children.

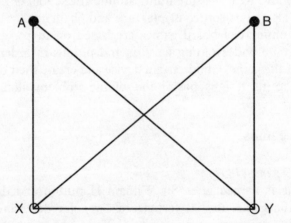

Fox and geese

This is a 'hunt' game which goes back at least 700 years and which Queen Victoria is said to have enjoyed.

It is played on a solitaire board:

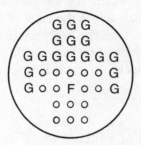

The fox (**F**) must try to catch 17 geese (**G**).

- The fox has first move. It can move forward, backward, diagonally or to the side and catches a goose by jumping over it into a vacant hole.
- When a goose is caught it is removed from the board.
- The geese may move only forward or sideways and must attempt to corner the fox so it cannot move.

Who should win? What would happen with different numbers of geese (originally the game had only 13).

Crossing the river
Many versions of this problem exist[7] (see the *Canoe problem* p.88), and children may enjoy making up their own versions, with stories and illustrations to match. The earliest version is probably from *Problems for the Quickening of the Mind* by Alcuin of York (c.775) and is as follows:

> A wolf, a goat and a cabbage must be moved across a river in a boat holding only one besides the ferryman. How must he carry them across so that the goat shall not eat the cabbage, nor the wolf the goat?

A modern version can be found in *Mathematical Activities* by Brian Bolt, published by Cambridge University Press, 1985:

> An army on the march through the jungle came to a river which was deep and wide and infested with crocodiles. On the far bank they could see two native boys with a canoe. The canoe can hold one man with his rifle and kit or two boys. How does the army cross the river?

Another well-known version is the computer program *Farmer* (MEP Micro Pack) in which the farmer has to transport a dog, chicken and sack of corn across the river in his small boat.

Children may like to take the problem away from the computer or paper, and create models, or play-act their own versions – overcoming their own obstacles to reach their chosen objective.

All change

This is one of a family of games in which the aim is to interchange sets of counters. Here is the playing board with the counters in their starting positions:

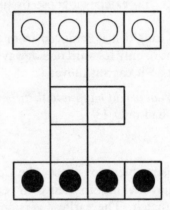

Each counter can move vertically or horizontally, but not diagonally. Only one may occupy a square, and they may not hop over each other. They may move forwards, backwards or sideways to an empty adjacent square. Children can work individually or co-operatively to solve this problem. They may also like to create their own problem-solving pattern shapes for the interchange of counters.

Hopscotch

There is a hopscotch diagram on the floor of the Forum in Rome, and the game is widely played in Great Britain, Russia, India and China. The word 'scotch' meant to mark or score lightly (as children might do with a stick on the ground). Here is one version of hopscotch:

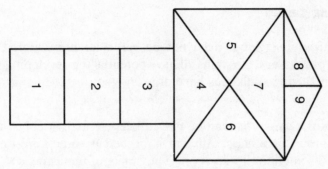

Can you design your own version of a hopscotch game for use in the playground? What other designs for playground games can you create?

Word games

Games such as *Scrabble* can create opportunities for strategic thinking. Word games can provide puzzles of logical and linguistic interest and can stimulate children to develop their own creative wordplay. One such game is *Jotto*, which is much older than similar commercial games like *Mastermind* and *My Word*.

- Each player writes down a secret word of four, five or six letters. The aim is to deduce the other player's word.
- In turn, players call out a word of similar length.
- The other player must tell you how many letters it has in common with his hidden word.
- The first to correctly identify an opponent's word is the winner.

Creating *word-squares* is a good way for children to generate problems using letter routes. For example:

P	R	O	B
R	O	B	L
O	B	L	E
B	L	E	M

How many ways can you make PROBLEM by following a letter-route through this word-maze? (This seven-letter word can be made in seven ways)

Try other words, other routes, other mazes. Share your problems.

Drawing games

Problem-solving games need not be verbal or numerical. Shape-games, puzzles and tangrams all have potential for developing visual problem-solving skills – as have drawing games.

Artists is a game that can be played between individual children, with a group or a class. All that is needed is something to draw with and something to draw on. The object of the game is to draw what an opponent is describing. Players take turns to be the artist. The other player describes an object in the room which the artist cannot see. They must not say anything about its use – only describe its shape, colour, texture and size and what it is made of. From this verbal description, the artist must try to draw the object.

Squiggles is another drawing game. Opponents are presented with identical squiggles, eg V   S   /   ? on pieces of paper, or halves of a blackboard. The aim of the game is for each player to complete a drawing incorporating the squiggle. The drawings can then be compared, and possibly judged.

Feeling games (tactile skills)

After the brain, the hands are probably our most important problem-solving tools. Feeling games can help develop tactile skills, challenging both fingers and brains.

The object of *Feeling Bags* is to guess the contents of the bag by feeling and saying (or writing) a list of contents within a time limit, say 30 seconds. Prepare a big fabric bag (a PE bag or pillowcase is ideal) containing objects of different kinds and shapes. Players take turns to feel the bag. The player who correctly identifies most objects wins.

The *Feeling Game* can help children understand the problems of blind people who have to 'see' with their fingers. One person is blindfolded, and turned round several times so that he loses his bearings in the room. He is then guided on a winding path to a mystery person. The object of the game is to recognise that person by sense of touch. *Feel the head, hair, features, clothes and size of the person. What clues can you feel? Who is it?*

Listening games (listening skills)

Since earliest times human beings have depended on listening skills to identify and to avoid problems.

A popular listening game for all ages is *Hunting*. One person is nominated to be the hunter, another the hunted. Both must keep their eyes closed or be blindfolded. The hunter starts at one end of the room or hall, the hunted at the opposite end. The object of the game is for the hunter to catch the hunted, before he can reach 'home' at the other end of the room. To locate the hunted, the hunter must *listen* for his footsteps, so absolute quiet and concentration is essential.

Adam and Eve begins with everyone sitting in a circle. One person is nominated as Adam and blindfolded, Eve is not blindfolded. The object of the game is for Adam to catch Eve. He calls out 'Where are you, Eve?' and she must reply 'Here I am Adam'. Adam has to catch her within a time limit of 30 seconds. Both must stay inside the circle. (To prevent sex-stereotyping, encourage role-reversal.)

Speaking games (verbal skills)

Verbal skills are needed in a variety of problem-solving situations.

In *One Minute Please* each competitor must talk for one whole minute on a given subject – sausages, school, holidays, TV, girls, boys, or any other real life problem! They must not dry up or wander off the subject. (For younger children *Thirty Seconds Please* may be more appropriate.)

Story games like *Story clues* help develop quick-thinking and verbal skills. A competitor is given a box containing three props, or story clues, for example a newspaper, a sock and an apple – and must make up a story bringing in these clues. *Carry-on stories* provide another sort of challenge. The teacher or first person starts off the story and talks for about half a minute. Then he or she passes it on to the next person with the link word 'and . . . ' The last person finishes the story. One word, or one sentence, carry-on stories are quicker versions of this. Children may like to tape-record their efforts, to review later.

Memory games

In *Kim's game* a number of common objects are placed on a tray. The player has one minute to study the tray before it is covered up or taken away. Then he is given a minute to see how many objects he can recall. (The number of items can vary according to the age of the child, perhaps 10 items for under 11 and up to 15 for 11 years and older.) *What strategies can help memory and visualisation?* Concentrating on shapes or initial letters can help.

Suitcase has a number of variants. In this game players are packing a verbal 'suitcase' for a long holiday. The first player packs the suitcase with anything he chooses. For example 'I packed my suitcase with a tennis racket . . . ' The second repeats these words and adds another item. Each player repeats the list, adding an item. When a player forgets an item he is out of the game. The winner is the last player to name all the items in order. Psychologists tell us that seven unconnected items is the maximum number that most people can remember. *What strategies could help us remember what we pack, or need to pack, for our holidays?*

Chess

The educational value of chess is widely recognised in primary schools. Chess stimulates the use of problem-solving strategies, it encourages logical and independent thought, it fosters a disciplined mental approach and develops capabilities in pattern recognition. Even very young children who do not know how to play enjoy investigating the pieces and creating their own – often very flexible – rules.

Older junior chess-players may well enjoy exploring the following variations:

Scotch chess Here, white plays one move, then black two, white three and so on. If a player gives check his turn ends there, even if he has not used all his moves. This variation has the advantage of being an extremely quick game!

Suicide chess The aim is to lose all one's pieces. The king can be taken like any piece, and captures are *compulsory*. The first to lose all wins.

Dominoes

The principle of representing numbers by patterns of round spots, as in dominoes, preceded the invention of numerals by many centuries. A Chinese manuscript dated 2200 BC shows the numbers from 1–9, as dots, arranged in a magic square. Dominoes are very useful for stimulating investigation and problem solving with pupils of all ages. Young children often begin by using dominoes to experiment with building, balancing and toppling – but they can also create some quite sophisticated games with them, such as matching, setting, making patterns, and shapes. Devising games, posing problems and exploring different patterns of dots are all part of the 'domino effect'.

Adapting games

Many of the best games are adaptations of old ideas. The game of *Ludo*, for example, was derived from a centuries-old Indian game. Try adapting a game for your children to create new problem-solving opportunities. Children often come up with challenging ideas of their own if they are in classrooms which stimulate experiment and enquiry. Here are some more ideas for ways in which you or the children could adapt existing games.

Snakes and ladders Cover some numbers with ? spaces and provide cards to turn over when players land on these spaces – like the *Chance* cards in *Monopoly*. On each card is a problem relating to current class projects – if a child can solve the problem he has another turn, if not, then he misses a turn.
Monopoly Devise a board of this type with local roads, industries and places of interest.
Boxes Extend the pencil and paper game, by putting positive or negative numbers in each space. When players make a box they either add or subtract the number 'boxed' from their score.
Darts Re-design the board to give a fairer or more even spread of numbers.
A marble rolling game Designed (by older children) to give younger children practice in recognising and adding numbers.

Trivial Pursuits This type of game can be adapted with an original board design and questions related to current class topics.
Card games These could be invented by older children to help younger children match letters, shapes and words.

The use of games can yield some entertaining, amusing and useful pieces of problem-solving. I hope this small collection of puzzles and games will provide some ideas for use by teachers in the classroom – or perhaps as a recreation at home after a stressful day in school!

Notes and references

1   *Intellectual growth in young children* (Routledge and Kegan Paul, 1930)
2   *Homo Ludens* J. Huizinga (Routledge and Kegan Paul, 1949)
3   *Structuring play in the early years at school* K. Manning and A. Sharp (Ward Lock, 1977)
4   *Mathematics Counts* Report of the Cockcroft Committee (HMSO, 1982)
5   *The GCSE Examinations: National Criteria for Mathematics* DES (HMSO, 1985)
6   *Mathematics from 5 to 16* DES (HMSO, 1985)
7   'Studies in a Continuing Investigation of the Cognitive Effects of Mathematics Instructional Games' M. M. Wheeler in M. Zweng *et al Proceedings for the Fourth IGME* Birkhauser, Boston, 1983, pp 652–4.
8   'Using Games to Retrain Skills with Basic Multiplication Facts' G. W. Bright, J. G. Harvey and M. M. Wheeler in *Journal for Research in Mathematics Education* 10, 2 pp 103–110, 1979.
9   'Using Games to Teach Fraction Concepts and Skills' G. W. Bright, J. G. Harvey in L. Silvery and J. R. Smart (eds) *Mathematics for the Middle Grades (5–9)* NCTM, Reston VA (1982) pp 205–216.
10 'Using Games to Teach some Probability Concepts' G. W. Bright, J. G. Harvey and M. M. Wheeler in D. R. Grey *et al Proceedings of the First IGOTS* (Volume 1, 1983) Teaching Statistics Trust, Sheffield pp 110–115.
11 G. W. Bright, J. G. Harvey and M. M. Wheeler 'Teaching Statistics Concepts through instructional games' *op cit* (1983) pp 158–168.

12 *Teaching Mathematics 7–13: Slow Learning and Able Pupils* E. Biggs (NFER/Nelson, 1985).
13 'Games moves as they relate to strategy and knowledge' G. W. Bright in *Journal of Experimental Education* (1980) 48, 3 pp 204–9.
14 *An exploratory study of the use of problem solving heuristics in the playing of games involving mathematics* W. H. Kraus (1980) Unpublished doctoral dissertation, University of Wisconsin, Madison.
15 *Problems with Patterns and Numbers* Shell Centre for Mathematical Education, University of Nottingham; Joint Matriculation Board, Manchester, 1984.
16 'The Effect of Instructional Gaming on Absenteeism: the First Step' L. E. Allen, and D. B. Main in *Journal for Research in Mathematics Education* (1976) 7 (2) pp 113–128

Further reading

Bell R. C. *The Boardgame Book* (Marshall Cavendish) *Board and Table Games from Many Civilisations* (Oxford University Press)
McConville R. *The History of Board Games* (Creative Publications)
Murray H. J. R. *A History of Board Games other than Chess* (Oxford University Press)
Stephen and Addison *100 other Games to Play on a Chessboard* (Peter Owen)

12 Teaching Problem Solving

'You cannot teach a man anything; you can only help him to
find it within himself'

Galileo

When teachers report on their experiences of teaching problem
solving, certain benefits are mentioned time and time again. These
include: pupil-centred learning; active participation; a growth of
independence and self-sufficiency; the revelation of talent and potential; improved relationships within the classroom; and a sense of
enjoyment and creativity. A problem-solving approach means that
the interests and enthusiasms which teacher and child bring to the
learning process can be exploited to the full.

Here are some comments by a group of infant teachers:

'We very quickly discovered interesting spin-off effects. Our
children were beginning to think more carefully for themselves,
they were accepting responsibility for their own actions, and
as a result the classroom was becoming a happier place, . . . a
democracy rather than a totalitarian state!

Although a good deal of time was spent in the initial stages
talking, learning the art of discussion, and kicking ideas around,
much time was saved in the long run as the children were
making sensible and relevant decisions for themselves. We now
have more time for positive thinking and we need less time for
negative nagging. The possibilities for developing social and
linguistic skills are enormous.

We are absolutely convinced of the value of Problem-Solving
in the Infants School. It is difficult to think of it in terms of
a package of learning materials; but if one looks at it as an
attitude which permeates right across the school's life then
there would be a great deal to be gained by including problem
solving in the training for already experienced teachers.'[1]

Another teacher, Carol Logan, reports on the educational benefits of problem solving with older children:

> 'Throughout the project the children were learning to work together as a team and all that that means. They had to accept decisions taken by another group and communicate their ideas from one group to another. The children recorded and wrote up all their discussions and decisions. The need for clear objectives and a well-planned system for achieving the objective was a lesson that was well learnt by those who took part.'[1]

Many, like Mrs Mai Monk, report on the improved motivation that teaching problem-solving can bring:

> 'One day as I entered the classroom one of my children asked, with a face full of hope, 'Have you a problem, Mrs Monk?' The topic had been a success as far as *all* the children were concerned. I set up a secret ballot and there was a 100% response of 'Yes' to the simple question of 'Do you like Problem-Solving and shall we keep it on?'[1]

A recent report identified several factors that contribute to effective Junior Schools[2] which have a direct bearing on the teaching of problem solving. Key factors of effectiveness included:

Structured sessions: where teachers organised a framework within which pupils could work, yet allowed them some freedom within this structure.

Intellectually challenging teaching: where teacher communication encouraged creative imagination and the powers of problem solving, and pupils were allowed some independent control over their work.

Work-centred environment: where teachers took time to discuss the *content* of work with pupils and gave feedback about their work.

Limited focus within sessions: where the focus was on one curriculum area, with variation in choice of topic and level of difficulty geared to children's needs.

Maximum communication between teachers and pupils: where teachers recognised the importance of speaking to the whole class so that intellectually challenging points could be raised with *all* pupils, as well as devoting time to individuals and groups.

Other key factors included the value of record keeping; purposeful leadership by the head teacher; the involvement of the deputy head, and teachers, in curriculum planning; parental involvement; and the positive atmosphere or ethos of the school.

Another factor, brought out in many reports, is the need for a *broad curriculum*, in which basic skills are exercised across a wide range of curriculum activities. Research into human intelligence adds weight to this finding. Instead of being a single aptitude, research suggests[3] that human intelligence is made up of a number of different abilities, such as linguistic, musical, logical-mathematical, spatial and bodily-kinaesthetic, as well as other forms of personal intelligence. The development of these different areas varies from individual to individual. We are not creatures of *general* intelligence, or of *general* problem-solving ability. We are a combination of many singular talents. The old IQ tests were mistaken in treating logico-mathematics as the general form of all intelligence. They did not do justice to the full range of abilities that humans possess. A broad curriculum which gives opportunities for classroom investigation and problem solving, is one in which children are most likely to develop their many abilities and to realise their full potential.

The learning environment

'Personally I am always ready to learn' said Winston Churchill, 'although I do not always like being taught'. A learning environment where problem solving can take place needs to be a 'prepared environment'. A wide range of materials should be available, to help stimulate children into activity, and to encourage them to reflect on what they are doing and the world around them. The slogan adopted by Maria Montessori was 'never do anything for a child that he can do for himself'. Children should be given freedom to investigate materials, develop ideas and tackle problems in their own way. However there are dangers in this approach. The HMI Report '*Primary Education in England* (1978) described the 'exploratory' approach as one in which 'the broad objectives of the work were discussed with the children, but where they were put in a position of finding their own solutions'. The Report went on to warn that, if lacking in guidance, the approach 'could lead to aimless activity and lack of progress' – the sort of situation typical of a wet playtime. Effective learning does not take place in a completely relaxed environment any more than in a tightly structured setting. There is a middle ground where problems are real and require contributions from both teacher and child.

Montessori's methods with pre-school children included many 'exercises of practical life' including washing up, dusting, and polishing – the children being made responsible for collecting and putting away appropriate equipment. The preparation and return of materials can be an important part of the problem-solving process. What and/or who do we need? Where is it? How is it to be used? Where and when will it be returned? The art of logistics ('everyone and everything in the right place at the right time') plays a vital role in industrial management, and in the management of successful learning environments. Making children responsible for the logistics of problem solving helps them develop planning and decision-making skills. However it does mean that the teacher will have to ensure easy access to materials, and unhindered movement round the room. The initial preparations can themselves be made part of the problem-solving process, if the teacher first discusses with pupils the logistical needs of the classroom. For example, when reception class teacher Doreen Macleod saw that children were slow to collect equipment from her neatly-labelled storage trays she put the problem to the class. 'Together we decided that if a picture of say, a piece of jigsaw or a shape, was put on the tray, as well as the words, it would help them find what they want more quickly'. Later the children improved this system by colour-coding the rows of trays.

A problem-table, problem-corner, problem-box, collection or display of problems, puzzles and questions – or the 'Problem of the Week' are all ways that different teachers have used to stimulate problem-solving ideas. A display area could be available for recording results, drawings and written work, so that children can share with others the results they have achieved. Schools may be centres of learning, but this learning often takes place in isolated cells; it is important to share experiences across age ranges, with other classes, children and adults. Valuing a child's creative problem-solving efforts will help to build up his or her self-esteem. Studies have shown how important the self-concept of ability is – 'I can do it' is often a better guide than any IQ test in predicting a child's future academic success.[4]

A child will only feel free to experiment, and to express ideas in new and spontaneous ways where there is a sense of *security* (what Carl Rogers calls 'psychological safety') in the learning environment. Fostering such a sense of security is part of the teacher's task in preparing the environment for problem solving.

The role of the teacher

When confronted with something new – a new toy, game, gadget, idea or word – the process of learning usually has two stages. First, we relate what is new and to be learned with what we already know. Then we take what is new and make it our own through using it, playing with it, and trying to make something new with it. When Piaget studied the spontaneous learning of children he found both these stages at work. He called the process *assimilation* – the child constructing his knowledge, solving problems, absorbing the new into the old. The job of the teacher is to provide opportunities for this to take place. There will, however, be blocks in the process, obstacles to overcome, conflicts in relating the different elements of the problem. The teacher needs to devise strategies to support children and help them cope with the stress of the new.

One way in which the teacher can offer help is by *sharing* in the problem-solving process – not by showing the solution to the child, but by inviting the child to participate in a problem that the teacher is trying to solve. An example of this happened when a teacher was re-tiling her kitchen. She shared the possibilities and problems with her class, and this provided the stimulus for investigations involving pattern-making and measurement. Papert says 'sharing the problem and the experience of solving it allows a child to learn from an adult not "by doing what the teacher says" but "doing what teacher does" '. It shows that there are different ways of approaching a problem and that co-operation is valuable in getting results. The teacher is an important problem-solving model for the child.

The teacher can also *support* the problem-solving process by directing and focusing the solver's attention on aspects of the problem that may not be obvious, asking such questions as: 'Are you trying every way/ using all the information/ considering all factors?' or 'What else does this feature/fact/ example tell you?' or 'What solutions are possible/impossible?' The teacher can encourage children to break down the problem, or suggest an easier way for them to get started on the main problem and show how drawings, diagrams and sketching out ideas can be helpful. The teacher acts as a guide, helping children to stop, reflect and talk about what they are doing and why they are doing it.

The teacher's role is also to ensure that *all* children become involved in and gain satisfaction from the problem-solving process. Often it is the sweet, conforming child that is rewarded in the classroom – we also need to reward the *risk-takers* – those prepared to 'take the plunge' 'have a go' and produce unusual solutions.

The role of the child

Piaget claimed that children were not able to think in a systematic or abstract manner until the 'formal operational period', which he identified as being around 12 years of age. This may be true of children placed in test situations, or those who have received a limited diet of formal teaching. However, most primary children are able to build up systems of related arguments and formal steps in a problem-solving process, both in talking and in writing. Young children can exercise many higher-order skills if presented with problems in contexts that are significant and relevant to them. Today it is commonplace to see in infant schools the sort of geometrical investigation once thought appropriate only to secondary children, and to see juniors tackle tasks in CDT – once the province of college students.

Children's minds resemble adults' minds more closely than was previously thought. What they lack is experience and knowledge. One of the common responses of teachers who have embarked on problem-solving activities is surprise at the way in which children previously regarded as backward and below-average in ability have produced highly creative and effective problem-solving solutions. What children need is to have problems set in a *context* that they can relate to. There is little value *to the child* in being set random puzzles, out of context, with no discernible purpose.

Children have an active role to play in learning from and helping each other, sharing experience and contributing in a co-operative task – sometimes by talking a lot, sometimes by looking a lot. Often, children take on the role of 'instructor' towards other children (although there are dangers here of encouraging dependency). If children are allowed some control over the direction of their work, co-operative instruction can be both sympathetic and successful.

The child brings to the problem a fresh mind and an urge to succeed in tasks that are seen to be worthwhile. The first task is to understand the problem, to be clear about what results can be expected and how to get started. Steps and strategies and the manner of representation (modelling, drawing, writing etc) will need to be planned. The child should be aware of the value of co-operation and also know how to seek help. Once the problem has been attacked and a solution found it may be necessary to review, evaluate and adjust different stages. Finally, because one problem often leads to another, the problem-solver should look beyond the immediate solution to see what could be added and investigated further. As a character in the N F Simpson play *A Resounding Tinkle* says 'And suppose we solve all the problems it presents? What happens? We end up with more problems than we started with. Because that's the way problems propagate their species. A problem left to itself dries up or goes rotten. But fertilise a problem with a solution – you'll hatch out dozens'.

Approaches to problem-solving

The work of Edward de Bono can provide stimulating starting-points for classroom use. It was de Bono who invented the term 'lateral thinking' to describe the way the mind can be made open and receptive to less obvious ideas and solutions. De Bono argues that we tend to have a rigid view of what can be altered in a problem situation. Our clichéd habits of everyday thinking cannot be bypassed using the step-by-step approach of vertical or logical thinking. What we need are thinking skills that will make it possible to arrive at unlikely, original and superior solutions to problems. Methods of training and practice in such 'thinking skills' appear in de Bono's books and lesson materials.[5]

The CoRT thinking lessons are designed to be used over a wide range of ages (from six years to adult) under the assumption that the basic thinking processes are the same at any age. The aim of the CoRT lessons is to 'broaden perception so that in any thinking situation, we can see beyond the obvious immediate and egocentric'. Many practical problems are suggested in the lessons but the aim is not to solve the problems, or achieve 'right' or 'wrong' answers, rather to encourage creative and divergent ideas.

Each of the lessons is aimed at introducing a 'thinking tool', describing its use and giving some practice questions. One of these 'tools' is the 'PMI' approach to the treatment of ideas. This is a useful *brainstorming* technique in which the good points of an idea are listed under P(Plus), the bad points under M(Minus) and points neither good or bad are I(Interesting). Another relevant 'tool' is CAF (Consider All Factors) in which students are asked to look at their own and other people's thinking to try and see what factors have been left out.

Emphasis in most CoRT lessons is on speed of thinking (the recommended time for group discussion being only two to three minutes) and on the rather abstract 'tools' labelled PMI, CAF, AGO, FIP, etc rather than on real or practical problem solving. However, many interesting ideas and approaches relevant to problem solving can be gleaned from de Bono's work.[6]

Much work has been done in the United States to develop 'tools' that will help develop cognitive and problem-solving abilities. The High-Scope Foundation pre-school curriculum is based on the premise that young children should be actively involved in planning their own activities.[7] Feuersteins Instrumental Enrichment programme is aimed at older, in particular 'slow-learning' or culturally deprived children who have not been taught how to utilise their thinking potential.[8] The Institute for the Advancement of Philosophy for Children (IAPC) produces materials to help children think more logically and meaningfully.[9] Science Research Associates (SRA) have produced *Thinklabs*, and other graded sets of puzzles and problems for use in the junior classroom, available in this country.

References to some of the books and materials relating to problem solving in various curriculum areas will be found in the relevant chapters of this book. Television programmes such as the BBC's *Mindstretchers* also provide starting-points for problem solving. Some of the best problem solving arises out of the self-initiated learning of individual children. In *Musical problems* (page 243) Margaret Hope-Brown presents a case study to show how this can happen through the solving of problems involving musical instruments. Patrick Easen and Denise Green show how a class tackled the real problem of improving their playtimes, in *Developing real problem solving in the primary classroom* (page 243). In *Bridges – an integrated and problem-solving approach* (page 257) Richard McTaggart illustrates how a topic can be used to extend problem solving across a whole range of curriculum activities. Finally, Mary Burns discusses what effects the introduction of problem solving has had in her school – *Reactions to problem solving* (page 260).

There is an obvious need for a lot more classroom research in the area of problem solving in primary schools – and teachers themselves are in the best place to contribute to this research. Not only can this experience lead to a better understanding of the ways in which children learn, it can provide stimulus and motivation for both teachers and children – and give them a lot of fun in the process. Through problem solving the task of teaching can, in a real sense, become an opportunity for learning.

Musical problems

Margaret Hope-Brown

One way in which *self-initiated learning* can be stimulated is by giving the child a classroom instrument, such as a xylophone or glockenspiel, to solve 'musical problems'. These 'musical problems' may be defined in terms of a given rhythm, restricted number of notes, and so on, providing a definite framework within which children can work. This is the musical equivalent of learning through problem solving in other areas of the curriculum such as mathematics, science, language, and so on.

The following account by a teacher illustrates the *commitment and perseverance* that children with special gifts may exhibit, as well as self-initiated learning.

It had been raining for days and the children had been unable to get out either to play or for games lessons. The sense of frustration of some of the fourth year junior children at being confined to their classroom day after day was becoming increasingly apparent. Kim, in particular, was becoming very bored with the usual 'playtime activities' that were taking place in the classroom and asked me if she could organise some group music-making. She and some of her friends collected together the classroom instruments and set about composing a piece of music which, Kim declared, would take the form of an improvisation around three notes. Within a very short while, she came to me to say that the piece had begun to take shape but was not finished, and could they have the instruments over the next few playtimes to complete their composition. Under her guidance the children created a piece which they invited me to hear. I was immediately impressed by the surprising originality and quality of the work that had been produced under Kim's direction. She had set herself the 'musical problem' of three notes and persevered until the piece met with her satisfaction. I rushed for the tape recorder in order to capture this piece which I found incredibly moving. It was later (at Kim's request) committed to paper.

Through the following years, Kim kept in contact with me. She eventually gained a place at Music college where she is training to be a professional oboist. She later told me that her love of music and the discovery that she could make music speak for her all began with that playtime experience.

From an unpublished dissertation by Margaret Hope-Brown for the MA degree of the University of London.

Developing real problem solving in the primary classroom

Patrick R Easen (*University of Newcastle upon Tyne*),
Denise A Green (*The Open University*)

You are a busy teacher and among the many problems confronting you are trouble in the playground and disappointing mathematical performance in the classroom. What do you do? Probably few people would answer 'Get the children to tackle the first problem and it will help you solve the second' but that's exactly what Ann Jones did with her class of 10-year-olds (see Figure 12.1).

These school rules were devised by Ann's children . . . and drawing them up gave the class plenty of opportunity to use their 'four rules'! That is not all they did. They built a marble area and a toy car track; they painted hopscotches, organised lunch-time clubs and instituted a football rota. In the process they used a considerable

Rules
Bad Behaviour
1. No swearing on school premises.
2. No spitting on school premises.
3. No fighting in playground.
4. No going through unit 2 unless going to the toilet

Trouble Makers
1. No going on school roofs.
2. No stealing peoples balls.
3. Never cut corners because grass is trying to grow.
4. You must never come into anyother cloakroom but your own.
5. No pushing off logs.

Prevent Accident
1. No going in sand or throwing sand on playground.
2. No running on paths round school
3 NO playing on logs in winter.

Figure 12.1

amount of mathematics in a way that helped them to see its relevance. The children were engaged in 'real problem solving'.

Real problem solving formed part of an Open University course, PME233: *Mathematics across the curriculum.* As members of the course team, we felt that the idea was sufficiently powerful to merit further attention in its own right. This article describes our attempt to explore the impact of real problem solving when it becomes a regular feature of classroom life. The classroom in question belonged to a mixed ability class of 28 10- and 11-year-olds at a school in Buckinghamshire. We began during the second half of the autumn term, and, for the rest of the academic year, the children spent a minimum of one session (morning or afternoon) a week on real problem solving.

What is real problem solving?

Real problem solving aims to build up the confidence and ability of children to solve just the kind of problems that are characteristic of a rapidly-changing society. Confidence in one's ability to cope, as any adult knows, plays a large part in tackling important problems. Again, as any adult also knows, the important problems are the real ones – the ones that will not go away on their own. While no-one would deny that adults should be capable of resolving their own problems, how well are children being prepared in the classroom for this need?

It is not as if children do not have real problems. These may well be different from those that concern adults, but many of the same characteristics remain. Real problems for adults are practical, immediate impediments to safe or satisfying living – and the successful resolution of such problems actually makes a difference to the life of the adult involved. Similarly, real problems for children are those that have an immediate, practical effect on their lives, and in which the children themselves can effect some improvement of the situation.

Where does it begin in the classroom?

Let's return to that class of 10-year-olds. Ann had tried to explain the idea of real problem solving to them, but was unsure whether they had really grasped what was involved. She left them to think about it, having asked them to write down the real problems that mattered to them. If a problem is to be real *and remain real* for the children, the work has to develop from their own responses. Nevertheless, Ann would be the first to admit that she was rather surprised by the children's comments. Some had written down more than one problem, but what was really striking was how much unspoken agreement there was about a particular area. Here is the final list:

Bullying	19
Cloakroom trouble	7
Swearing in playground	4
Spitting in playground	4
Football at playtime	3
Litter	2
Not enough to do	1
Shoes being hidden	1
Mud	1
Writing on walls	1

Clearly the children saw much that was wrong with playtimes. Was there scope here for some real problem solving? In the Open University course we suggested five criteria for judging a problem to be suitable for real problem solving:

1   it has immediate, practical effects on children's lives;
2   there is the possibility of children being able to do something to change and improve matters. In other words, it is 'actionable' rather than merely 'discussable';
3   there are neither known 'right' solutions nor clear boundaries;
4   it will require children to use their own ideas and efforts to resolve the problem;
5   it is 'big' enough to require many phases of class activity for any effective resolution. In other words, the process of working upon the problem requires a considerable amount of different activities and the possibility of stages of partial resolution.

As far as both Ann and the headteacher were concerned 'playtimes' would meet these criteria. The children talked it all through and eventually agreed that the 'challenge' for them was 'Getting a better and safer playtime' . . . they had begun their real problem solving.

Children tackling real problems

In adult life the process of solving a real problem, from the initial discontent with an existing state of affairs through to a satisfactory resolution, is rarely smooth. Initial strategies for dealing with a complex problem are often inadequate and may lead to frustrating dead ends. The value of these cul-de-sacs is that they usually provide new insights into the nature of the problem. Often we need to be in the position of being able to make *in situ* experiments with the problem and *reflect on what happens*, so that we may come to change our understanding of the problem, our possible strategies for action and even our framing of the problem. Indeed, in thinking about a problem we always seem to start from our prejudices. What really matters, however, is whether we are able to move on from this position in a constructive manner.

So it is with children. For example, working from negative criticisms through to a more positive view – based on the understanding that boredom was a major factor in their playtime problem – was an essential (but slow) process for the 10-year-olds discussed in this article. In the early stages they identified five areas they felt needed to be tackled and so they split themselves up into groups to do this. Since the class was looking for improvements, it was suggested that they should establish a 'brief' for each group. Eventually, after much uncertainty, they decided on the ones in Figure 12.2.

Area for Investigation	Brief for this group
Bullying:	Ways to stop bullying.
Mud and grass	Ways to stop people going on the grass.
Football.	How to organise the football.
Cloakroom:	How to stop people playing in the cloakroom.
Rule-Breaking	What set of rules to have

Figure 12.2

The *bullying* group observed patterns of bullying and kept charts indicating who the bullies were, why the victims were bullied and what effect resulted from the presence of a teacher. They quickly came to the decision that a system of punishments was needed to solve their part of the problem. As time wore on, however, their initial perceptions grew into a deeper understanding that boredom contributed to much of the bullying at playtime. This enabled them to develop a more positive approach to finding a solution. Consequently, their revised attempt to reduce bullying was in the form of providing more interesting playtime activities. Playing marbles on the playground was forbidden so a piece of waste land was cleared for use as a marble area. A mound was built adjacent to a disused concrete base nearby. The mound was concreted and the entire area (mound and base) painted with white lines. This created a very effective miniature car track. As there was a nagging feeling among some of the class that the activities planned were rather 'boy-orientated' a hopscotch was painted on one of the patios. After all, their data told them that some girls also bullied!

The group with the brief to *stop children hanging around in the cloakroom and causing trouble* had a similar experience. They spent hours collecting data, making charts and generally investigating the extent of the problem. However, their original ideas of 'policing' the cloakrooms was dropped when it became apparent that the reason for children frequenting cloakrooms during playtimes was boredom. Now they were in a position to develop their approach. Surveys were made to establish areas of interest. As a result a stamp club, a pony club and a 'sitting down' games club, all organised and run by the children, were established in lunch hours.

The *football* group certainly didn't expect much mathematics to be required in their investigations. All the boys really enjoyed football, so why did it give rise to so much friction? Initial observation revealed that the footballers unfairly monopolised the playground. The group considered that a third of the playground space would be a fair share, so a green line was painted to show the section allocated to football. Of course this meant that fewer people could play. They decided to devise a football rota organised by year groups – each year group would be entitled to play on particular days.

The experience of this group was very telling. It illustrates that the bolder and more definite an idea is, the better it can be tested. The boys knew their subject so well that they quickly developed an idea for improving things which had a high information content.

They didn't just want to try a rota – they had an idea of what the rota would be like and what it would entail. They had distinguished which factors or variables within the problem could change – in this case the numbers of people playing football – and had been able to define that variable operationally. In other words, they could specify what they meant in practice and they could express their idea in a way which enabled it to be tested. By undertaking opinion surveys and organising a trial period they managed to find a system that eventually worked. Even when the space had been reallocated and a rota instituted they had not finished. In order to implement their plans it had been necessary to resite the football goals. The new position, in front of a classroom window, soon presented new difficulties. To break a window once may be regarded as a misfortune; to break it twice looks like carelessness (apologies to Oscar Wilde). Once more they needed to draw on their mathematics in order to make a protective frame for the window as they measured up and then costed the materials.

The frustrations inherent in solving real problems were fully appreciated by the *rules* group. They first devised a carefully classified set of rules. But then they had to find a way of ensuring that the rest of the school knew and used them. They tried all manner of techniques – lists of rules on doors, announcements and class quizzes – before deciding to record the rules on cassette tape and play the tape in school assemblies. Slowly it began to dawn on them that the mere existence of rules did not guarantee that these were either 'known' or, more importantly, 'used'.

Solving real problems often involves retracing steps and trying new strategies, as the *mud and grass* group discovered. Their plans to returf the muddy patches in the playground, which were unsightly and dangerous, had to be postponed because they had not ascertained what caused the muddiness in the first place. After further investigation they decided that some of the paved areas were too narrow. The children researched the cost of the various ways of extending these areas, raised the necessary cash and acquired extra paving slabs. The next stage involved getting round the Dads – paving slabs are very heavy!

It is impossible, in the space of a short article, to convey the richness of the work arising from this project or to describe in detail the events involved. Suffice it to say that eventually the work of each group began to fit together and the children were very satisfied with the new style of playtimes. It seems that, given the opportunity, children can solve real problems which matter to them. Further-more, in doing so they can naturally bridge the gap between the abstractions of the school curriculum and the world of the child.

What other real problems have children tackled?

The range of real problems tackled by primary children has been enormous. Almost anything seems to be grist to the mill – organising a Christmas party; planning an assembly; reorganising the class-room; organising a day's outing; improving 'wet playtimes'; starting a school magazine; creating a school garden; reclaiming a school pond; running children's games at the school fete; tackling the litter problem; improving the tuck shop; raising money to buy classroom pets; organising the sports day; forming a junior youth club . . . the list seems endless. It is remarkable what children of this age can do when given the opportunity.

Nor is real problem solving the type of activity which is restricted to one particular age range or type of school. Teachers have tried it successfully with pupils from reception age to 'non-examinable' school leavers. The variety of educational contexts where real prob-lem solving has been undertaken has surprised even ourselves. One thing that we are keen to ensure is that our approach makes no extra demands on resources. There are no special text-books or apparatus needed. By making use of the normal classroom resources the only facilitation needed to develop our approach is attitudinal – and here we mean on our own part as teachers. This, of course, is the nerve ending, for real problem solving can only be made operable in the classroom through the teacher.

The teacher and real problem solving

In essence, the demand on the teacher during real problem solving is to protect and foster independent reasoning. Children, as our experience suggests, are persons capable of autonomy (albeit not fully developed) in the here and now of the classroom. We must avoid what Seligman has described as 'learned helplessness', ie a state of being in which people come to accept that no action they can possibly take will alter what happens in their lives. Consequently, we feel that it is important to consider one particular dimension of teaching-learning, namely, the degree of intellectual dependence or independence of the learner with respect to *what* he or she is permitted to do and *how*. This can operate at two levels:

1 in relation to the overall control of approaching the problem (a 'macro-level');
2 in relation to accessing the necessary resources (facts or techniques) to service that approach (a 'micro-level')

If an environment with a large amount of freedom of choice is to be created in the classroom – a facilitating environment rather than a hampering one, then we, as teachers, need to do three things:

- we must not force our own 'real problems' on the children. Careful preparation may help to ensure that what we select to introduce into the classroom is based on the concerns of the children. If the children do not recognise and accept the problem then it can never be real to them.
- we need to let go of the problem so that it becomes the children's own rather than remaining ours. If the problem really matters to the children they will inevitably have ideas about what to do and why. The flow of ideas and their decision making should not be impaired by the knowledge that we, as teachers, intend to retain full control and will manipulate their work to suit some pre-planned pattern of our own. Solving real problems in adult life is not a game of guessing what solution is in somebody else's mind!
- we should be careful not to take the problem away from the children at any stage of the problem-solving process. This could happen if teachers insist that children make their investigations or collect information in a certain way. The children must be allowed to find their own route to a solution even if we, as more experienced problem solvers, can see a better way. For us to impose our own way is to take the problem back and render it no longer real for the children.

If teachers act according to these guidelines the initiative for resolving the problem moves to the children. With it comes the responsibility for taking decisions and exercising their own judgment, both important elements of good adult problem solving. For the teacher in the classroom, however, this can be extremely demanding. We need to look at the constraints that we tend to impose (intentionally or unintentionally) on childrens' thinking by virtue of our authority position; we need also to conceptualise our experience in order to guide our own decision-making and actions in the classrooms.

Frameworks for conceptualising experience

At first, it may be difficult to distinguish the approach advocated here from that of other forms of project work. Typical of the latter is a strategy which could be described as 'micro-open and macro-directed' ie the pupil is encouraged to openly investigate materials, or a situation during a lesson, but the expected results are then evaluated by the teacher and then another prescribed situation placed before the children. If we are to protect and foster independent reasoning through real problem solving, this strategy is clearly inappropriate. Indeed, it should be reversed, so that it becomes a strategy of 'macro-openness and micro-structuring'. By this we mean a large amount of freedom of choice for pupils, based on a small amount of directed learning. This mirrors real life where it is possible for the problem solver to get 'micro-direction' – facts and techniques (eg how to conduct an opinion survey) – from outside sources, while maintaining overall control of how to approach the problem and what to do.

If they are to put this into practice, teachers need to be helped to find ways of managing group problem solving. Two main components need to be considered:

1   *the social relationship* which will assist the achievement of group real problem solving, ie mutual trust and respect;
2   *the process* through which the task is accomplished (ie the real problem-solving process) in particular, the structure of critical points within that process, such as decision-making.

Below we offer some simple conceptual frameworks for analysing and interpreting phenomena in the classroom. These can help teachers through enabling them to structure their experience. The frameworks are intended to be descriptive *not* prescriptive and have been distilled from practice.

Framework 1
Real problem solving requires the class as whole to co-operate in defining the task and working for its completion. *The flow between*

whole class and small group interactions is impor
the approach to the problem. Each unit has fairly
The whole class establishes objectives by de
develops a co-ordinated plan of action, reviev
the overall decisions. The small groups are t;
on behalf of the whole class and responsibl
may decide which aspects of a problem neea ...
is the small group which actually does the investigating a...
reports back (see Figure 12.3).

In our experience, once the children get used to the idea of
planning and making decisions together, then entrusting the execu-
tion of the jobs to sub-groupings, they organise themselves remarkably well. Indeed, the process is often self-correcting, so that groups
going astray may be sorted out quite helpfully in the report-back
sessions.

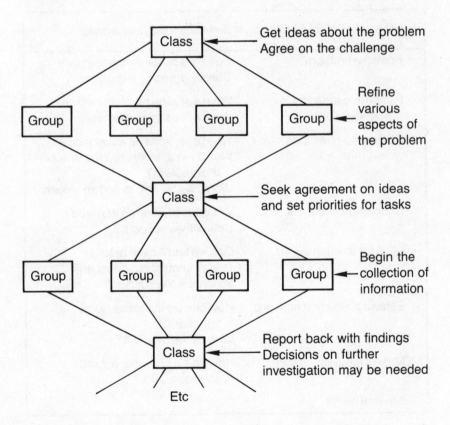

Figure 12.3

...process of tackling a real problem can be encapsulated in an ...ronym – *PROBLEMS* (see Figure 12.4).

This is a simplified but useful framework for describing what happens when a group engages in real problem solving. It is one possible way of analysing what is going on. In this acronym the component taks of real problem solving are matched to a series of self-organising questions which guide the learner through the task. We are not suggesting that these questions be forced upon the children, but they represent a generalised approach to the component task which may enable us, as teachers, to help the children decide upon what needs to be done. Of course, as the children gain more experience at problem solving, they should become able to cope with such questions for themselves and internalise the essential tasks.

Stage of 'PROBLEMS'	Self-organising questions
Pose the problem	Does this problem concern us? Can we agree on a challenge?
Refine into areas for investigation	What does the problem involve? What needs investigating?
Outline the questions to ask	What questions do we want to ask? Would the answers help us to solve the problem? Would we be able to find an answer?
Bring the right data home	What information do we need? How will we collect it?
Look for solutions	Can we find a clear result? Does it answer our question? So what is the solution?
Establish recommendations	How can we fit the solutions together? Who will be affected?
Make it happen	How do we know our overall solution works?
So what next?	

Figure 12.4

Framework 3
Reality is never as simple as the models we offer; many complications can be expected during the problem solving process but these can often be put to good use. The complicating phenomena most likely to occur during real problem solving is 'looping'; by this we mean back-tracking through the process and doing something again. The need to revisit again and again stages already passed is in the very nature of problem solving. Again, it can be helpful to pose self-organising questions appropriate to various forms of looping. For example, when moving back from the 'Look for solutions' stage to the 'Outline the questions to ask' stage, the 'loop' looks like the one in Figure 12.5.

The acronym PROBLEMS and possible forms of looping can then be formalised into a flow-chart in order to help teachers to analyse the progress of the work.

It is important, however, to consider the implications of such looping. For many children, going back over ground already covered will be strongly associated with a sense of failure. They need a great deal of support and encouragement throughout the process. A need to loop may also suggest that children require an opportunity to develop their thinking to cope with the task. The teacher must judge whether the children are ready to acquire the necessary concept or skill, or whether they would do better to alter their approach to the problem.

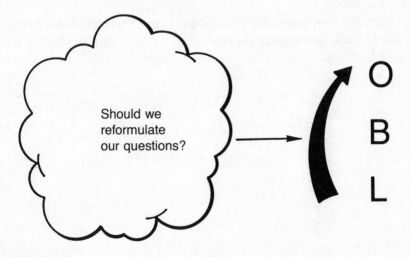

Should we reformulate our questions?

O
B
L

Figure 12.5

Conclusion

The examples in this article were drawn from one particular class-room where the approach could be incorporated into the curriculum on a regular and coherent basis. Furthermore, we chose to concentrate on one particular aspect of the primary curriculum – mathematics – when evaluating the work. Nevertheless, real problem solving provides opportunities for learning in other aspects of the curriculum, as many other teachers have reported.

The full potential of real problem solving has hardly begun to be exploited. Freire calls the process of learning to take charge of the world for yourself 'conscientisation'. Education is clearly part of the process of conscientisation. Perhaps, therefore, the acid test of the real problem-solving approach will be what happens for the children *beyond* the classroom and the curriculum.

We want children to become involved with issues with which they can grapple, at a level in which they can get real evidence, *do* real things and *learn* what real action-research and real problem solving is all about. Learning and doing are not different kinds of acts but part of the same process. We can learn to do something by doing it. We feel that the most effective way for children to learn how to solve real problems is by solving real problems. If we attempt to prevent children making mistakes or to stop them using unconventional strategies, we often perpetuate dependence on adults and lack of confidence in themselves. We are unwittingly teaching them to be 'incapable'.

Give children 'problems' – real ones to experience and the acronym to help them develop the process – and we can begin to educate for the real world.

'BRIDGES' – an integrated and problem-solving approach

R McTaggart (*Cypress Junior School, Croydon*)
'We've done it before!' was the children's surprise response to my proud announcement of the term's project. No record of their work was to be found in the archives and as I had attended a DES course in Craft, Design and Technology during the summer, I was raring to approach the term's work through personal and group problem-solving activities. A class assembly, I soon discovered, was the extent of the children's work on the subject, so our *Bridges* project got under way. Certain key lessons were class taught throughout the project, but the main emphasis was on individual and group discovery through problem-solving activities.

Decision making is at the core of CDT. Decide on a hypothesis, formulate the practical solution, then finally test and evaluate. A child or group should recognise the problem, analyse it, then gather or research relevant information in order to reach a decision as to the solution. During this period of decision-making the teacher should advise, initiate and provide appropriate stimuli, becoming a *question poser*, not a solution giver. This often presents the teacher with the problem of knowing when to give help and advice and when not. A long, involved path to failure can have beneficial aspects, but the children will not realise or value them.

But back to the problem of crossing the bridge. As our project was to centre on CDT, the introductory activity was to give the groups three sheets of thin card and a 'brief' which required them to 'bridge' a span of 30cm. The card could be rolled, bent, folded or joined in any way. The groups' decisions were influenced by an introductory talk about structures, looking at existing bridges and the ways in which they had been designed to withstand forces. Testing took the form of 'weights until destruction' (lots of maths here!) then the solutions of corrugated, rolled and arched card were evaluated. The results were looked at scientifically, applying the practical discovery to the concept of forces.

After looking at a set of slides of world-famous bridges, groups were asked to select one and research it. Facts as to siting, history, designer, location etc were recorded. The groups presented their information to the rest of the class, and then entered the data into an information-handling program on the computer.[10] I wanted to use this opportunity to show the class how a computer can sort data in seconds, and to discuss the implications this has for industry. The questions to be asked were not worked out in advance, but after programming their data the children altered the key-line of the computer to discover 'Which bridges were built this century?', 'Which bridges were designed by Isambard Brunel?' etc. Each group was also asked to devise two questions for other groups to present to the computer.

In addition to scientific and computing problems, bridges also lend themselves to initiatives in curriculum integration. The presentation of a project folder provides an ongoing outlet for written language. The children painted a bridge of their choice, and a detailed plan of the bridge they were to construct required a basic form of technical drawing – some groups were able to draw this plan to scale. Geography can be brought in by visiting local bridges and discussing the requirements of particular sites. Another geographical task involved 'placing' the famous bridges on a traced map of the world. Similar entries were made on a map of Britain, and this led on to historical research into the style and period of the bridges.

Building 'physical' bridges was the problem tackled in educational gymnastics. How could the children travel across a set distance without touching the 'shark infested' gym mats?

The central and most exciting part of our bridge experience was an extension of the first activity, a problem requiring the groups to design and create, from any material, a bridge to span a 50cm gap. We had already established an easy method of joining centimetre-square wood,[11] but groups decided for themselves whether or not to use this technique. Group size and composition were also left to the children. Then, after a short design period, the 'hands on' experience began.

Problems were constantly arising as first designs were discarded or amended. I was amazed and excited as the groups began to develop their work. The range of designs was vast. Syringes of water formed the basis of a rising 'bascule' bridge (since operated by Ministers for Education Keith Joseph and Kenneth Baker!). Copper wire lifted a suspension bridge, and the wood-joining technique was used to make a remarkably strong railway bridge. Aluminium foil rolls formed strong towers, when joined, and two groups used a winding handle/pulley method to lift the bascules on their model.

The interaction within the groups and the discussion when a

problem arose seemed endless, and many children displayed an extensive vocabulary. The children's interest, and the time they took on the project, far exceeded my expectations. The experience was possibly even more enriching and enlightening for the teacher than it was for the pupils!

Reactions to problem solving

Mary Burns

In two years' experience of problem solving I have noticed that the children gain greater self-reliance, learn to think before acting, become less dependent on the teacher and develop an appreciation that results may vary, yet be 'correct' if feasible – and all this leads to enhanced self-concepts. The children also realise that the rank order of intellectual ability in subjects such as Maths and English does not reflect their results in problem solving. This is a factor I always stress when introducing the subject to other teachers.

I persuaded other staff to try teaching problem solving itself, as I find that to introduce the system directly into subject areas becomes much easier if the process is first learnt and understood in a variety of contexts: practical, imaginary and/or immediate. The timetable was arranged so that two rather different types of teacher could participate (both teaching children of 10 and 11). One was a general subjects class teacher, orientated towards the arts, and rather didactic in teaching style. The other was a science specialist with a formal background but a flexible approach to lessons.

My first task was to convince them that they could enjoy teaching problem solving. The Arts teacher was very doubtful of her ability to cope, but she is a great knitter, and she gave her class the problem: 'I must knit a large sweater in the next few weeks. All the wool factories and shops are empty of wool. Show me what I might do.'

The children jotted down ideas individually. Then the class discussed the merits of the different ideas and the obstacles which might arise, eg use different yarn; collect wool in the fields and process it; ask other knitters for left-over wool, etc. The idea which seemed most plausible and appealed most to the teacher was to collect jumble-sale woollens, unravel them, and then re-cycle the wool. This was practical, cheap and could be put into effect quite easily.

The immediate reaction of the teacher was surprise that the lesson had been fun and delight at the children's ability to help her with such a wide range of ideas. After two terms I asked this teacher for her comments.

> Problem solving has changed my opinion with regard to the intelligence of the children. Some have the most amazing ideas, and it is obvious that the difficulties of writing hold back their creativity and ingenuity.

With regard to the originality of ideas she went on:

> I am very pleased and surprised, constantly amazed by the
> ideas they come up with. Quite an eye-opener. They are often
> far more mature than we give them credit for.

I asked if she found it difficult not to impose her ideas and
opinions. 'I did at first but the class have trained me to shut up!'
This is the area I find most difficult to put across – that most
children are capable of problem solving given time and encouragement. I ask teachers not to give any ideas at all unless it is to guide
the class thinking in response to direct questions from the children.
I prefer to answer questions by posing a further question. So often
the children then answer it for themselves, and this helps them
become more self-reliant.

When I asked this teacher if she could relate problem solving to
wider social issues she replied:

> It is good for children to think for themselves, to solve prob-
> lems. The classroom situation is often 'boring' for some (if not
> all) at times. Perhaps if they learnt how to sum up a situation
> and think it through to the end the consequence of their actions
> might stop them from behaviour such as vandalism. I think
> we don't spend enough time on personality and character
> development and extension. These lessons are one way. . . to
> this end. However it depends considerably on the teacher hand-
> ling the situation of problem solving.

She saw the advantages to be gained by giving children control
over decisions as a way of extending self-confidence.

> Being able to do it themselves and not being told by adults for
> once! . . . when a child has been naughty, get them to solve
> the problem of punishment and/or solving the argument.

I gave the second teacher involved (the science specialist) the
following 'material' for her first lesson:

> 'I have to get this class to the cross-roads in the next village
> and there is no public transport. We need to do it as quickly
> and efficiently as possible.'

The children's suggestions ranged from bikes, go-karts, skates,
local supermarket trolleys (two passengers and one pushing), to

testing how many children could cram into the teacher's car. By doing simple maths to compare numbers of children and 'trips' they produced varied results and ideas.

The teacher's comment was that the children had far more ideas that she expected them to produce and she enjoyed the lesson. It was interesting that the children could jot down ideas in cartoon form and label them in sequence rather than writing more lengthy notes. She named a few children who had excelled at verbal reasoning but whose bookwork she had found poor in her other lessons.

All the teachers who have been involved so far have commented on the need to understand the system and theory of the lessons. All see the value of using the technique in other lessons, as two further comments emphasise:

> 'I realise that in science I still judge by quite blinkered standards – intelligence is reflected by giving the accepted answer' and 'I now realise that children who score badly in traditional written tests are not necessarily unintelligent.'

From *Problem-Solving News*, July 1985

Notes and references

1   The Bulmershe-Comino Problem-Solving Project Report 1983
2   *The Junior School Project* (ILEA Research and Statistics Branch, 1986)
3   *Frames of Mind* Howard Gardiner (Heinemann, 1985)
4   *Self-Concept and School Achievement* William W. Purkey (Prentice-Hall, 1970)
5   Edward de Bono: *Thinking Course for Juniors 5–12; Think Links* (a set of card games); *CoRT Thinking Lessons* (Direct Education Services Ltd., Blandford Forum, Dorset)
6   See *Teaching Thinking: an Evaluation of Edward de Bono's Classroom Materials* Elizabeth Hunter-Grundin (Schools Council / SCDC, 1985)
7   See *Young Children in Action* Mary Hohmann, Bernard Banet, David Weikart (USA)
8   See *Making up our minds: an exploratory study of instrumental enrichment* (Schools Council, 1983)
9   See *Philosophy in the Classroom* Matthew Lipman, Ann M Sharp, F S Oscanyan (Temple University Press, Philadelphia, 1980)
10   A Six Line Program developed in Croydon
11   A technique developed by David Jinks, see *Design and Technology 5–12* by Pat Williams and David Jinks (Falmer Press, 1985)

Further reading

Nickerson R., Perkins D., and Smith E.E., *The Teaching of Thinking* (Lawrence Erlbaum, 1985)

The Institute for the Advancement of Philosophy for Children publishes a thinking skills programme for junior, middle and secondary children; books of teaching philosophy for children; and a quarterly magazine for teachers entitled *Thinking* (available from IAPC, Montclair State College, Upper Montclair, New Jersey 07043, USA)

Index